Moving to
Ubuntu Linux

Moving to
Ubuntu
Linux®

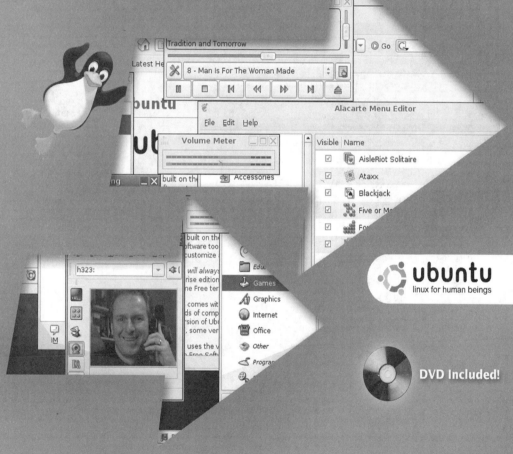

ubuntu
linux for human beings

DVD Included!

Marcel Gagné

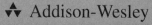
Addison-Wesley

Upper Saddle River, NJ   Boston   Indianapolis   San Francisco
New York   Toronto   Montreal   London   Munich   Paris   Madrid
Capetown   Sydney   Tokyo   Singapore   Mexico City

Many of the designations used by manufacturers and sellers to distinguish their products are claimed as trademarks. Where those designations appear in this book, and the publisher was aware of a trademark claim, the designations have been printed with initial capital letters or in all capitals.

Ubuntu, the Ubuntu logo, Canonical, and the Canonical logo are all registered trademarks of Canonical Ltd.

The author and publisher have taken care in the preparation of this book, but make no expressed or implied warranty of any kind and assume no responsibility for errors or omissions. No liability is assumed for incidental or consequential damages in connection with or arising out of the use of the information or programs contained herein.

The publisher offers excellent discounts on this book when ordered in quantity for bulk purchases or special sales, which may include electronic versions and/or custom covers and content particular to your business, training goals, marketing focus, and branding interests. For more information, please contact:

> U.S. Corporate and Government Sales
> (800) 382-3419
> corpsales@pearsontechgroup.com

For sales outside the United States, please contact:

> International Sales
> international@pearsoned.com

This Book Is Safari Enabled

The Safari® Enabled icon on the cover of your favorite technology book means the book is available through Safari Bookshelf. When you buy this book, you get free access to the online edition for 45 days.

Safari Bookshelf is an electronic reference library that lets you easily search thousands of technical books, find code samples, download chapters, and access technical information whenever and wherever you need it.

To gain 45-day Safari Enabled access to this book:

- Go to http://www.awprofessional.com/safarienabled
- Complete the brief registration form
- Enter the coupon code L3JV-TFWK-ERY6-6TL7-AC55

If you have difficulty registering on Safari Bookshelf or accessing the online edition, please e-mail customer-service@safaribooksonline.com.

Visit us on the Web: www.awprofessional.com

Library of Congress Cataloging-in-Publication Data
Gagné, Marcel.
  Moving to Ubuntu Linux / Marcel Gagne.
    p. cm.
  Includes bibliographical references and index.
  ISBN 0-321-42722-X (pbk. : alk. paper)
  1. Linux. 2. Operating systems (Computers) I. Title.

  QA76.76.O63.G3455 2006
  005.4'32—dc22

                              2006021595

ISBN 0-321-42722-X
Text printed in the United States on recycled paper at Courier in Stoughton, Massachusetts.
First printing, August 2006

*This book is dedicated to
Chris Kelly,
my great friend of more than thirty years
and the only guy crazy enough to fly
5,000 kilometers in a Cessna 172, with me as the pilot.*

Contents

Acknowledgments

Before you embark on your journey through *Moving to Ubuntu Linux*, allow me a few moments to thank some of the people who have made this book possible.

First and foremost, I want to acknowledge my wonderful son, Sebastian, and my beautiful wife, Sally, the two most important people in my life. I love you both dearly. Sally is my love, my life, my inspiration, and my strength. She is also my best friend and confidante. Sebastian, meanwhile, has given me new eyes with which to see the world. I can't imagine a greater gift.

To my family and friends, thank you for believing in me, for your love, and for your support. I love you all.

Many thanks to Mark Taub, my editor, and to Heather Fox, my publicist. Thanks also to Lara Wysong, Kelli Brooks, Michelle Bish, and to everyone at Addison-Wesley and Pearson. Many thanks also to my agent, Richard Curtis, working hard for me in the wilds of Manhattan.

My sincere thanks to those people who reviewed my book along the way. They are (in alphabetical order by last name) AEleen Frisch, Peter Garrett, Arnav Gosch, and Sally Tomasevic. Your hard work, sharp eyes, and suggestions have helped make this a better book. Special kudos to Peter Garrett who went above and beyond to provide his invaluable comments and insight.

Finally, I would like to recognize and thank the Linux community: the developers and software designers, the members of Linux user groups (including my own WFTL-LUG), the many who share their experiences on Usenet, and all those unnamed folk who give free advice under pseudonyms in IRC groups.

—Marcel Gagné

Foreword

To the newcomer, the computer world can seem pretty forbidding. The secret codes for operating these metal beasts are under the control of mysterious geeks who speak some language that sounds like English but makes no sense. Even if you manage to master some corner of the computer continuum, the rug can be pulled out from under you without warning. A program that seemed tame will suddenly grow fangs. The way you've been doing things for months will stop working without notice.

Once you've managed to tame the beast even a little it seems like masochism to consider switching to another operating system, but for many of us who use, and suffer with, Windows, the choice to continue to use that spawn of Microsoft may seem masochistic, too.

Spyware, viruses, blue screens of death, confused user interfaces, buggy programs, security flaws, the list of problems with Windows seems endless. Many Windows users wonder if there's a better way, but dread the idea of learning to tame another beast.

Well, as Marcel Gagné has been showing us for years in his superb books, his "Cooking with Linux" columns, and on my TV show, *Call for Help*, there is a better way, and it's called Linux. Until recently Linux was the choice of cellar-dwelling computer geeks and four-eyed server administrators. The idea of a normal person using Linux on his or her desktop for day-to-day work was far-fetched to say the least. All that is changing, due in part to the success of Ubuntu Linux.

Ubuntu was created with one goal: to make a desktop version of Linux that everyone can use, and I think the team has succeeded marvelously.

Finally there's a version of Linux I'd feel comfortable giving to my mom. It comes with a great range of applications without falling prey to the common "everything including the kitchen sink" approach of many other Linux distributions. You'll find just what you need on your Ubuntu installation, with little or no fatty excess. Oh, and by the way, there's a version for you server geeks, too.

Of course, because Ubuntu, as all Linux distributions, bundles applications from the Free Software Foundation, the Apache Software Foundation, OpenOffice.org, and many other open source software groups, you get a great variety of powerful well-designed programs. Ubuntu includes more than 16,000 individual applications (even though it fits on one CD). You'll find tools for almost anything you can think to do with a computer including a full office suite, Web server software, and programming tools. Yet all that power and complexity is wrapped in a very slick, easy to use user interface that's, frankly, a whole lot better than Windows.

It's pretty mind-blowing that a free operating system can best one that costs hundreds of dollars and is backed by a hundred-billion-dollar corporation, but it's true. The essential verity of the open source software movement is that programmers who are doing what they love will always do a better job than programmers who are working merely to make a living.

As well designed as Ubuntu is, however, it's still terra incognita for the Windows user. Where's my Start menu? they plead. What happened to the Control Panel and My Network Neighborhood? Fear not intrepid operating system explorer, this book will clear a path in the jungle, and you'll find yourself at home with Ubuntu in just a few short weeks.

So come on in. No secret knock is necessary. The only password you'll need is the one you create yourself to secure your system. The Linux and free software community welcome you with open arms. There is a better way, and this book is your first step toward freedom.

Les Laporte

Petaluma, California
June 2006

Chapter

1

Introducing Ubuntu!

Welcome to the Ubuntu Linux universe, one and all!

So, what is Ubuntu Linux? I could tell you that Ubuntu Linux is currently one of the hottest Linux distributions around with one of the most active and dedicated user and development communities. We could also take a look and see what the Ubuntu Web site has to say.

> "Ubuntu" is an ancient African word, meaning "humanity to others." Ubuntu also means "I am what I am because of who we all are." The Ubuntu Linux distribution brings the spirit of Ubuntu to the software world.

Ubuntu Linux (and Kubuntu Linux) are funded and supported by the Shuttleworth Foundation, headed by billionaire Mark Shuttleworth. I mention this to say that Ubuntu Linux is a solid organization backed by solid financial support. With this support, the Ubuntu Foundation will ship free Linux CDs to anyone anywhere in the world (visit https://shipit.ubuntu.com). This is quite impressive, but it does not answer the question: What is Ubuntu Linux? The official Ubuntu site goes on to say the following:

Ubuntu Linux is a complete desktop Linux operating system, freely available with both community and professional support. The Ubuntu community is built on the ideas enshrined in the Ubuntu Manifesto: that software should be available free of charge, that software tools should be usable by people in their local language and despite any disabilities, and that people should have the freedom to customise and alter their software in whatever way they see fit.

If you are new to Ubuntu Linux and to Linux in general, this might be time for a little Linux Q&A. These days, the first question I get is not, "What is Linux?" but rather, "What do I have to do to get Linux on my system?" And in the case of Ubuntu Linux, people know enough to point to a specific distribution and ask for it by name.

But What Is Linux?

For those who want clarification, Linux is a fully multitasking operating system based on UNIX—although technically, Linux is the *kernel*, the master program that makes running a Linux system possible. That kernel, by the way, was written by a young Finnish student named Linus Torvalds. On August 25, 1991, Torvalds posted this now famous (perhaps legendary) message to the Usenet group comp.os.minix:

```
From: torvalds@klaava.Helsinki.FI (Linus Benedict Torvalds)
      Newsgroups: comp.os.minix
      Subject: What would you like to see most in minix?
      Summary: small poll for my new operating system
      Message-ID:
<1991Aug25.205708.9541@klaava.Helsinki.FI>
      Date: 25 Aug 91 20:57:08 GMT
      Organization: University of Helsinki
      Hello everybody out there using minix -
      I'm doing a (free) operating system (just a hobby,
won't be big and professional like gnu) for 386(486) AT
clones. This has been brewing since april, and is starting to
get ready. I'd like any feedback on things people like/
dislike in minix, as my OS resembles it somewhat (same
physical layout of the file-system (due to practical
reasons) among other things).
```

```
    I've currently ported bash(1.08) and gcc(1.40), and
things seem to work. This implies that I'll get something
practical within a few months, and I'd like to know what
features most people would want. Any suggestions are
welcome, but I won't promise I'll implement them :-)
    Linus (torvalds@kruuna.helsinki.fi)
    PS. Yes - it's free of any minix code, and it has a
multi-threaded fs. It is NOT protable (uses 386 task
switching etc), and it probably never will support anything
other than AT-hard disks, as that's all I have :-(.
```

Much has happened since then. Linus somehow captured the imagination of scores of talented programmers around the world. Joined together through the magic of the Internet, they collaborated, coded, tweaked, and gave birth to the operating system that is now revolutionizing the world of computing.

These days, Linux is a powerful, reliable (rock solid, in fact), expandable, flexible, configurable, multiuser, multitasking, and completely free operating system that runs on many different platforms. These include Intel PCs, DEC Alphas, Macintosh systems, PowerPCs, and a growing number of embedded processors. You can find Linux in PDA organizers, digital watches, golf carts, and cell phones. In fact, Linux has a greater support base (in terms of platforms) than just about any other operating system in the world.

What we call the Linux operating system is not the work of just one man alone. Linus Torvalds is the original architect of Linux—its father, if you will—but he is not the only effort behind it. Perhaps Linus Torvalds's greatest genius lay in knowing when to share the load. For no other pay but satisfaction, he employed people around the world, delegated to them, worked with them, and asked for and accepted feedback in a next generation of the model that began with the *GNU project*.

GNU, by the way, is a recursive acronym that stands for GNU's Not UNIX, a project of the Free Software Foundation, started in 1984 by Richard M. Stallman. The aim of the project was to create a free, UNIX-like operating system. Over the years, many GNU tools were written and widely used by many commercial UNIX vendors and, of course, system administrators trying to get a job done. The appearance of Linus Torvalds's Linux kernel has made the GNU dream of a completely free, UNIX-like operating system a reality at last.

Is Linux Really FREE?

In any discussion of what *free* means in relation to software, you'll often see the expressions "free as in speech" or "free as in beer." In this case, free isn't a question of cost, although you can get a free copy (as in *free beer*) of Linux and install it on your system without breaking any laws. As Robert A. Heinlein would have said, "There ain't no such thing as a free lunch." A free download will still cost you connection time on the Internet, disk space, time to burn the CDs, and so on. In the case of Ubuntu Linux, you can have a free CD mailed to you, so free in this case starts to feel pretty, well . . . free.

Linux is also free, as in speech, in that you have the right to view the source code and modify it to suit your needs. This is very unlike other operating systems when looking at or changing the code could get you in legal trouble.

Perhaps this is where a little French helps. You'll also see the delineations free (*libre*) and free (*gratis*). The first, *libre*, means free in the sense that you have freedom of expression, the freedom of speech, and the freedom to think. The second, *gratis*, refers to no cost. Imagine yourself at a friend's party. Your friend walks up and hands you a beer—*gratis.*

What's a Distribution?

Linux comes in many flavors, often referred to as distributions. Ubuntu Linux is just one of many distributions out there. You have probably heard of Red Hat, SUSE, or Mandriva (formerly Mandrake). These are all popular and well-respected distributions. A distribution is a collection of software, usually free software, with the Linux kernel at its core and hundreds, sometimes thousands, of applications. Different manufacturers may offer boxed sets that come with documentation, support, and CDs, the latter saving you time and energy downloading and burning discs. Furthermore, there are boxed sets of varying prices, even within a distribution. For instance, you can buy a Red Hat personal or professional edition. The difference is there may be additional software, documentation, or support.

Ubuntu Linux is a distribution based on yet another, very popular distribution known as Debian. Debian's popularity has spawned a number of distributions including Xandros, Linspire, Knoppix, and several others.

What sets one distribution apart from another is not always easily defined, but there are some basics. For instance, most distributions provide their own administrative interfaces. They include their own unique desktop themes and organization of applications in a menu.

Speaking of applications, this is one of Ubuntu's strengths and something that attracts many people. Ubuntu has selected a simplified core set of applications that makes sense. To understand why this is such a great idea, you need to understand that some distributions give you three terminals, five Web browsers, two word processors, and so on. Ubuntu Linux makes it easy with intelligent choices for applications that do the job.

Linux and the GPL

Linux is distributed under the GNU General Public License (GPL), which, in essence, says that anyone may copy, distribute, and even sell the program, so long as changes to the source are reintroduced back to the community and the terms of the license remain unaltered. Free means that you are free to take Linux, modify it, and create your own version. Free means that you are not at the mercy of a single vendor who forces you into a kind of corporate servitude by making sure that it is extremely costly to convert to another environment. If you are unhappy with your Linux vendor or the support you are getting, you can move to the next vendor without forfeiting your investment in Linux.

In other words, it's "free as in speech"—or freedom.

The GNU GPL permits a distributor to "charge a fee for the physical act of transferring a copy, and you may at your option offer warranty protection in exchange for a fee." This is further qualified by the statement that the distributor must release "for a charge no more than your cost of physically performing source distribution, a complete machine-readable copy of the corresponding source code." In other words, the GPL ensures that programs like Linux will at best be free of charge. At worst, you may be asked to pay for the cost of a copy.

You should take some time to read the GNU GPL. For your convenience, I've reprinted it in Appendix A of this book.

What Do I Gain?

No operating system is perfect, and nothing comes without some hassles, but as time goes on, Linux is getting closer and closer to perfection. These days, Linux is even easier to install than your old operating system, and you don't have to reboot time and again as you load driver disk after driver disk. I won't bore you with everything I consider an advantage but I will give you a few of the more important points.

Security

Say goodbye to your virus checker and stop worrying. Although Linux is not 100 percent immune to viruses, it comes pretty close. In fact, to date, most so-called Linux viruses do not exist *in the wild* (only under tightly controlled environments in *proof-of-concept* labs). It isn't that no one has tried, but the design model behind Linux means that it is built with security in mind. Consequently, viruses are virtually nonexistent in the Linux world, and security issues are dealt with quickly and efficiently by the Linux community. Security flaws are well advertised. It isn't unusual for a security hole to be discovered and a fix created within a few short hours of the discovery. If something does present a risk, you don't have to wait for the next release of your operating system to come along.

Stability

The stability of Linux is almost legendary. Living in a world where people are used to rebooting their PCs one or more times a day, Linux users talk about running weeks and sometimes months without a reboot. Illegal operations and the Blue Screen of Death are not part of the Linux experience. Sure, programs occasionally crash here, but they don't generally take down your *whole* system with them.

Power

Linux is a multitasking, multiuser operating system. In this book, I concentrate on the desktop features of Ubuntu Linux, but under the hood, Linux is a system designed to provide all the power and flexibility of an enterprise-class server. Linux-powered Web site servers and electronic mail gateways move information along on the Internet and run small to large businesses. Under the friendly face of your graphical desktop, that power is still there.

Money

It is possible to do everything you need to do on a computer without spending any money on software—that means new software and upgrades alike. In fact, free software for Linux is almost an embarrassment of riches. In Chapter 8, I'll show you how to install (or remove) additional software on your Linux system. You won't believe how easy it is.

Freedom from Legal Hassles

When you run Linux, you don't have to worry about whether you've kept a copy of your operating system license. The GNU GPL, which I mentioned earlier, means you are legally entitled to copy and can legally redistribute your Linux CDs if you wish.

Keep in mind, however, that although Linux itself can be freely distributed, *not all software that runs on Linux is covered* by the same license. If you buy or download software for your system, you should still pay attention to the license that covers that software.

What Do I Lose?

Nothing ever seems to be perfect. By moving to Linux you gain a great deal, but I would be doing a disservice if I did not mention the disadvantages.

Hardware and Peripheral Support

The hardware support for Linux is, quite honestly, among the best there is, and Ubuntu Linux's hardware support is among the best in the Linux world. In fact, when you consider all the platforms that run Linux, its hardware and peripheral support is better than that of the Windows system you are leaving behind. Unfortunately, there are some consumer devices designed with Windows specifically in mind. Consequently, certain printers or scanners may have limited support under Linux because the manufacturer is slow in providing drivers. That said, the vast majority of standard devices work very well and you aren't likely to run into too many problems.

On the upside, you'll find that where you always had to load drivers to make something run in your old OS, Linux automatically recognizes and supports an amazing number of peripherals without you having to do anything extra or hunt down a driver disk. Furthermore, the Linux community is vibrant in a way that few businesses can ever hope to be. If you have your eye on a hot new piece of hardware, you can almost bet that some Linux developer somewhere has an eye on exactly the same thing.

We'll talk about devices and device drivers later in Chapter 6.

Software Packages

There is a huge amount of software available for the Linux operating system. Amazingly, most of it is noncommercial and free for the download. There are *thousands* of games, tools, and Internet and office applications available to run on your system. You don't have to go far either. Most modern distributions come with several hundred packages on the CDs, more than enough to get you going, working, and playing without having to look elsewhere. Once again, much of the software out there will cost you nothing more than the time it takes to download it.

And installation? With the Synaptic package manager included with Ubuntu, you'll be asking yourself why it wasn't this easy to install software in your old OS!

On the other hand, commercial, shrink-wrapped software, including those hot new 3D games at your local computer store, are still hard to come by. As Linux grows in popularity, particularly on the desktop, this is starting to change.

There are ways around this issue, however. For instance, you can pick up a package called Cedega that lets you install and run Windows games.

A Step into the Unknown

Let's face it. For some, moving to Linux is a step into the unknown. Things won't be exactly as they were with your old operating system, and for the most part, this is a good thing. You will have to do a little relearning and get used to a different way of doing things.

Even so, if you are used to working in your Windows graphical environment and you are comfortable with basic mousing skills, writing the occasional email, surfing the Web, or composing a memo in your word processor, moving to Linux won't be a big deal. Your Linux desktop is a modern graphical environment, and much of what you have learned in your old operating system can be taken with you into this new world.

Some Tips on Using This Book

My intention in creating this book was to provide a simple transition from your old OS to Ubuntu Linux. I'll cover things such as installation shortly, but the majority of the book has to do with working (and playing) in your new Ubuntu Linux environment. I want to show you how to do the things you have grown used to doing: surfing the Net, writing emails, listening to music, printing, burning CDs, and so on. Furthermore, I am going to tell you how to take those Word documents, Excel spreadsheets, and music files you have collected over time and start using them with Linux. In short, my plan is to have you move as effortlessly as possible from your old OS to Linux.

Working your way through the chapters, you'll notice that I am constantly inviting you to try things. That's because I believe the best way to learn anything is by doing. Yes, you're going to learn to work with a new operating system, but it doesn't mean you can't have fun. As everyone knows, all work and no play will make anyone pretty dull. Later in this book (in an effort to avoid dullness), I'll take you into the world of Linux fun and games.

Quick Tips and Shelling Out

Throughout the book, I occasionally provide you with boxed asides, tips that should serve as little reminders or simpler ways to do things.

You'll also notice boxes that start out with the phrase "Shell out." Although I intend to concentrate on working with graphical tools and in a graphical way, much of the power of Linux comes from working with the command line, or the *shell*. The Shell Out boxes will guide you in working with the shell.

Learning to wield the command line is akin to getting a black belt in a martial art or earning a first aid certificate. It doesn't mean that you are going to run out and take on all comers or that you are going to be facing daily crisis situations. Working with the shell does give you the means and the confidence to step outside the confines of the graphical environment. The shell is power, and it is always there for you, so you should not fear it.

Meet Your Desktop

Your Ubuntu Linux system comes with a modern, advanced, and easy-to-use desktop environment known as GNOME. There are many such environments, and in time, you will learn about them. Part of that freedom I spoke about is the freedom to do things your way, and that extends to the type of graphical environment you may want to work in. The most popular desktop environments today are the K Desktop Environment (KDE) and GNOME, but WindowMaker, IceWM, XFCE, and others have quite a following, as well.

Ubuntu Linux is just one face of a handful of simplified, fine-tuned, Linux distributions. There is another version of Ubuntu being distributed called Kubuntu, the difference being that it uses KDE as its default desktop environment. In Chapter 20, I'll tell you how to install and run the Kubuntu default environment, the KDE desktop. Don't worry; you won't be giving anything up. You can easily switch from one to the other as you so desire.

 Note This may sound repetitious, but it is important. Kubuntu *is* Ubuntu. It just happens to be Ubuntu Linux running KDE as its desktop environment. It is not a fork of Ubuntu, nor is it a different distribution.

When you become comfortable with GNOME and Ubuntu Linux, I invite you to experiment with other desktop environments. *Exercise your freedom to be yourself.*

Help Me!

After you are done working with this book, I am confident that Ubuntu Linux will be your operating system of choice for the foreseeable future. That doesn't mean you won't have questions that aren't answered in this book. To that end, I give you a Web site address that will link you to the support pages for this book on my own Web site:

```
http://www.marcelgagne.com
```

My site has links to a number of other resources, including many articles I have written on using and administering Linux, links to other information sites, and much more. Click the Moving to Ubuntu link (or its cover), and you'll be transported to the support pages for this book.

I also run a few mailing lists for readers, which you'll find under the WFTL heading. WFTL is a short form I've used for years now. It stands for Writer and Free Thinker at Large (computer people love acronyms). It's also the hierarchy for the lists I'm talking about. One of those lists is the WFTL-LUG (a LUG is a Linux User Group), an online discussion group where readers can share information, ask questions, and help each other out with their various Linux adventures. I invite you to join any of the lists I offer there. There is *no cost*, and you can unsubscribe at any time.

If you check under the Linux Links menu of my Web site, you'll find a useful list of additional links to Linux information sources. One of these is the Linux Documentation Project (LDP).

 More Help In Chapter 3, I'll introduce you to your GNOME desktop's help system. It's a great tool with tons of additional information right at your fingertips.

The Ubuntu Community

One of the very best places to turn for additional information on your Ubuntu system is the Ubuntu community. You will find a large number of people with considerable knowledge and information in doing things the Ubuntu way. This community includes developers, documentation writers, and perhaps most importantly, Ubuntu users. This is a vibrant, growing community, providing many different options for locating the help you need.

The first place to start is the Ubuntu Linux Web site (www.ubuntu.com). Closely tied to the Web site is the Ubuntu Wiki, a regularly updated, community-supported source of information. The Wiki is at `wiki.ubuntu.com`. Also on the Web are the Ubuntu forums at `ubuntuforums.org`.

Log on to the #ubuntu IRC channel on irc.freenode.net (see Chapter 9 for information on IRC), and you'll find between 500 to 600 people logged on at any time of the day or night. Ask your questions and it's very likely that somebody has answers.

You can also join the Ubuntu Users mailing list by visiting this site:

```
https://lists.ubuntu.com/mailman/listinfo/ubuntu-users
```

Finally, you can also check Yelp, the included help documentation browser included with your Ubuntu Linux system. For more information on using Yelp, see Chapter 3.

The Linux Documentation Project

The Linux Documentation Project (LDP) is a dynamic community resource. On your Linux distribution CD, you probably have a collection of documents known in the Linux world as *HOWTOs*. These are user- or developer-contributed documents that are maintained and updated by one or more individuals. You can find the latest version of these documents at the LDP site

```
http://www.tldp.org/
```

The mandate of the LDP is essentially to provide a comprehensive base of documentation for all things Linux. If you've been looking high and low for information on installing that bleeding-edge FTL radio card on your PC and still haven't found what you are looking for, try the LDP. The LDP also makes a point of offering the latest versions of the man pages, as well as user guides that tend to cover more ground than standard HOWTOs.

Linux User Groups

A few paragraphs back, I made reference to Linux User Groups, or LUGs. Let's put technology aside for a moment and explore something else you may have heard about: the Linux community. Yes, there really is a Linux community. All around the world, you will find groups of enthusiastic Linux users gathering for regular meetings, chatting over beer and pizza, and sharing information. This sharing of information is part of what makes Linux so friendly.

LUGs tend to run electronic mailing lists where informal exchanges of information take place (just as I do with my online LUG). New users are welcomed, and their questions are happily answered. These users range from newbies getting their feet wet to seasoned kernel developers. Should you find yourself stuck with nowhere to turn, seek out your local LUG and sign on to the mailing list. Today, someone will help you. As you grow more knowledgeable in administering your Linux system, maybe you will return the favor.

Locating a LUG in your community is as simple as surfing over to the Linux Online Web site (`http://www.linux.org/`). Once there, click the User Groups button, and you are on your way. The list is organized by country, then by state or province, and so on.

About the DVD

Included with this book is a full Ubuntu Linux distribution that you can run entirely from your PC's DVD-ROM drive (though slower than if you actually install Ubuntu Linux). That's right. You can run Ubuntu Linux on your system without having to change your system or uninstall Windows.

This DVD includes a complete Ubuntu system with tons of great software that I will be covering in this book. You'll have access to your email, manage your contacts, keep organized, surf the Web, write letters in your word processor, use spreadsheets, play games, and more. In fact, you should be able to follow along with this book and do most of the things I talk about without having to install Linux at all.

Furthermore, the DVD also contains an archive of all Ubuntu supported packages, including many not available in the live session. I'll show you how to install additional software from the DVD in Chapter 8.

The bootable DVD is a fantastic introduction, but remember what I said about performance. The DVD does run *much slower* than a hard-disk install, so keep in mind that the performance you experience from the DVD is not indicative of the performance you can experience from a Linux hard-disk install. At their fastest, DVD drives are no match for even the slowest hard disk drive. Furthermore, when you run from the DVD (as opposed to installing Ubuntu Linux on your hard drive), you are limited to the packages on the DVD. In other words, you can't add or install any new software.

Ready to take Ubuntu Linux for a spin? The bootable DVD is a *perfect* introduction. I'll tell you all you need to know in the next chapter.

When you are truly ready to make the move to Ubuntu Linux, you can install it right from the same DVD. I'll tell you about that as well.

It's My Philosophy

I have a philosophy. All right, I have *many,* and this is just one of them.

Every once in a while, people tell me that desktop Linux is just crazy, that it is just too complicated for *the majority of people*.

I don't know about you, but I am tired of being told that people can't learn to use something that is both good and powerful. With a certain amount of training and a little proper guidance, *anyone who is familiar with a computer can learn to use Linux*.

That isn't to say that working with Ubuntu Linux is difficult (it is not), but as you go along, you will be learning new things. This book is meant for users at every level of experience. It is meant to be read for fun, as well as for reference. And because I'll ask you to try things throughout this book, it's a training guide, as well.

I'm delighted and thrilled that you've decided to join me in *Moving to Ubuntu Linux*. It's not just Linux for human beings; it's an operating system for real people doing real things.

Resources

Linux Documentation Project

```
http://www.tldp.org
```

Linux.org List of LUGs

```
http://www.linux.org/groups/index.html
```

Linux User Groups Worldwide

```
http://lugww.counter.li.org/groups.cms
```

Marcel (Writer and Free Thinker at Large) Gagné's Web site

```
http://www.marcelgagne.com
```

ShipIt Free Ubuntu Linux Service

```
https://shipit.ubuntu.com
```

Ubuntu Linux Forums

```
http://ubuntuforums.org
```

Ubuntu Linux Mailing List

```
https://lists.ubuntu.com/mailman/listinfo/ubuntu-users
```

Ubuntu Linux Website

```
http://www.ubuntu.com
```

Ubuntu Linux Wiki

```
https://wiki.ubuntu.com
```

2

Running and Installing the Ubuntu Live DVD

Included with this book is a full-featured Ubuntu Linux distribution that runs entirely from the DVD-ROM drive. That's right. You can run Linux on your system without having to change your system or uninstall Windows. Then, when you are ready to make the jump official, the live DVD comes with a friendly installer that makes the process virtually painless.

Note Because it is running from the DVD drive, Ubuntu Linux live DVD runs slower than if you actually install Linux and run it from the hard disk. Keep in mind that the performance you experience from the DVD is not indicative of the performance you can experience from a Linux hard-disk install. At their fastest, DVD-ROM drives are no match for even the slowest hard disk drive.

Running Ubuntu Linux is as easy as putting the DVD in the drive and booting. A couple of minutes later, you are working with a great looking, modern desktop (see Figure 2-1). This DVD is full of great software. There are tons of applications and literally thousands of programs on the disk. You'll be able to send and receive email, surf the Web, write documents in your word processor, put together a budget using the spreadsheet package, play a

Figure 2–1   Meet your new Ubuntu Linux live desktop!

few games, and a whole lot more. In fact, you should be able to follow along and play with the software you'll explore in this book and do most of the things that are covered without having to install Ubuntu Linux at all.

The bootable DVD is a fantastic introduction to Ubuntu Linux, providing you with a no-commitment way to take Linux out for a spin; but there are limitations.

I've already covered one issue related to DVDs, that of performance. The other limitation is also DVD related. Because this bootable Linux does not install itself on your hard drive, you are limited to the packages on the DVD. In other words, you can't add or install any new software. After you install Ubuntu Linux to your hard drive, this limitation will vanish and you can choose to install from thousands of great packages. In fact, the DVD includes all of the Ubuntu supported packages so you'll have thousands more programs to choose from—all this without having to download from the Internet.

Ready to Try Ubuntu Linux?

Loading the Ubuntu Linux live DVD is easy because there is no installation required.

Take your DVD and insert it into your DVD-ROM drive. Shut down Windows, and select Restart. Make sure your PC is set to boot from the DVD. Ubuntu Linux boots up to a nice, graphical screen with a simple menu (see Figure 2-2). Booting from the disk is the first option; just press Enter or wait. After a few seconds, the system will boot automatically. Before you do that, however, notice the menu option labeled Check CD for Defects. This is a very good idea if you plan on installing Ubuntu to your hard drive, and I highly recommend that you run this step.

 Note Most modern systems are set to boot directly from the DVD-ROM drive if a bootable DVD is found there. If your system does not, you may have to change the BIOS settings on your PC to allow this. This is generally done by pressing <Delete> or <F2> to enter Setup as the system is booting. (You will usually see such a message before the operating system starts to load.) Because the menus vary, it is impossible for me to cover them all, but look for a menu option that specifies the boot order. You'll see something like A: first, then C: (i.e., your floppy drive, then the hard disk). Change the boot order so that it looks to the DVD first, save your changes, and then restart your system.

Figure 2-2   The boot menu provides a means of checking the DVD for defects.

The boot process takes a few minutes as Ubuntu identifies devices, disks, network connections, sound cards, and so on. At some point, the screen will go dark as your video card is configured and X, the Linux graphical user interface, is started.

If the screen doesn't respond instantly, don't panic. Give it a few seconds. If nothing has happened even after you've waited awhile, it is possible that your video card is one of the rare ones not included in the distribution. Never fear, most (if not all) modern cards support VESA, and Ubuntu should fall back to this setting.

HELP!

Problems, problems . . .

The DVD is amazingly good at automatically booting and running on a huge number of systems, but it isn't perfect. There is only so much software that you can pack on one DVD and that includes drivers for hardware. That said, most problems with booting the Ubuntu live DVD can be resolved.

You might have noticed when the boot screen came up (refer to Figure 2-2) that there were a number of options at the bottom of the screen: <F1> Help, <F2> Language, and so on. Some of these are fairly obvious. Pressing <F1> gives you further assistance. If you don't want to run Ubuntu with English as the default language, press <F2> and select an alternate from the list. Closely related is <F3>, which lets you select an alternate keyboard for the language of your choice.

Getting a proper graphical display is not generally a problem, but if all else fails and you still can't get a good, clear screen, try pressing <F4> and selecting VGA as your video type. Ordinarily, Ubuntu scans for and assigns the proper video driver based on your card. Several accessibility options are also built in to the boot screen that allow users with visual impairments of varying degrees to choose a more suitable environment. There are also settings for users with minor motor difficulties who may have trouble with a mouse or other pointing device. You can access these at boot time by pressing <F5>.

As the system boots, most everything is done for you. This is what is referred to as *Normal mode* and it is the best choice, 99.9 percent of the time. For those who might want total control over every aspect of the boot, device detection, hardware configuration, and so on, it is possible to switch to *Expert mode* by pressing <F6>.

Boot Level Options

The biggest set of boot changes are those that can be added to the boot command prompt itself, directly beside the Boot Options label. For instance, it is possible that you might experience lockups on boot or strange hardware glitches that stop the system from booting, a not uncommon problem with buggy APIC controllers (Advanced Programmable Interrupt Controller). To disable the APIC, press <F6> to bring up the boot prompt, then add this line to the end of the existing options:

```
noapic
```

Press <Enter> and the machine will boot normally but with the APIC disabled. Some of the prompts do not deal with actual problems. They just speed things along. An example of this has to do with network configuration. Normally, the Ubuntu live DVD will configure its network card for DHCP with the idea that an address will automatically be provided by another machine on the network. You can always change this after the system is up (networking is covered in Chapter 7), but it is possible to force a static IP address at boot time.

```
disable_dhcp=true
```

To see a much more comprehensive list of boot parameters, press <F1> to enter the help screen, then press <F5> for an overview of boot parameters, <F6> for parameters dealing with specific machine hardware, <F7> for parameters related to disk controllers, and <F8> for those related to the boot process itself.

Taking a Tour of Ubuntu Linux

After the system has booted, you can start playing with Ubuntu Linux. From here, you can follow along in the book and try the various programs covered. To get you feeling at home quickly, however, let me give you a quick tour of the menus and I'll show you what your system has to offer.

Looking at your Ubuntu desktop (refer to Figure 2-1), you can see that there is a gray panel running along the bottom and along the top of your screen. I will cover all the details of those panels, what they are, what they can do for you, and how you can modify them to suit your needs in Chapters 3 and 5. For the time being, I want you to look at the labels along the top panel and to the left. One says Applications, followed by Places, and finally, System. Each of these represents a menu of possibilities, granting you access to the great programs included with your Ubuntu Linux system, your computer's hardware, storage devices, peripherals, and the tools you need to customize every aspect of your Ubuntu Linux experience.

Start by clicking the Applications button. Then, pause your mouse cursor over the Accessories menu, where you'll see some handy system tools (see Figure 2-3).

The Alacarte Menu Editor (sounds yummy, doesn't it?) is a program designed to let you add or remove, or even modify, menu items. Sometimes, a program doesn't appear where you would like it to go or another program that you use regularly isn't available there. Alacarte is how you change things. Calculator is a simple calculator when it starts, but it also provides advanced functions, including business, financial, and scientific functionality. Character Map is a program that makes it easy to insert international and special characters not directly available from your keyboard (useful when your last name has an **é** at the end).

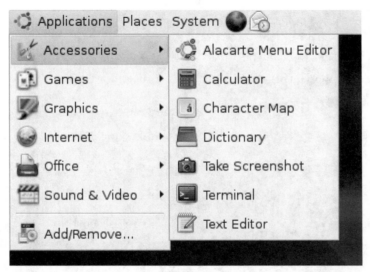

Figure 2–3   The Accessories submenu includes a number of useful tools.

The Dictionary looks up words using Internet accessible resources from dict.org. In Chapter 5, I'll show you how to change the appearance of your desktop. If you feel like sharing your desktop's new look with friends, Take Screenshot is the tool for you. Terminal is a means to access your system's text command line. You'll learn more about that as we progress through the book. Finally, the Text Editor provides a simple, yet powerful, means of editing and manipulating text files.

Move that mouse cursor down one and let's have a look at the Games submenu (see Figure 2-4).

At some point, everybody needs a break, some time to relax and enjoy a little down time. How about trying one of the many solitaire games included in AisleRiot, or spending some time at the Blackjack table? A little Mahjongg, perhaps?

The collection of games included with your system is just the beginning. In Chapter 8, I'll show you how to install hundreds of other games from dungeon crawlers to first-person shooters, high-end 3D action, puzzles, and strategy. Your Ubuntu Linux system could be the game machine you've been looking for.

Figure 2–4   An operating system without games is like a day without sunshine—or something like that.

Next, we are on to the Graphics submenu (see Figure 2-5).

Figure 2–5 *Graphics applications distributed with Ubuntu include the amazing GIMP.*

The GIMP Image Editor is an almost legendary piece of software, a powerful graphic manipulation package with dozens of built-in filters, special effects, and every tool you need to produce high-quality images. I cover the GIMP in detail in Chapter 17. The gThumb Image Viewer provides an easy-to-use way to navigate your folders and view your collection of digital art. Finally, if you have a scanner, the XSane Image scanning program will scan, copy, and fax.

The Internet submenu (see Figure 2-6) starts off with the Ekiga Softphone, a VoIP communication program that provides both audio and video. Those of you keeping track of such things will know that Ekiga started out as GnomeMeeting. For email, contact management, and a great way to stay organized, Evolution Mail handles these beautifully. You can read all about Evolution in Chapters 11 and 12.

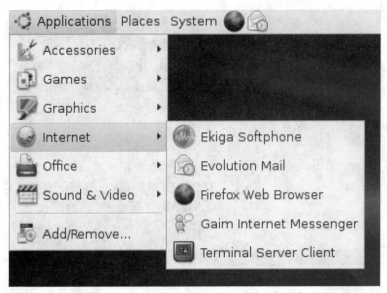

Figure 2–6 The Internet menu has everything you need to surf, email, chat, and connect to the world.

The hottest Web browser in cyberspace doesn't come out of Redmond. No, it's the Firefox Web Browser and after Chapter 10, it may well become your new best friend. An instant messaging client for AOL, another for MSN, and yet another for Jabber? Never! After learning about the Gaim Internet Messenger in Chapter 9, you'll wonder how you ever used anything else. The Terminal Server Client is a great program that makes it possible to take control of another computer using VNC (Virtual Network Computing) or Microsoft Terminal Server.

I'll wrap up this rapid-fire Internet tour by letting you know that Chapter 9 is also the place to learn about the XChat-GNOME IRC Chat client.

Let's move down and have a look at the Office submenu (see Figure 2-7).

First on the menu is Evolution, which you saw back in the Internet menu with Evolution Mail. Because Evolution is so much more than just an email package, it qualifies as an invaluable office application. OpenOffice.org version 2 is a superb, and free, alternative to Microsoft Office, compatible with Microsoft Word, Excel, and PowerPoint files. It also does a whole lot more. OpenOffice.org Base is a powerful, integrated database application, which you'll learn about in Chapter 16. OpenOffice.org Calc (see Chapter 14) is

Figure 2–7 Ubuntu's collection of office applications has you covered with Evolution and the feature packed OpenOffice.org suite.

your spreadsheet program, similar to Microsoft Excel, whereas OpenOffice.org Draw is a flexible drawing program you can use to create all sorts of images including flow charts, organizational charts, logos, and so on. Impress, covered in Chapter 15, is a presentation package, compatible with Microsoft Powerpoint. Think of OpenOffice.org Math as a word processor for creating complex scientific formulas and equations, handy for the students out there. Finally, we come to what is perhaps the most important office tool of all, at least to this writer: OpenOffice.org Writer, a truly excellent word processing package.

Let's look at the last of these submenus, Sound & Video (see Figure 2-8).

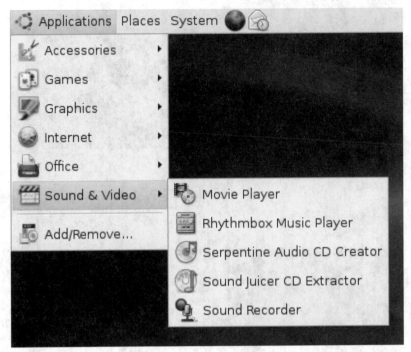

Figure 2–8   The Sound & Video submenu. Watch videos, listen to your favorite songs, and create your own music collections.

At the top of the list is the Movie Player, and its purpose is self-explanatory. With the Rhythmbox Music Player, you've got a great little jukebox program to organize your digital music, keep your ears entertained, and your spirit dancing. When you need to take your music with you, use the Serpentine Audio-CD Creator to build music CDs with collections of your favorite songs. Most of us have tons of music CDs in our collections. Getting them transferred to your PC is the job of the Sound Juicer CD Extractor. Sound Juicer is also an easy-to-use CD player. We wrap up this tour of multi-media applications, and applications in general, with the Sound Recorder, a simple program for recording sound clips.

What? I'm not done yet?

You are right; I'm not done. There is an Add/Remove menu item in that list. If you want to find out how incredibly easy it is to install software in Ubuntu Linux, get your Internet connection set up (see Chapter 7), and then read all about installing software in Chapter 8.

Famous Places on the Menu

Next to the rather rich landscape of the Applications menu and its submenus, we find the Places menu (see Figure 2-9). Places primarily is a menu of physical storage locations, most of them disks or folders on your own system.

Figure 2–9 The Places menu provides quick access to your system's local and network storage locations.

From here, you can quickly jump to your home folder, navigate the computer's disks, create a CD or DVD using your writer, and search for files on your system. These storage resources don't need to always be connected to your system. For instance, if you plug in a USB storage key, it will appear in the Places menu and you can access it without additional fuss.

Places can also show resources a network jump away, either on your local area network or on the Internet. If you have Windows machines with shared drives on your network, Network Servers will get you there with a click.

Administering and Personalizing Your System

The final set of menus are both listed under the System label on the top panel. Before I tell you a bit about them, I would also like to let you know that the GNOME help system is available from the System menu. You can also lock your screen with a password (when you run off for coffee or a muffin) or log out of your current Ubuntu Linux session.

Now, let's take a look at the Preferences submenu (see Figure 2-10).

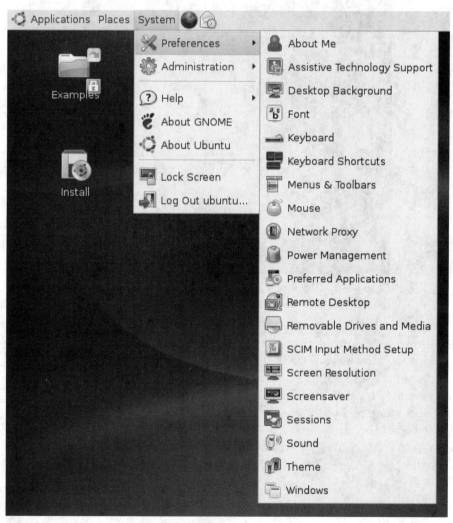

Figure 2–10   The Preferences submenu allows you to change your personal settings.

Tip Near the top left of your screen are two very interesting icons. The Examples folder contains a number of sample documents, spreadsheets, images, and multimedia files to try with your Ubuntu Linux system. The Install icon, meanwhile, is your starting point for installing the Ubuntu Linux live DVD permanently onto your hard disk. I'll discuss those steps shortly.

The Preferences menu is all about personalizing the user experience, something I'll cover in greater detail in Chapters 3 and 5. Because these are personal options, none of them require administrative privileges. You can set a screensaver, change the background, window decorations, or play with the colors. Pick one of the included themes and give your system a whole new look.

If the fonts look a little small, there's a simple option for changing the size of what you see on the screen. And speaking of your screen, changing the screen resolution is easy and doesn't require that you restart your graphical environment.

Okay, let's wrap up this tour of your system menu with the Administration submenu (see Figure 2-11).

System administration may sound like something most people would rather stay away from, but it's not all that scary. From time to time, you will want to do things on your system that affect everyone who logs in equally. Changes made under Preferences don't affect anyone but the current user, and if your niece, Stephanie, chose some garish desktop colors, it wouldn't affect you when you logged in.

Administration functions cover the gamut from setting up a printer to configuring your Internet access. You can share folders (so others on your home or office network can use them), look at system logs, change the look and feel of the login screen, and add users.

Perhaps one of the most important functions here involves updating and maintaining the packages on your system. Keeping up-to-date is one of the best ways to keep your system humming along nicely, and securely.

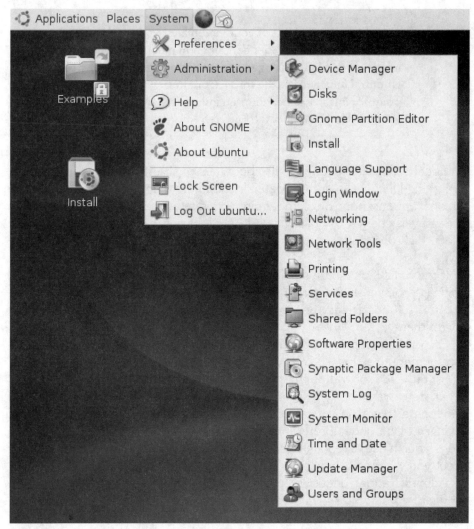

Figure 2–11   Ubuntu's Administration submenu is your starting point to configure your network, check logs, install software, and more.

Installing the Ubuntu Live DVD

After you have played with your Ubuntu Linux live DVD for awhile, I'm confident that you are going to want to make the experience permanent. Linux is far superior to your old OS in many ways and after you install it to your hard drive, Ubuntu Linux will run much faster. Luckily, the process of installing Ubuntu Linux is practically pain free with Ubiquity. Answer a few simple questions and in a few minutes, you'll have Ubuntu installed on your hard disk.

On your desktop, directly below the Examples folder, is an icon labeled Install(see Figure 2-12). Double-click the icon to start the Ubiquity Installer.

Figure 2–12 Double-click the Install
icon to start the Ubiquity installer.

When you do this, the Ubiquity Installer window appears. The first screen is a welcome screen, but it is also a warning that installation is a process that will overwrite your current hard drive configuration (see Figure 2-13).

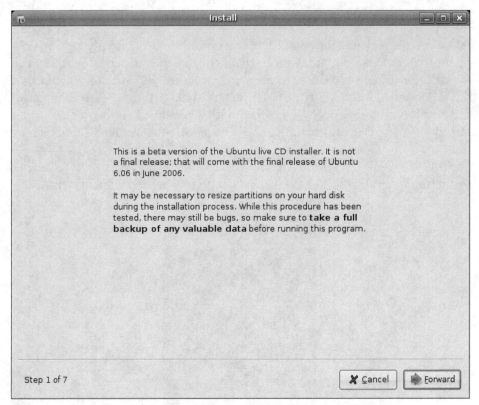

This is a beta version of the Ubuntu live CD installer. It is not a final release; that will come with the final release of Ubuntu 6.06 in June 2006.

It may be necessary to resize partitions on your hard disk during the installation process. While this procedure has been tested, there may still be bugs, so make sure to **take a full backup of any valuable data** before running this program.

Step 1 of 7   ✗ Cancel   ➡ Forward

Figure 2–13   Ubiquity's first screen is mostly a welcome screen, but take note of what it has to say, especially when it comes to backups.

The warnings about making sure you have taken a backup of your data cannot be repeated too many times. Make a backup, then make another backup.

Click the Forward button and you are taken to the installation language selection screen (see Figure 2-14). This language will also be the default language when the system is fully installed. English is selected by default, but Ubuntu has been internationalized for dozens of languages. There's no Klingon here, but Esperanto is available.

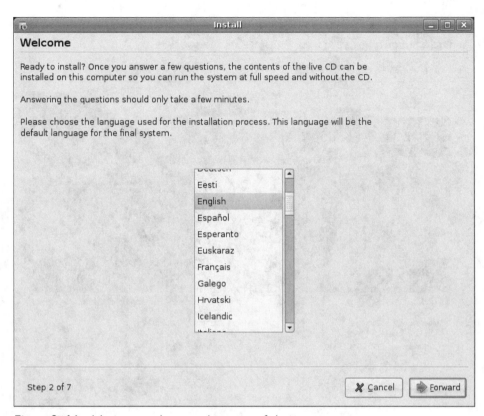

Figure 2–14   It's time to select your language of choice.

Make your choice, then click Forward to continue. The next screen is labeled "Where are you?" This is where you set your location and time zone. Select your location by clicking on the map. One click will zoom you in to an area from which you can fine tune your selection. There's also a drop down box labeled "Selected City" that you can use to the same effect but clicking on the map is more fun. Click Forward to continue.

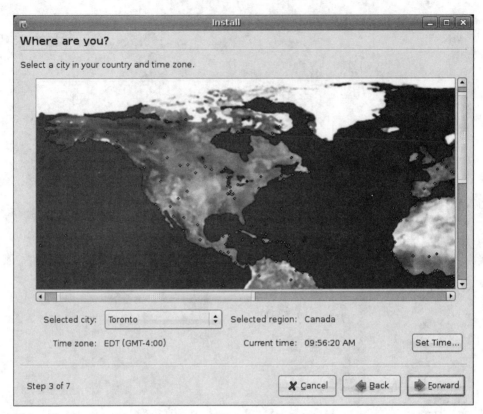

Figure 2–15   *Select your location and time zone by clicking the map.*

The next screen, labeled "Keyboard layout" sounds very much like the language selection screen (see Figure 2-16). Nevertheless, your keyboard layout may not necessarily reflect your language of choice. As a bilingual Canadian, I still use a keyboard with an "American English" layout because that selection most closely reflects my notebook's keyboard. If you have an alternative keyboard, make your selection, then use the input box at the bottom of the screen to test your selection.

Figure 2–16 The keyboard selection screen provides a text box so you can test your hardware.

When you are satisfied, click Forward. A new window labeled "Who are you?" will appear. This is the personal identification window from which your initial user login will be created (see Figure 2-17).

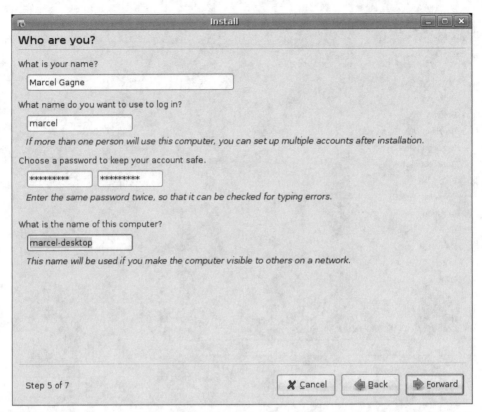

Figure 2–17 Both you and your computer need a name. The username you specify here is that of the primary user. You can add users later.

Enter your full name in the "What is your name?" field. In the second field labeled "What name do you want to use to log in?" select a username, preferably eight characters or fewer (although this isn't a hard and fast rule), and tab to the Password field. When you enter the password, it is echoed back as stars (or asterisks) so don't worry if you can't see what you are typing. After this, you must enter the password again. This is to make sure that you typed what you thought you typed in the first password field. Finally, under the heading "What is the name of this computer?" enter a hostname for your system. By default, the installer will append "-desktop" to your username, but you are free to select something else.

Click Forward and Ubiquity's partitioning tool starts. A small window appears titled Starting up the partitioner. A progress bar keeps you posted as your disks are scanned and analyzed. A few seconds later, the main partitioning window appears. It is labeled "Select a disk." Most people will have just one disk but if you have multiple disks, select one here and click Forward. The next window, labeled "Prepare disk space," lets you select the amount of space you are willing to allocate (see Figure 2-18).

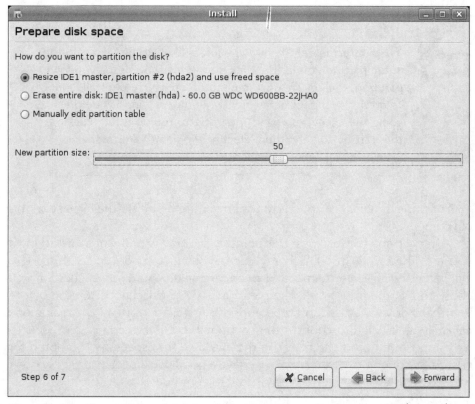

Figure 2–18 The partitioner's job is to help you create a place on your disk (or disks) to install your Ubuntu system.

The information you see on the partitioning screen will vary from system to system. My test system has two hard drives to choose from. Yours may have a single drive with a Windows partition that you are happy to overwrite. Notice the first option in the list. It provides an option for resizing the current partition. This is particularly useful for those who are running Windows on their system and would like to have Ubuntu and Windows co-exist (yes, it is possible). If you select this option, the slider at the bottom of the list activates and you can use it to select the percentage of space you would like to have freed up.

Tip Unfortunately, Windows is just as likely to be taking up the entire partition table. The trick is to *shrink* the existing Windows partition, thereby creating some space on which to install Linux. To do this, you must defragment your disk in Windows before going ahead and resizing your partitions. You do this by clicking the Start button and then selecting Programs | Accessories | System Tools | Disk Defragmenter.

For this example, I've chosen to use the entire first disk (the biggest on this old computer).

After clicking forward past this point, a warning window appears asking if you are "Ready to install." The choices you have made up to this point, including language, username, and so on, are all repeated for you here. If you chose to use the entire disk, like me, this is your last chance to stop before your hard drive is erased in preparation for installation. Read the dialog box carefully as it will also confirm the partitions to be created—this is particularly important if you chose to use the available free space or you opted for custom partitioning. If you are ready, have a good backup, or you simply don't care about what's on the PC, click Install to continue.

Tip Have I mentioned that you should have a good backup of your system, in particular, your personal data?

A dialog box appears informing you of the progress as your disks are partitioned and formatted (see Figure 2-19).

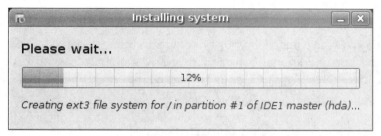

Figure 2-19 A status bar informs you of the progress as your disks are partitioned and formatted.

Although the excitement may be running high at this point, what happens next is only so exciting, and the amount of time it takes depends largely on how fast your processor is, how much memory your system has, and how fast your disk drives are. This is usually a good place to walk away and get a snack and something to drink. If you feel so inclined, you can watch the progress bar as your system is prepared and installed (see Figure 2-20).

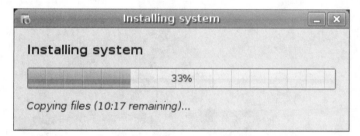

Figure 2-20 Besides providing a graphical status on the install process, the window also tries to provide a time estimate to completion.

Some time before that bar hits 100 percent, you'll see a message at the bottom of the progress window informing you that it is configuring the system, creating the user, and configuring hardware, network, bootloader, and so on. These are the final steps in creating your new Ubuntu Linux system from the live DVD.

When the installation completes, a final dialog appears. Click "Reboot the computer" to finish the process. The system shuts down and the DVD is ejected. Make sure you remove the DVD, then press Enter to reboot your system.

Remember to Share

Now that you have installed your system from the included DVD, feel free to make and burn additional copies of this disk and share it with friends. The license under which Ubuntu Linux is covered makes this perfectly legal.

Resources

Ubuntu Linux on the Internet

`http://www.ubuntu.com`

Chapter

3

Getting Your Hands Dirty (Desktop Overview)

Welcome to the multiuser, multitasking, multieverything world. Linux is designed to run multiple users and processes concurrently. This means your system is capable of doing many things, even while it appears to be idle. This is the reason so many businesses and organizations use Linux as a Web server, email server, file server, print server . . . well, you get the idea.

From the perspective of the individual user, this means that all users in your family (or office) can have desktop environments that are truly theirs and theirs alone. Your desktop can be configured and modified to let you work the way you want, with different backgrounds, icons, colors, or themes, depending on your mood. It also protects your personal information from others, meaning that the kids can totally change their desktops and reorganize things but you won't be in any way affected when you log in.

I'll have you logging in very shortly, but for the moment, I want to say a few words about your new desktop.

Getting to Know You . . . GNOME

Linux is extremely flexible. Linux makes it possible to run in a number of different desktop environments. The plus side of this is that *you* decide how you want to work. Your system works the way you want it to and not the other way around. The down side is exactly the same. Let's face it, being told what to do is often easier, even if it means getting used to working in a way that you may not particularly like at first—not necessarily better, but easier.

On that note, at some time when you've gotten comfortable with your Linux system running the GNOME desktop, you may want to try one of the other graphical desktop environments that are available to Linux users. You may have already heard of the K Desktop Environment (KDE) desktop. Between it and GNOME, you've got the two most popular desktop environments in the Linux world. There's another version of Ubuntu called Kubuntu that uses the KDE desktop by default; in Chapter 20, I'll show you how to add the Kubuntu desktop to your Ubuntu Linux system. The beauty of this is that you can then flip back and forth between the different desktop environments. Why would you want to do this? Quite simply, you may find yourself totally taken with a different way of doing things. All your programs will still work as they did, but the *feel* of your desktop—the *experience*, if you prefer— will be all yours. For now, we'll stick to GNOME.

Note I've covered the KDE desktop in detail in some of my other books including the latest version of *Moving to Linux: Kiss the Blue Screen of Death Goodbye!*

A Few Words About X

After I start showing you around your desktop, what I am telling you now will fade into the background of your memory, but I still think you should know: GNOME, that great-looking desktop system, is the friendly face that rides above your Linux system's real graphical engine. That engine is called the *X window system*, or simply *X*. GNOME, your desktop environment, provides control of windows, borders, decorations, colors, icons, and so on.

When you installed your system, you went through a graphical desktop configuration step of some kind. That wasn't GNOME, but X.

X is what the desktop—and every graphical program you run—*really* runs on. Let's log in and see what the excitement on the desktop is all about.

Logging In

Your workstation will boot up to a graphical login screen known as a *login manager*. More specifically in this case, it is the *GNOME Display Manager*, or GDM (see Figure 3-1). Near the center of the screen, there is a box labeled Username. Entering this information changes the label to Password. Remember that both the username and the accompanying password are case-sensitive, so you must type both as they were created. You can always change the password at a later time. (I'll tell you about it a little later in the chapter.)

Aside from logging in, this screen also lets you select a language and a session type. You do this by clicking the Options button in the lower left of the screen. The session type is GNOME, by default. If you do wind up installing KDE at a later time, you can click the Session button to switch to a different desktop. With a standard Ubuntu install, you do also have the option of logging in to a failsafe desktop with limited options. For now, we'll skip that and log in using the default GNOME desktop.

Figure 3–1   The Ubuntu graphical login manager.

Enter your username and press <Enter>. The login manager then asks you to enter your password. Ubuntu logs you in to a default desktop with a given look and feel that you can change to suit your needs and tastes, something we'll talk about in detail in the next chapter.

Becoming One with the Desktop

Your Ubuntu Linux screen has two panels, one at the top of the screen and one below. Each provides quick access to different functions, which I'll cover individually. Let's start with the top panel (see Figure 3-2).

Figure 3–2   This is the Ubuntu/GNOME top panel. The right and left sides of the panel are zoomed in for more detail.

The Applications starter in the top left is similar to the Start button on that other OS. Clicking here drops down a menu of menus, a list of installed applications that you can run with a single click. Two other menus follow, one labeled Places, and the other System. Places concerns itself with your storage media including disks, mounted CDs, USB storage keys, and so on. System covers system functions such as logging out, shutting down, changing personal preferences, and administering your Ubuntu Linux system. Finally, to the right of the System menu, there may be one or more icons providing ready access to a popular application. In a standard Ubuntu installation, you'll see one for Firefox (the Web browser) and one for Evolution (an email client).

Let's move to the far right of the top panel, just before the clock. As you run more and more programs, you might notice small icons embedded in the panel, next to the speaker icon. These icons also represent programs, but running programs hidden more or less out of sight (this saves clutter in the panel). These applications have been iconified (*swallowed*) by the panel and can be called up with a click. That mini-icon area is called the *notification area*. In Figure 3-3, you can see the Rhythmbox music player, the Gaim Instant Messenger icon, and the system update notification applet.

Figure 3–3 The three icons on the left side are in the notification area of the top panel.

Speaking of running applications, let's take a look at the bottom panel (see Figure 3-4). When you start an application, you see it listed in a portion of the bottom panel known as the *window list* (you may know it as the taskbar). This not only shows you what you have running on your desktop, but it also provides a quick way to switch from process to process. Just click the program in the window list. Alternatively, you can press <Alt+Tab> to switch from one running program to another. The window list can be configured to list all processes from all desktops, group similar processes together, or simply show you what is on your current workspace.

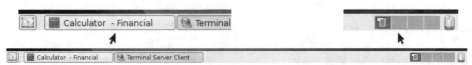

Figure 3–4 The bottom Ubuntu/GNOME panel. Once again, the left and right sides of the panel are zoomed to show detail.

Workspaces, sometimes referred to as virtual desktops, are one feature you are going to absolutely *love*! On the default installation, you'll notice four little squares on the right side of the bottom panel. This is your desktop switcher, allowing you to switch between any of the four virtual desktops with a mouse click. Think of it as having a computer monitor that is four times as large as the one you already have, with each desktop running different things. You can leave each one the way you want it without having to minimize windows so that you can come back to the virtual desktop later and see everything as you left it. It gets better: You can have four, five, six, or even more virtual desktops if you find that four aren't enough for you (see Figure 3-5).

To change the number of workspaces, right-click any of the workspace squares and select Preferences from the pop-up menu. A window labeled Workspace Switcher Preferences appears listing, among other things, the number of workspaces. Change that number to whatever you like.

Figure 3–5   The desktop switcher with six virtual desktops.

Finally, there's a little wastebasket icon to the far right. You can drag and drop files and folders into the trash can, but you can also click the trash can to see the contents (that is, items you deleted). We'll talk further about the wastebasket shortly.

Your First Application

It's time to really get into this, nail down some terminology, and get you working with the system. Starting a program or opening up an application is as simple as clicking an icon. Let's do that. In fact, let's open up *the* great GNOME application, *Nautilus*.

You'll be using Nautilus a lot. This is the GNOME file manager and it lets you work with files and folders. Nautilus makes it easy to create folders (or directories, as they are known in the Linux world), copy, delete, and move other folders and files around by dragging and dropping from one to the other. Nautilus is also a universal file viewer so you can view and organize your photo collection, preview documents, and much, much more.

There are several ways to get Nautilus running on your desktop, but let's start by clicking Places in the top panel and selecting Home Folder from the drop-down menu. This opens the Nautilus file browser in your home directory. The window that opens looks something like Figure 3-6, minus a few folders and documents, of course.

On the left, Nautilus shows a small list of important places on your system, primarily in your home folder. This side panel is the *navigation panel*. Pressing <F9> hides (or brings forward) the navigation panel. Beside the Places label, there is an arrow, alerting you to the fact that this is actually a button with a drop-down list of options. Click here and you can switch between a list of your places, information on the current folder, notes regarding the information in those folders, and an easy-to-navigate tree-like view of your file system.

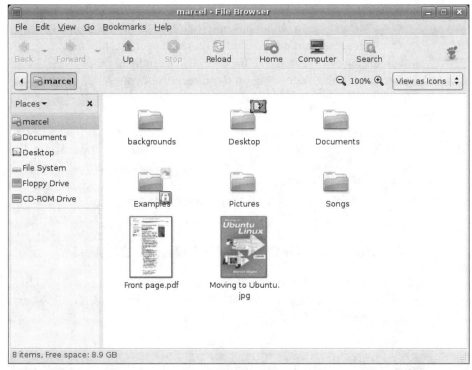

Figure 3–6 Introducing Nautilus, the all-purpose file manager, also called the File Browser.

On the right, the contents of the current place (or location) are displayed. If this is a directory (like your home directory), the various directories appear as folder icons. Depending on how Nautilus is configured, images in your folders may appear as little thumbnails. Would you like to see the full-sized image? Just click the thumbnail, and Nautilus calls the right application to do the rest.

Quick Tip I've made the icons large, which makes the thumbnail images easy to view. To change the icon size, click View on the menu bar, then select Zoom In until the icons are the size you prefer. Just what is the menu bar? Read on.

Quick Tip Got a wheel mouse? Then try this tip for changing the icon sizes. Hold down <Ctrl> and scroll over the files and folders in your Nautilus file browser. The icons increase or decrease in size depending on the direction of your scroll.

Nautilus is flexible, powerful, and definitely worth your time to get to know. In fact, it will likely become your most used desktop application. I'm going to give the Nautilus File Browser the focus and consideration it deserves in the next chapter. For the moment, leave Nautilus where it is and read on as we discuss windows—and I don't mean the operating system.

Windows, Title Bars, and Menus, Oh My!

Each graphical program that runs on your desktop has certain common characteristics. Have a look at the top of your Nautilus File Browser window, and you will see something like Figure 3-7.

Figure 3–7   Most windows have a title bar, as well as a menu bar.

The Title Bar

The top bar on a running program is called the *title bar*. Depending on the application, it may display a program name, a document you are working on, a location on the Web, or a nice description explaining what you are running. Left-clicking the title bar and dragging it with the mouse moves the program window around on your desktop.

Quick Tip Most modern desktops assume a monitor running at a resolution of at least 1024×768, and a number of applications assume this to be a universal truth. This plays havoc when your monitor is smaller than this (say, 800×600) and the buttons you need to click are offscreen. Clicking the title bar and dragging the window gets you only so far, especially if the title bar is offscreen.

Don't despair. By pressing the <Alt> key and left-clicking a window, you can drag it anywhere you want, including beyond the boundaries of your desktop. This is particularly handy if you need to get at a hidden OK button.

Double-clicking the title bar maximizes the program window—the application suddenly takes up the whole screen. Double-click it again and the window returns to its original size.

The title bar also has a number of small icons. Pause your mouse cursor over them, and a tooltip informs you of their functions. Starting at the left corner of the title bar is a small icon that a tooltip identifies as a *Window Menu*. Clicking here brings up a small drop-down menu that makes it possible to move the program to another workspace, and to minimize or maximize the application (among other things).

One of the other items in the drop-down menu is labeled On Top. Selecting this makes the window lighter, so it always floats above the others, regardless of which one you have selected. Okay, so it doesn't really float, but it will always appear above any other window, even if you click that window.

The other item I want you to notice is related to the whole workspace concept and that's the entry labeled Always on Visible Workspace. The best way to understand this one is to try it. Click one of your other three workspaces. If you haven't already excitedly opened dozens of other programs on each one, you should find yourself with a nice, clean desktop. Now, go back to your first workspace. Click the window menu and select Always on Visible Workspace. Now, jump to workspace 2. Nautilus is there. Click workspace 3, and it is there also. In fact, if you had 10 workspaces defined, Nautilus would be waiting for you on all of them.

Here's a cool bit of information. You are still running only *one* instance of Nautilus. It's just that it is available to you on every workspace. Finally, let's assume that you made Nautilus available to every workspace while you were on workspace 1 and you are now on workspace 3. Click the window menu and select Only on This Workspace. Workspace 3 is now Nautilus' new home, and it ceases to be available on the other workspaces, including workspace 1, where it started.

All of the things I've mentioned—maximizing, minimizing, and making an application visible on all desktops—can be implemented from the window list icon for any running application. Right-click the window list icon and select what you need from the pop-up menu (see Figure 3-8).

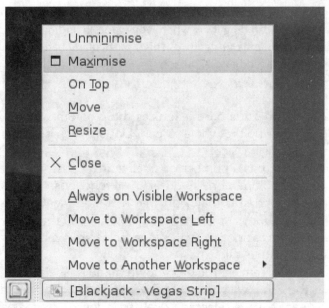

Figure 3–8   Right-click window list icons in the bottom panel to bring up the window action menu.

Before we move on to other things, we need to look at the buttons on the right side of the title bar. You use the leftmost icon, the one with an *underscore* (or a small straight line, if you prefer), to minimize a window (remember that you can pause over the top with your mouse button to get the tooltip). The icon with a square in the center maximizes a window, causing it to take up every bit of space on your desktop except for the space taken up by your panels. Finally, the X does pretty much what you would expect it to: It closes a running application.

On to the Menu Bar

Directly below the title bar is the *menu bar*. The menu bar generally has a number of labels (such as File, Edit, View, and so on), each grouping the various tasks you can do into some kind of sensible order.

Every program has a different set of menu options, depending on the nature of the application. Clicking a menu label drops down a list of options for that function (see Figure 3-9).

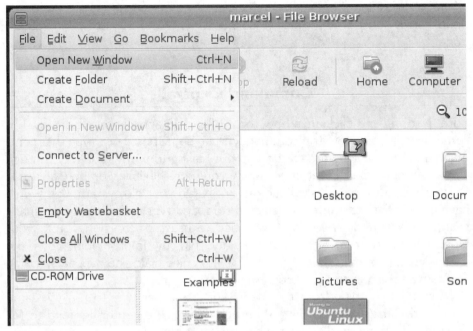

Figure 3–9   The File drop-down menu.

And the Wastebasket?

Yes, I did say that I would talk further about the wastebasket. I want to give you a taste of what I am going to cover in the next chapter. If you haven't done so, close Nautilus. Now, look down to the wastebasket icon in the lower-right corner of the bottom panel and click it, just once.

A Nautilus window appears labeled Trash - File Browser. That's because the wastebasket is just another folder on your system and Nautilus can browse it as easily as your home folder. We'll be seeing a lot more of Nautilus in Chapter 4.

Resizing Windows

The last thing you should know is that (for the most part) you aren't stuck with the default window size. By grabbing any of the corners of an application window, you can drag that corner and stretch the window to a size that is more comfortable for you. The same applies to the top, bottom, and sides of a program window.

As you position the cursor on a corner or a side, you'll see it change to a double arrow. Just drag the side or corner to where you want it, and you are done.

Command Central

Sure, pointing and clicking is how most of us run applications. It's easy, but sometimes, if you know the command, it can be faster to just type that command and tell the program to run without having to work your way through all those menus. Better yet, it can allow you more flexibility on how an application runs, but I'm getting ahead of myself. On your old system, you would have clicked the Start button, selected Run, and typed something in, usually **setup** because that is when you tended to use the Run option. On your Ubuntu Linux system, you can do the same thing by simply holding down the <Alt> key and pressing <F2> (<Alt+F2>). A nice dialog box appears, asking you to type the name of the program you want to run.

Clicking something from the menu is just another way to run the same command. That's why, as we go through this book together, I intend to tell you what the command name is whenever possible. (If you really aren't interested, you can just skip over it.) Are you wondering what those programs are called? Well, just as there is more than one way to, er, um, feed the proverbial cat (this is a friendly book, folks), there is more than one way to find out what a running command is called. If you are curious to discover everything there is to know about running processes, check out the advanced command-line chapter, Chapter 21. At this moment, I'll tell you about one, graphical way.

 Tip In case you are curious, the program name for Nautilus is `nautilus`.

On the top panel, click System, Preferences, and finally Sessions. A three-tabbed Sessions window appears. Click the middle tab, the one labeled Current Session, and you'll see a list of currently running programs for your graphical session. This isn't a list of every program running on your system, just the ones associated with your GNOME session. Scroll down to the last command in the list (it will vary from system to system). After you've done that, click the Applications menu, navigate to Accessories, and start the Calculator program. Now, look back at your Sessions window and the list of running programs. (You may have to scroll down again.) A new program called `gcalctool` should have appeared at the bottom of the list (see Figure 3-10). That's what the calculator program is called.

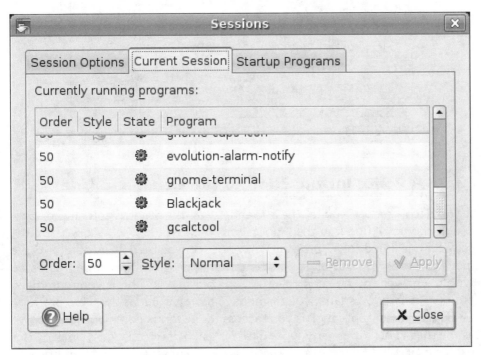

Figure 3–10   The Sessions Preference tool can show you what programs are running under GNOME.

The Sessions Preference tool isn't meant to be a process listing tool. In fact, it is designed to control what programs are running during a session, whether those programs should automatically be started when you log in, and what the state of those programs should be at session start. Nevertheless, it's a quick and interesting way to see programs come and go and to identify them by name.

To recap, when you know the program name (for example, the calculator), pressing <Alt+F2>, typing **gcalctool** in the dialog box, and pressing <Enter> is the same as going through the menus. Have a look at Figure 3-11 for an example.

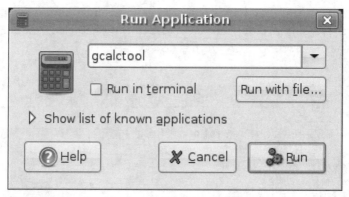

Figure 3–11   Running a command with <Alt+F2>.

A Polite Introduction to the Command Line

It's time to introduce you to a new friend. Okay, the friend is actually an application and you'll find it in the Applications menu under Accessories. On the surface, this friend (okay, *program*) may not seem as friendly as others you've met, but after you get to know the *terminal* program, you'll be impressed with the power and fine control it puts in your hands. This is your command prompt. In Windows-land, you might have thought of it as the DOS prompt.

The terminal application is your access to the Linux command line, known as the shell. There are many types of shells, each of which works similarly (for example, all allow you to run commands), but each may have different capabilities. The default on Linux is called bash, the *GNU Bourne-Again SHell*.

The shell is powerful, and learning about its capabilities will make you a wizard of the Linux world. Become one with the shell, and nothing can stop you. The shell is the land of the Linux systems guru and the administrator. For the most part, you can do just about anything you need to do by staying and working with the X window system and your Ubuntu GNOME desktop. Here's another treat. Although the graphical interface makes things friendly and easy-to-use, there are times when working from the shell can be so much faster. Despite the fact that you can do pretty much everything you need to do from the graphical desktop, every once in a while, I will ask you to do something from the shell prompt.

As time goes on, you too will *feel the power* of the Linux shell.

Give Me More!

For those of you who get to the end of the chapters in this book and find yourselves wanting to know *more* about the shell, check out Appendix A.

Here's our polite introduction. Click the Terminal menu item and a rather empty window appears. Along the top is a menu bar with some quick access items arranged according to how they affect the terminal session. Below that, in the larger part of the window, you see a flashing cursor sitting beside a dollar sign prompt. This is the shell prompt. Whenever you find yourself at a shell prompt, the system is waiting for you to type in a command. Remember the calculator example from earlier? You could type **gcalctool** here and have it start up just as easily. For now, type **date** at the shell prompt, and press the <Enter> key (see Figure 3-12).

Figure 3–12   The GNOME terminal program with the results of the date command.

Now that you know the date and time that I wrote this paragraph, when you try it, you'll get your current date and time. That's what date is: a command that displays the date and time. You'll also find yourself back at the shell prompt as your system patiently awaits your next command. Type **exit** and press the <Enter> key.

The terminal program disappears. That's it. We'll use the shell again as we go through this book, but for now, your polite introduction to the shell ends here.

 Funny Tip Be careful not to type **ddate** instead of **date**. You will wind up with the Discordian Date, a numbering system from the Church of the Subgenius. For instance:

```
$ ddate
```

Today is Sweetmorn, the 46th day of Chaos in the YOLD 3172

Changing Your Password; It's All About You!

It is good security policy to change your password from time to time. Look along the top panel and click System, Preferences. Right at the top, you should see an entry labeled About Me. A personal information window appears, from which you can change or fill in a great deal of personal information (see Figure 3-13). You can also run the command as in the calculator example above by using your <Alt+F2> run sequence and typing the command **gnome-about-me**.

You might be asking why Ubuntu provides a space for all these details about you. You don't have to fill in any information here, but several applications do look here. For instance, in Chapter 11, I'll tell you all about the Evolution email package and its contact management functions. In your Evolution address book, there's an entry created for you, which you can send as a virtual business card. The real point of this exercise, however, is to change your password. Click the Change Password button in the top right corner. Doing so brings up the Change Password dialog shown in Figure 3-14.

Notice that, like the login manager, your password is not visible. Instead, each key you press is echoed as an asterisk. When you have successfully entered your password, the system asks you for a new password. Then, you are asked for the password again, for confirmation. That's it. Be sure to remember your new password. You'll need it the next time you log in.

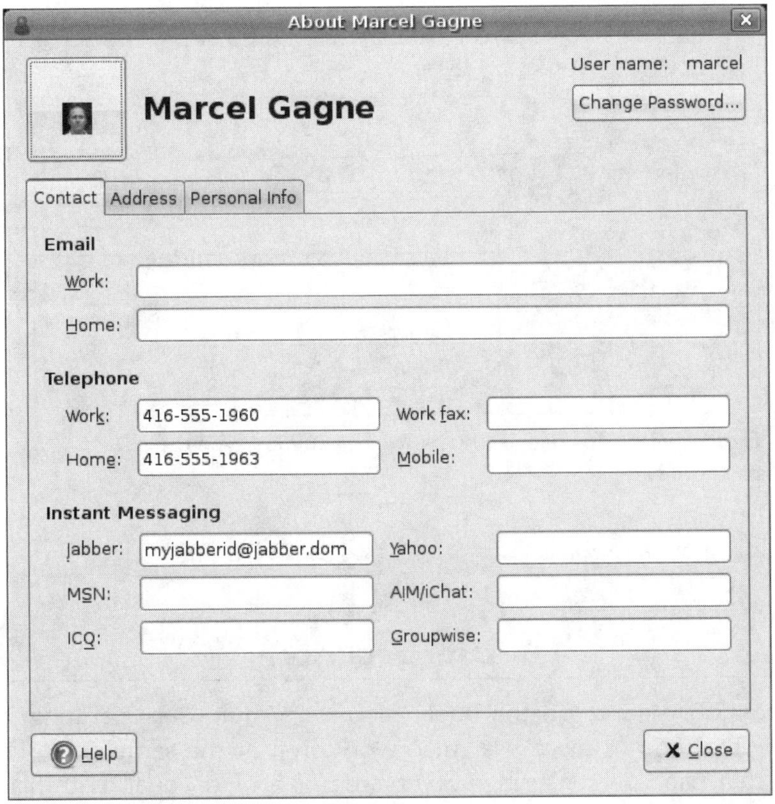

Figure 3–13 The About Me dialog provides quick access to your personal information. It also happens to be a way to change your password.

Shell Out You can easily change your password from the command line as well. Just open a shell prompt and type the command:

```
[marcel@mysystem marcel]$ passwd
Changing password for user marcel.
Changing password for marcel
(current) UNIX password:
New UNIX password:
Retype new UNIX password:
passwd: all authentication tokens updated successfully.
```

Although the steps are essentially the same, the wording of the actual password change dialog can change from system to system.

Figure 3–14   To change your password, you must type the new password twice.

Speaking of passwords . . .

User Security

As I mentioned earlier in the book, Linux is a multiuser operating system, meaning that one or more users can work on it at the same time. This *also* means that each person using your system is an individual, with his or her own home directories, files, menus, and desktop decorations. By creating a login for each member of your family or office, you not only protect the files that belong to each user, but you also protect yourself. If little Natika deletes all her icons or changes the desktop to a *garish green and purple*, it doesn't affect you. Similarly, this is a great opportunity to create a play world for the kids.

Each user is referenced by a username. Each username has a *user ID* (UID) associated with it and one or more groups. Like usernames, group names are also represented by a numeric identifier, this time called a *group ID* (GID). A user's UID is unique, as is a group's GID.

Adding users requires that you operate as root, so when you launch the GNOME users administration tool (command name `users-admin`), you are asked for your password. When the program starts, a window appears like the one in Figure 3-15. There are two tabs, one for Users and the other for Groups.

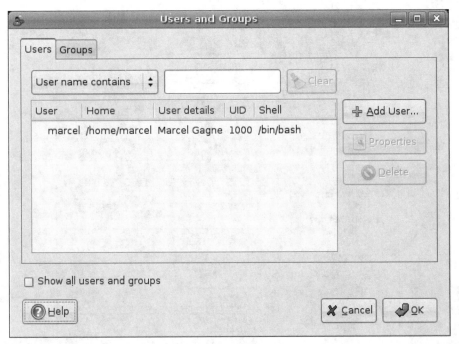

Figure 3–15 The GNOME users administration tool.

By default, only nonadministrative user accounts are shown. With a fresh Ubuntu installation, that generally means only one user, the one you set up at install time. To see all users on the system, click the Show All Users and Groups check box at the lower left. To add a user, click the Add User button on the right. A new window, the User Account Editor, appears (see Figure 3-16).

Most of the information on this page is optional. In fact, all you need to enter is a username and a password. The other fields are provided to further identify the person for whom you are creating the login. For instance, you can choose to enter his or her full name, office location, phone number, and so on.

The most important part of this process has to do with entering the password information. By default, you have the opportunity to Set Password by Hand. The radio button for this area should already be selected. Choose a password and enter it into the User Password field. You must enter it twice, the second time in the Confirmation field. Note that when you do enter the password, you don't actually see it, but rather stars echo your keystrokes. You can also ask the program to generate a random password by selecting the last radio button, then clicking the Generate button. When you are done, click OK.

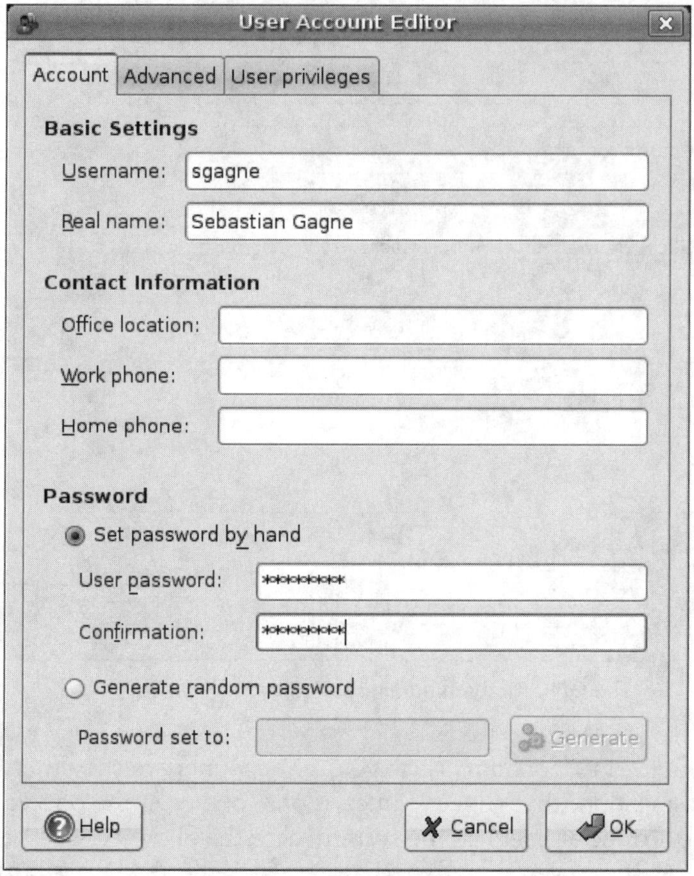

Figure 3–16 Setting user properties.

This takes you back to the Users and Groups screen, where you can simply click OK to finish. Of course, you can also add more users.

Much Ado About sudo

When you start a graphical command that requires administrative privileges, a dialog appears asking you for your password. This dialog is actually a command called gksudo. In turn, gksudo is a wrapper for a shell command called sudo.

For those of you who may have used other Linux (or UNIX) systems, you may have had access to an account called root. This is the superuser account with ultimate power over the system. Ubuntu locks down the root account and does not allow a direct login. To execute commands with root privileges, Ubuntu makes use of the sudo command.

When you run a program with sudo (or gksudo), you are asked for your password to confirm access. After entering your password, your account can execute additional root-level commands for the next 15 minutes without having to reenter your password. That said, you still need to preface your commands with sudo or gksudo.

To run a command inside a GNOME terminal session, or a command shell, preface the command with sudo.

```
sudo command_name
```

From time to time, you may need to run several commands with root privileges. At those times, it may get a little tiring to prefix each and every command with sudo. To get around this, you can enter a session with administrative privileges by typing the following.

```
sudo -i
```

When you are through with your admin session, type **exit**.

In Chapter 21, I give an extended tour of the command shell. There, you will have additional opportunity to see sudo in action.

 Note Always use gksudo when running graphical applications that need administrative privileges.

I Need More Help!

Way back in the introduction to the book, I gave you a list of places that you might look to for help, some online and others in the community. As it turns out, your desktop has a very handy and fairly impressive collection of help, right at your fingertips.

The GNOME documentation browser, or Help Center, if you prefer (command name yelp) is something you've probably already guessed at.

Look at your top panel and click the System menu where you'll find a sub-menu for Help. The documentation browser is labeled System Documentation. To start the program, click the icon. When the documentation browser opens, you'll see something similar to Figure 3-17.

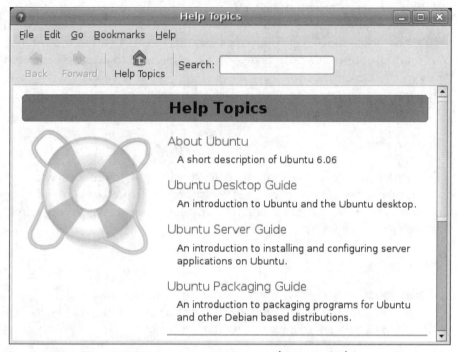

Figure 3–17   The GNOME documentation browser (Help Center).

The documentation browser is very much like a Web browser with left and right arrow keys for navigation and a quick return Help Topics button that takes you back to the start. The documentation browser provides online help for basic individual applications, a command reference (manual pages), as well as some tutorials. Just click the links to go to highlighted sections, or click the forward and back arrows to navigate the documents.

Logging Out

I started this chapter by having you log in to your Ubuntu system, and it seems fitting that I end it by having you log out. Take a look at the right corner of your top panel. You should see a little icon that looks like an open door with an arrow pointing out. When you are done your work and it's time to log out, click the door and the Exit dialog appears offering you a handful of choices (see Figure 3-18).

Figure 3–18   The Exit dialog provides a lot of options for logging out or shutting down your system.

The first and most obvious choice is to Log Out, which returns your system to the log on screen I discussed at the beginning of this chapter. You've come full circle.

Switch User is probably the most interesting option here. This option takes you back to a login screen so another user can log in and start using the system, but leaves your current session active. To switch back to the first user logged in, press <Ctrl+Alt+F7>. To switch to the second user, press <Ctrl+Alt+F8>, and so on. Why would you want to use this feature? Because it lets you quickly switch from one user's desktop to another without having to go through all the steps of logging out and logging back in. In a busy family, this can be a real time saver.

The final four options are all variations on the theme of shutting down. It's just a question of how far and how long you take this shutting down. For starters, you can Restart (or reboot) your system. You can also send it into

Sleep or Hibernate mode. The difference between the two is that your system effectively powers off in hibernate mode but with your session saved until you power your system back on. If you were in the middle of typing a document, you'll be back in the middle of that document when you restart your system. Sleep is a reduced power mode where you can just hit any key to bring your system back to life.

 Note Not all computer hardware supports Sleep or Hibernate modes.

Finally, the Shut Down option is a total shut down of all your processes followed by a power down (if your hardware supports it). The system stays off until you power it back on. Unlike hibernation, you find yourself back at the main login screen.

Navigating Your Ubuntu Desktop

Now that you and your system have been *properly* introduced, it is time to do some exploring. In the next chapter, you are going to learn to wield Nautilus to navigate, work with, and otherwise unlock the mysteries of your Ubuntu Linux system.

Resources

The Ubuntu Document Storage Facility
    http://doc.gwos.org

The Official Ubuntu Documentation Site
    http://help.ubuntu.com

4

Navigating Nautilus

Nothing on your computer is more important than data. Other than playing games (and even there), computers are about storing and dealing with information. That's why being able to work well with that data—moving, copying, renaming, and deleting it—is vitally important to getting comfortable in your Linux world.

That means it is time to revisit your new old friend, Nautilus, the GNOME file browser.

Files, Directories, and the Root of All Things

There's a saying in the Linux world that "everything is a file" (a comment attributed to Ken Thompson, the developer of UNIX). That includes directories. Directories are just files with lists of files inside them. All these files and directories are organized into a hierarchical file system, starting from the root directory and branching out.

 Note Folders and directories are the same thing. The terms can be used interchangeably. I tend to think of them as directories, but if you are more comfortable thinking of them as folders, don't worry. Depending on the application, you'll see both terms used.

The root directory (referred to as *slash*, or /) is aptly named. If you consider your file system as a tree's root system spreading out below the surface, you start to get an idea of just what things look like. Under the root directory, you'll find folders called usr, bin, etc, tmp, and so on. Let's open Nautilus and have a look at this structure.

Click Places on your top panel and select Home Folder. This brings up the file browser in your home folder. If your navigation panel isn't up (Nautilus' left side panel), press <F9> to open it. You'll see a number of entries, including your home directory. On the left, Nautilus shows a small list of important places on your system, primarily in your home folder. This side panel is the *navigation panel*. Pressing <F9> hides (or brings forward) the navigation panel. Beside the Places label, there is an arrow, alerting you to the fact that this is actually a button with a drop-down list of options. Click that button now and select Tree for your view. In all likelihood, you'll see two entries: one for Home Folder and another for File System. To the left of each entry is a small arrow. Click the one beside File System (or double-click the folder) to get a top-down view of your Ubuntu Linux system (see Figure 4-1).

On the right, the contents of the current place (or location) are displayed. If this is a directory (like your home directory), the various directories will appear as folder icons. These are all system directories, and they will contain all the programs that make your Linux system run, including documentation, devices, and device drivers. For the most part, you aren't going to be touching the files under File System. Accidentally changing things around in this part of your system probably isn't a good thing (it could render your system inoperative), which is why everyone logs in with their own accounts.

Figure 4–1   Nautilus, the GNOME file browser, with a top-down view of the Ubuntu Linux file system. This view is selected from the navigation panel on the left.

Tip   When you look at your files and folders in Nautilus, they are arranged alphabetically. Usually, this is what you want, but you can also sort them by size, modification date, file type, and more. Just click View on the Nautilus menu bar and check out the Arrange Items submenu. You can even choose to arrange them manually.

One of the directories under the root is called home and inside that directory, you'll discover other directories, one for each login name on your system. These are the individual home directories, and it is where you'll find your personal files and directories. If you want to store personal documents, music files, or pictures, this is the place. Once you are in Nautilus, you can jump to your home directory by clicking the Home icon or clicking Go on the menu bar and selecting Home (keyboard jockeys can just press <Alt+Home>). This is your $HOME.

> *Quick Tip* My use of $HOME isn't just to be silly. The system can recognize some things based on environment variables, symbolic names that can refer to text, numbers, or even commands. In the DOS/Windows world, you had similar variables—for instance, the PATH in your AUTOEXEC.BAT file. $HOME is an environment variable assigned to every person who logs in. It represents a person's home directory. If you want to see all the environment variables assigned to your session, shell out and type the following command:
>
> ```
> env
> ```

Try this. Over on the left side of the Tree view, click the small arrow beside the home directory. As you saw earlier, the Tree view expands to show the folders in your own personal directory. Notice that the right-pointing arrow is now a down-pointing arrow. If you click it again, the directory view collapses. With the home directory expanded, click your personal directory. You should see a few items appear in the right-side view, including one icon labeled Desktop. For an example, see Figure 4-2. On the left side, the home folder is expanded, and the right-side view shows the same folder collapsed.

Before you do anything else, I want you to reopen Nautilus in your home folder (click Places and select Home Folder). There's a very special folder there called Desktop. Now, look down in your bottom panel, over on the far left side of the screen. Do you see the Desktop icon there? It looks like an old-fashioned desktop blotter with a pencil and a piece of paper on it. Pause your mouse cursor over it, and the tooltip displays Click Here to Hide All Windows and Show the Desktop. Click it, and your desktop appears, free of windows. Click it again, and everything returns to normal.

Now, I'm going to briefly jump ahead in the book and have you create a folder on your desktop. Right-click anywhere on that empty desktop and a pop-up menu appears. The top entry in that menu is Create Folder. Click that and a folder appears on your desktop with the label Untitled Folder beneath it (see Figure 4-3). Type in a name and press <Enter>.

Home Expanded   **Home Collapsed**

Figure 4–2   Expanding and collapsing folders in Nautilus'
Tree view.

Figure 4–3
To create a folder on the desktop, right-click
and select New Folder. Then, change the
name of the untitled folder.

I am having you do this because I want you to remember something later when I have you create icons on your desktop. The desktop you are looking at when you work with your Ubuntu system is that Desktop folder in your home directory. If you create a folder on the desktop, use Nautilus to view your home folder, and then double-click the Desktop folder, you will see your newly created folder in the Desktop folder. The same is true for image files or songs or video clips. If it's on your desktop, it's in the Desktop folder. Even those icons on your desktop are files or directories. Cool? Let's move on.

 Shell Out Open a terminal shell by selecting Terminal from the Accessories submenu under the top panel Applications menu. At the shell prompt, type `ls Desktop`. The `ls` command lists the contents of your Desktop directory. Compare what you see there with the icons currently on your graphical desktop. Do the names look familiar? When you are done, type **exit** to close the terminal.

Directories (and subdirectories) usually show up as folders, although this isn't a hard and fast rule because you can customize this. Nevertheless, some directories have different icons right from the start—the Desktop icon you just visited being one of them.

Wherever You Go . . .

To move from folder to folder, you can simply click a folder in the Tree view or double-click a folder icon in the right pane or the Places view. You can also move around the directory tree by using your *cursor keys*. You'll see the highlight bar move from directory to directory. To see the contents in the main window, move to a folder and press <Enter>. To go up a level in the directory tree (rather than folder by folder), press <Alt+Up Arrow>.

There's another way, as well. If you look up at the menu bar, you'll see an up arrow, a left-pointing arrow, and a right-pointing arrow (see Figure 4-4). Next to that is an icon to stop a listing (if it is taking a long time), to reload a location of folder, and finally, and icon labeled Home. Clicking that house icon always takes you back to your personal home directory. Clicking the up arrow moves you up the directory tree, and the left arrow takes you back to whatever directory you were last visiting.

Figure 4–4 The Nautilus file browser's main navigation toolbar.

Tip When you look at your home folder using Nautilus, there are more files and folders than you actually see. So-called hidden files (those prefixed by a dot) aren't shown in the default view. Star Trek fans can think of it as a cloaking device for files. To see all files, including hidden files, click View from the menu bar and select Show Hidden Files. Keyboard jockeys can just press <Ctrl+H> to cycle back and forth between the views.

Sometimes, the quickest way to navigate your file system (assuming you know the folder you want to be in) is simply to type it in the location bar. Looking at Nautilus, you might be wondering where this location bar is. Click Go on the menu bar, then select Location (or press <Ctrl+L>). An empty field labeled Go To appears just below the navigation toolbar (see Figure 4-5). From here, you can type in whatever you want—for example, `/home/marcel/Songs/Rock`. Press <Enter> and the location bar vanishes.

Figure 4–5 To jump quickly to a known folder, open up the location bar and type in the path to that folder.

Search Me . . .

Your Ubuntu Linux system may not have a lot of files in your home folder, but that won't last long; I promise. There's an old adage that suggests, "data will grow to fill all available disk space." In my experience, that's a fact. In time, that big drive of yours just won't seem big enough.

This means that at some point, you are going to have some trouble finding the files you created. It's a good thing Nautilus has a quick find built in. I've got a lot of music ripped on my Linux system (see Chapter 17). I like to listen to it when I work. Let's pretend that I want to find out in which folder my Pink Floyd songs are stored. Just press <Ctrl+F> and a Search box appears. Type in some part of the filename you are searching for (for example, **Pink Floyd**) and press <Enter>. Nautilus displays the results in the main window (see Figure 4-6).

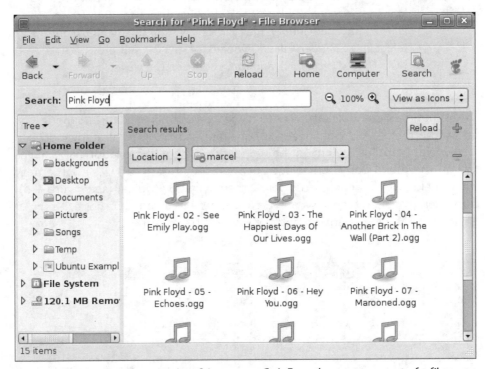

Figure 4–6   Looking for something? Just press <Ctrl+F> and enter some part of a filename to let Nautilus do its thing.

Navigating the Side Panel

We should spend a couple of minutes looking at the left panel—or as I like to call it, the navigation panel. You've already seen how to use it to switch from a Places view to a Tree view of your file system. But wait (as they say on television), there's more. As you recall, there is a drop-down list that lets you change the way you look at your system. I've already had you switch from Places view to Tree view and that has affected how you navigate your file system. However, there are other interesting options in that list and I'd like to look at them now (see Figure 4-7).

Figure 4–7
The left panel provides a number of ways to view, catalog, and identify the content in your folders.

Because we've already covered Places and Tree, I'm going to continue with Information. When you click here, the side window displays information about the current folder. That includes the name of the folder, its icon (you can change the default icon for each folder, which is covered later), the number of items in that folder, and the date it was last modified (when files were added or removed).

The next possible selection is History. Clicking here shows you recent folders you have visited (in the order you visited them), network folders, FTP sites, and any searches you may have performed. This last item is particularly cool because if you need to, you can revisit a particular search by double-clicking it in the history listing. The same holds true for folders. Double-click and there you are.

Tip If you want to be able to quickly come back to a particular folder or site, you can bookmark that location by clicking Bookmarks on the menu bar and selecting Add Bookmark (you can also press <Ctrl+D>). To go back to a bookmark, click Bookmarks again and select it with a click.

Now, we come to Notes. With every folder, you can add notes about the content. This is free-form text that helps you identify the contents or alert you that there is something of note there. For instance, let's say you've got a folder named Holiday Shots and inside that folder is where you keep those really embarrassing photos from the company Christmas party. You might want to add a note to that effect as a reminder a few months later. When you do that, a small note appears to be pinned to your folder (see Figure 4-8).

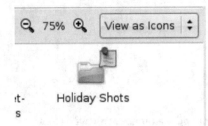

Holiday Shots

Figure 4-8
When you add a note to a folder, a note icon is tacked to the folder icon.

This little added decoration on the folder segues very nicely into the last choice in our little side panel list, and that's the Emblems selection. Click here and the side panel fills up with a list of graphical icons (see Figure 4-9). These are designed to give you a quick way to identify the importance or relevance of a particular file or folder.

All you have to do is click one of those icons and drag it over to a file or folder. There are tons of these emblems with names like Art, Certified, Cool, Favorite, Important, Oh No!, and more. Should you find that you have added too many emblems (since you are doing that right now!), drag the Erase icon (located at the top of the list) onto your file or folder. The emblems you added there vanish.

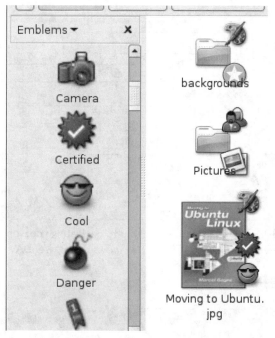

Figure 4–9 Emblems provide a quick and visually interesting way to identify files or folders.

Navigating Networks

When I was telling you about history and bookmarks, I casually tossed out the idea that you could use Nautilus to visit FTP sites and other network locations, including Windows shares, WebDAV servers, and more. To establish a network connection, click File on the Nautilus menu bar and select Connect to Server. A connection dialog appears, from which you can establish your connection (see Figure 4-10).

Next to the Service Type label, there is a drop-down box from which you can select the type of server. Your options are SSH, Public FTP, FTP (with login), Windows share, WebDAV, secure WebDAV, and custom location. For this example, let's choose a public FTP server, one with an anonymous login. In the Server field, enter the name of the server you are trying to connect to (for example, `ftp.ubuntulinux.org`). That's really all you need to do. Click Connect and Nautilus opens that network folder (see Figure 4-11). Navigation of that remote folder is the same as it would be on your own system.

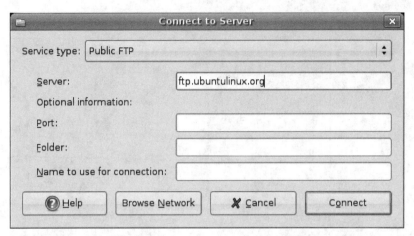

Figure 4–10 Nautilus doesn't limit you to navigating your local file systems. It is also easy to connect to FTP sites, Windows shares, WebDAV servers, and more.

Figure 4–11 After you are connected to a remote server, navigating it is as easy as navigating any locally connected folder.

Another way to do this is to click Go on the menu bar, then select Location (or press <Ctrl+L>. I told you about this a little earlier for local folders but it works here as well. To get to the same FTP site, you could type the following URI (Universal Resource Identifier) in the location field.

```
ftp://anonymous@ftp.ubuntulinux.org/
```

The best way to discover the format of these connections is to connect to a network resource, then press <Ctrl+L>. The current URI will be visible.

Another way to access network resources is to select Network Servers from the Places menu. This is particularly useful if you have Windows machines connected into your network. A Nautilus window appears with a Windows Network icon. Double-click that icon and the Windows domains and workgroups on your network appear (see Figure 4-12). Double-click any of the workgroup icons and you can browse individual machines in that workgroup.

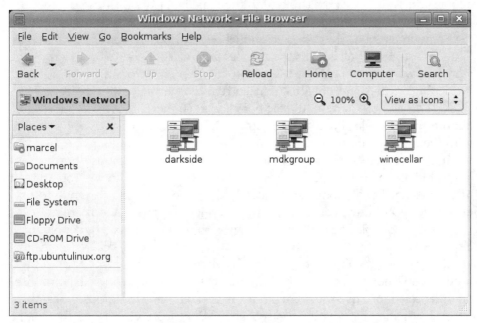

Figure 4–12   Selecting Network Servers from the Places menu makes it easy to navigate Windows shares on your network.

To get to the Windows share browser directly, press <Ctrl+L> in any Nautilus window, then enter **smb:///** in the Location field.

Uh, Roger, Copy That . . .

You can create, copy, move, rename, and delete files and directories by using Nautilus, but before you can do any of these things, you need to *select* a file or directory. Selecting files is something you will be doing a lot, so let's start with that. Place your mouse cursor just outside one of the icons of your choosing. Now, drag the cursor across the icon and notice the highlight box you are creating as you drag. You'll know a file is selected because it becomes *highlighted*. Right-clicking also selects a file but in a somewhat different way, bringing up a menu dialog that then asks you what you want to do with that file.

Don't forget your cursor keys either. Moving left, right, up, or down highlights whatever file or directory you happen to be sitting on. You can then click on Edit in the menu bar (or press <Alt+E> to get to the Edit menu) and decide what it is you want to do with the file. I'll talk about those decisions in a moment.

Sometimes, one file just isn't enough—you need to *select multiple files*. The easiest way of all is with the mouse. Left-click to the top and left of the icon you want to start with, then drag your cursor across a series of icons. Notice again the highlight box that surrounds the files and directories you select. Perhaps you just want a file here and a file there. How do you pick and choose multiple files, you ask? Simply hold down the <Ctrl> key and click with the mouse. Let's say that you have selected a group of four files, and you want one further down in your directory. Let go of the mouse button (but keep holding down the <Ctrl> key), position your mouse to the top and left of the next group of icons, and select away. As long as you continue to hold down the <Ctrl> key, you can pick up and select files here and there at will.

It is also possible to do all these things with the cursor keys by simply moving your cursor over the file you want to start with, holding down the <Shift> key, and moving the cursor to the left (or whatever direction you like). As you do this, you'll notice file after file being selected. Try it for yourself. For nonsequential selection, use the <Ctrl> key as you did with the mouse. Select (or deselect) the files by pressing the spacebar. When your cursor is sitting on the file you want, press the spacebar, and your files will be highlighted.

Finally, and probably quite important for the future, you can also select by extension. Let's say that you want to select all the files with an .mp3 or .doc extension in your directory. Click Edit on the menu bar, then click Select Pattern. A small window pops up, asking you for an extension. If you want all the .mp3 files, you enter *.mp3. The .mp3 extension limits your selection to a certain type of file, whereas the asterisk says, "give me everything" that matches.

Creating New Folders

If you aren't already running Nautilus, start it up now and make sure you are in your personal home directory. In the main Nautilus window, right-click any blank area and look at the menu that pops up. Click the first item on that menu, conveniently labeled Create Folder. Of course, this is a refresher of what I told you earlier in the chapter, but instead of your desktop, this is happening inside the main Nautilus window. An Untitled Folder appears waiting for you to give it a more appropriate name. This folder can be pretty much anything you like. If this directory will house your music files, perhaps its name should be Music.

 Tip Cool trick time. Earlier I had you create a folder on the desktop, then look at the Desktop folder in Nautilus. Why not double-click on the Desktop folder in Nautilus, create a folder, then go back and look at your desktop?

Just remember that you can create folders inside other folders, and you can start organizing things in a way that makes sense. For instance, you might want to create folders called Rock, Jazz, Hip Hop, and Classical in your Music folder.

"I've Changed My Mind" (a.k.a. Renaming Files)

You created a folder called Classical, and you really meant Opera. To rename a file or directory, select it, right-click to get the menu, and then choose Rename. The name is highlighted under the appropriate icon—just type the new name and press <Enter>. Alternatively, select it and choose Rename from the Edit menu in the menu bar. The easiest way of all is to press <F2> after you have selected the file or directory.

Shell Out Open a terminal shell and type **ls** to see your directories. Renaming a file or directory from the shell is easy using the mv command. Why move to rename? Because renaming involves copying to a new location first, then deleting the old file. Type **mv oldname newname** and press <Enter>. For instance, to change your Classical directory to Opera, you would type the following command:

```
mv Classical Opera
```

Copying Files and Directories (and Moving, Too!)

Ah! This is where you learn another great trick with Nautilus. An easy way to copy a file from one directory to another is to fire up two versions of Nautilus. (I usually close the side navigation panel in one version.) You can also right-click a folder in the Tree view and select Open in New Window from the pop-up menu. In the first window, you find the file (or files) you want to copy. In the second Nautilus window, you locate the directory to which you want those files copied. Hold down the <Ctrl> key and simply drag the file from one window into the other. Your file is copied.

Copying and moving files is similar, but instead of holding down the <Ctrl> key, you just drag the file or folder into the new location. Both copying and moving involve a copy. The difference is in what happens *after* the copy is done. In one case, you copy the file over and keep the original, thus giving you two copies of the same file but in different places. A move, on the other hand, copies the file and deletes the original from where it was.

Here's an interesting trick for you. Click the file or folder you want to move, then before you drag it anywhere, hold down the <Alt> key. A little menu pops up, asking whether you want to copy the file here or move it here (see Figure 4-13).

Another easy trick is to select the file you want, right-click to get the menu, and then click Copy. Now, go into the folder where you would like this file to appear, right-click somewhere on a blank space of Nautilus' main window, and click Paste from the pop-up menu. You can also specify the Copy and Paste options from the menu bar under Edit.

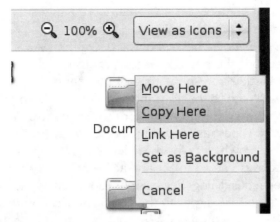

Figure 4–13 Confirmation when moving or copying files.

Shell Out The Linux command to copy is cp. If you want to copy a file called big_report to notsobig_report, you would type the following command:|

```
cp big_report notsobig_report
```

If you want to play it safe when copying files, use the -i flag and the cp program will warn you before it overwrites another file by the same name.

```
cp -i big_report notsobig_report
```

Wait! What About Links?

If you're following along, you probably noticed that the pop-up menu for dragging and dropping a file offered a Link Here option. A link is a kind of copy that doesn't take up much space. In the world of that other OS, you probably thought of links as *shortcuts*. Links let you create a pseudo-copy of a file or directory that doesn't take up the space of the original file. If you want a copy of a particularly large file to exist in several places on the disk, it makes more sense to point to the original and let the system deal with the link as though it *were* the original. It's important to remember that deleting a link doesn't remove the original file, just the link.

Let's say that you copy a file by holding down the <Alt> key and that you select Link Here from the pop-up menu. When the icon shows up on your desktop, there is a little arrow in the top-right corner of the icon indicating that this is a link. The full path to the file is the name or the file you just linked to.

If you want to see a different name for this file, right-click the link you just created and select Properties. A dialog appears with seven tabs, the first of which is labeled Basic, which holds the link name (see Figure 4-14). Emblems, the second tab, allows you to select and add emblems (which I covered earlier) from the Properties dialog. Permissions represents security-related information. Open With lets you specify the default application that opens this file when you double-click it. Notes allows you to attach comments to files or folders. Finally, the Image and Document tabs are strictly informational.

Figure 4–14   To view the properties of a file in Nautilus, right-click the file and select Properties. The Desktop icon properties dialog appears.

Tip You can change the properties of any file or folder, not just links, in this way. The number of tabs, however, may vary depending on the file type or whether you are dealing with folders or files.

On the Basic tab, you should see an icon next to the name of the file you are linking to. If the file is an image, you'll see a thumbnail, as in Figure 4-14. You can change that icon by clicking it and selecting a new one using the Select Custom Icon dialog that appears (see Figure 4-15). The idea here is that you navigate your disk looking for an icon that suits you. To make that job a little easier, there's a preset location on the left for pixmaps. Click here and you are taken to the part of your system where icons are generally stored.

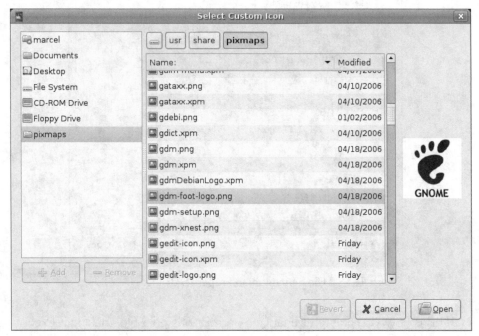

Figure 4–15   The Select Custom Icon dialog lets you search your file system for an appropriate icon.

To see if an icon is right for you, click the icon in the main listing (center) and look to the right in the preview area. When you have something that appeals to you, either double-click it, or click the Open button.

Which Brings Us to Permissions

This is your first look at Linux security—this time at the file (or directory) level. Under that Permissions tab, you'll see a list of access permissions (see Figure 4-16).

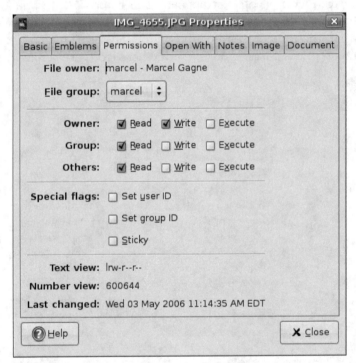

Figure 4–16   File permissions in Properties dialog.

This is how you go about changing permissions on a file, making it executable or providing read and write access to another user (for a more detailed exploration of file permissions, see Chapter 21). There are, however, a couple of other ways to identify file permissions that don't involve opening up a properties dialog for every file. When you look at your file listing in the main Nautilus window, you see a name listed under the file or folder and nothing else. Try this.

Click Edit on the Nautilus menu bar and select Preferences. A five tabbed window appears. Click the Display tab and look near the top under the Icon Captions header. There are three buttons, each of which is a drop-down list. The first has None selected. Change that to Permissions (as you can see, there are several options here). Instantly, any file displayed in the main Nautilus window will have the permissions listed next under the name.

Before you click Close, click the List Columns tab. This defines what information gets listed when you choose Nautilus' list view as opposed to the icon view. Click Permissions here and then click Close. Look at the Nautilus menu bar on the far right. Directly below the icon bar on the right, there's a button labeled View as Icons. Click this button and a drop-down list appears allowing you to change the view from icons to text (see Figure 4-17).

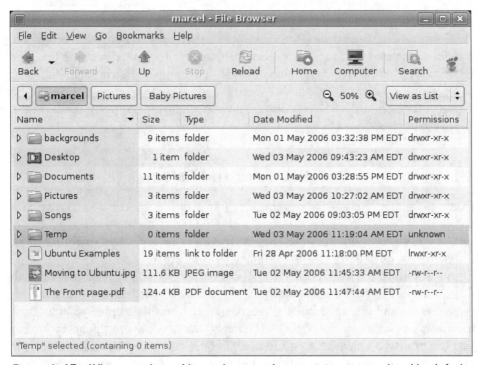

Figure 4–17 When you choose View as Icons mode, permissions are not listed by default. You need to activate that view in the Edit menu Preferences dialog.

There are actually 10 columns describing permissions for a file. For the most part, you'll see either a hyphen or a d in the first column, representing a directory. The next nine columns are actually three sets of three columns.

Those other nine characters (characters 2 through 10) indicate permissions for the user or owner of the file (first three), the group (second group of three), and others or everyone else (last three). If you look at an image and see `-rw-rw-r--`, you'll see that the user and group have read and write permissions. All others have *read-only* permission, the same permission everyone else has. The `r` stands for read, the `w` for write, and the `x` (not seen above) for executable.

Shell Out Want to see the permissions at the shell prompt? Simply add `-l` to the `ls` command, like this:

```
ls -l directory_name
```

From time to time during your Linux experience, you have to change permissions, sometimes to give someone else access to your directories or files or to make a script or program executable. By using the Permissions tab, you can select read, write, or execute permissions for the owner (yourself), the group you belong to, and everyone else by checking off the permissions in the appropriate check boxes.

Deleting Files and Folders

Every once in a while, a file or directory has outlived its usefulness. It is time to be ruthless and do a little cleaning of the old file system.

As you've no doubt come to expect, there are several ways to get rid of an offending file or directory. The friendliest and safest method is to drag the file from Nautilus to the *wastebasket icon* over on the right side of your lower panel. For the novice, this is a safer method because items sent to the trash can be recovered—until you take out the trash, that is. Until that time, you can click the trash can icon and (you guessed it) a Nautilus window appears, showing you the items you have sent to the trash. These items can then be moved (or copied) back to wherever you need them. To remove files from the trash permanently, right-click the trash can icon and click Empty the Wastebasket.

Note After you empty the wastebasket, those files are gone forever.

I did say that there are other ways of deleting a file. From inside Nautilus, you can select a file or directory, right-click, and select Move to Wastebasket. There's also the command line if you need a break from all that clicking.

Other Interesting Places to Visit

You now have a pretty good grasp of Nautilus and what it can do for you. Starting from the Places menu on the top panel is the best way to take Nautilus where you want it to go. There are, or can be, some other interesting places in that menu.

For instance, select Computer from the Places menu and Nautilus opens up with a bird's eye view of your system. A Filesystem icon starts you at the top level of your file system tree. Your floppy drive appears here as does another icon representing your CD-ROM or DVD drive. There can be several icons depending on how many drives are on your system (see Figure 4-18). These days, it's not unusual for people to carry around a USB key or USB pen drive. If you plug one of these in to your Ubuntu system, it becomes one of the interesting places you can visit.

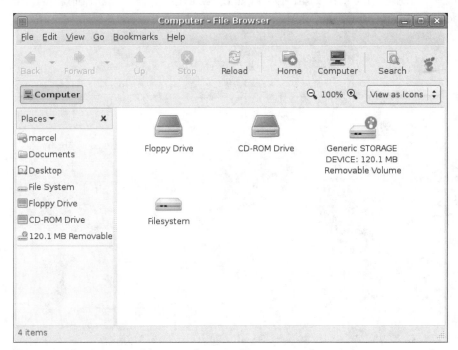

Figure 4–18 Selecting Computer from the Places menu shows you an overview of devices connected to your system.

My World, My Way

I'm hoping that you are walking away from this chapter with an appreciation for the power and flexibility of the tools you have at your disposal. Nautilus may well become your most important application by the time you are finished reading this book. I've barely touched on some of its capabilities. Never fear; you'll see more of Nautilus as we progress through the book. From the file browser, you can play music, launch video clips, read PDF files, burn a CD, and more.

Making Your Home a Home

By now, you're starting to feel like this isn't so difficult after all. In fact, it's probably starting to feel pretty familiar. After all, there are many similarities in desktop environments, and working with GNOME isn't like working in a totally alien environment. Well, it's time to make your new virtual home even more of a home. It is time to personalize your desktop experience.

In the next chapter, we'll talk about changing your background, adding icons, setting up a screensaver, and all those other things that help make your desktop yours and yours alone.

Chapter

5

Customizing Your Desktop (or Making Your World Your Own)

After having taken the first steps into the Linux world, you are probably thinking, "Hey, this is pretty easy," and "I wonder what the fuss was all about." For what it's worth, I'm thinking the very same thing. Now that the fear of dealing with a new operating system is gone, it's time to get really comfortable.

In this chapter, I'm going to show you how to make your system truly your own. I'll show you how to change your background, your colors, your fonts, and anything else you need to create a desktop as individual as you are. Would you like some icons on your desktop? Perhaps some shortcuts to programs you use on a regular basis? No problem. I'll cover all those things, too.

I Am Sovereign of All I Survey . . .

As I've already mentioned, working in the Linux world is working in a *multiuser* world. This means that everyone who uses your computer can have his or her own unique environment. Any changes you make to your desktop while you are logged in as yourself will have no effect on little Sarah when she logs in to play her video games. If she happens to delete all the icons on her desktop or change everything to a garish purple and pink, it won't affect you, either.

Let's start with something simple. The first thing most people want to change is their background. It's sort of like moving into a new house or apartment. The wallpaper (or paint) that someone else chose rarely fits your idea of décor. The same goes for your computer's desktop. Let's get you something more to your liking.

Changing the Background

Start by right-clicking somewhere on the desktop. From the menu that appears, choose Change Desktop Background and the Desktop Background Preferences dialog appears (see Figure 5-1). You can also access the Desktop Background dialog from the System menu in the top panel under Preferences. Look for the item labeled Desktop Background.

The top half of the dialog displays a list of desktop wallpapers available to the system. The default list available with Ubuntu is rather small, basically a choice between no wallpaper and two different resolutions of the same background. I'll tell you how to add more in a moment, but for now I want you to click the No Wallpaper setting. Notice that the change to your background is immediate. No need to click OK or Apply here.

Directly below the Desktop Wallpaper area, there's an area labeled *Style*. There is a drop-down list here with *Fill Screen* selected as the default. This tells the system how to treat the image you select. Some images are only small graphic *tiles*, designed to be copied over and over until they fill your screen. For these, you change the mode to Tiled. If the image you are using is a bit small for your screen but you want it as your background anyway, choose Centred and it will sit in the center surrounded by whatever background color you choose. If you just want the image to fill your screen and you don't care what it looks like, go for Scaled. Play. Experiment. These are *your* walls.

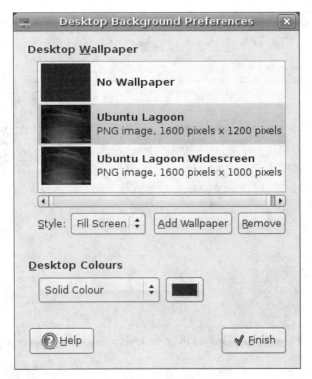

Figure 5–1   Choosing a background image for your desktop.

To add a wallpaper to the small default list, you first need to have some available. Click the Add Wallpaper button and the GNOME file selector appears (see Figure 5-2).

You can then use it to navigate to whatever folder contains your pictures and select from there. Find something you like and double-click it (or click and then click the Open button), and you'll find yourself back at the Desktop Background Preferences dialog from which you can choose an image that suits your mood. Incidentally, these images remain as wallpaper choices from here on in.

I know I'm repeating myself, but you don't *have* to have a background. You can create a nice, plain background by clicking No Wallpaper. Then, in the Desktop Colors section at the bottom of the dialog, you can select a solid color or create a vertical or horizontal gradient based on your choice of color. Make your selection from the drop-down box, then click the color button to the right to select from a color wheel (see Figure 5-3).

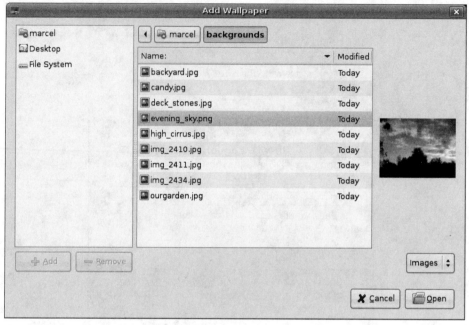

Figure 5–2   Use the file navigator to locate and add new wallpaper for your desktop.

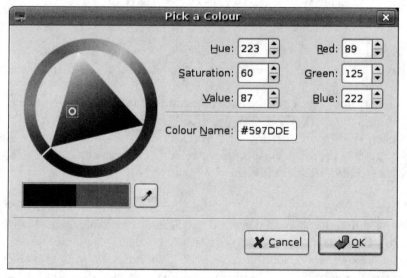

Figure 5–3   Use the color selector to create your own custom background color.

Here's a cool trick. Let's say the color you want is already somewhere on your screen and you'd like to have that as your background. No problem. See that eyedropper icon just below the color wheel? Click that and you can use the eyedropper that pops up to select any color already on your screen.

When you are happy with your choice, click OK to banish the dialog.

Save My Screen, Please!

Okay, screensavers don't really do much screen saving these days. Once upon a time, the idea was to protect screens from phosphor burn-in. Old-style monochrome screens were particularly bad for this. In time, the letters from your menus (we were using text in those days) would burn in to the phosphor screen. Even when you turned off the monitor, you could still see the ghostly outline of your most popular application burned into the screen itself. As we moved to color screens and graphics, that changed somewhat, but the problem continued to exist for some time, partly due to the static nature of the applications we were using.

Time passes, and some bright light somewhere got the idea that if you constantly change the image on the screen, that type of burn-in would not be as likely. What better way to achieve this than to have some kind of clever animation kick in when the user walked away from the screen for a few minutes (or hours). Heck, it might even be fun to watch. The screensaver was born. Modern screens use scanning techniques that all but banish burn-in, but screensavers did not go away. Those addictive fish, toasters, penguins, snow, spaceships, and so on have managed to keep us entertained, despite the march of technology. Let's face it, we are all hooked.

Ubuntu Linux has the screensaver turned on by default. In fact, if you wait long enough (10 minutes) without doing anything on your computer, the screensaver kicks in. Let it go for more than 10 minutes and you'll see that a different screensaver starts up. That's because Ubuntu's default screensaver cycles randomly through a number of preselected screensavers. As you might expect, I'm getting a little ahead of myself.

Start by clicking System in the top panel. From the Preferences menu, select Screensaver. The Screensaver Preferences dialog appears (see Figure 5-4). The main window has a list of screensavers to the left and a larger preview window to the right. At the top of the screensaver list is an option for a Blank Screen and another, the selected default, for Random. In the lower portion of the window, there's a check box labeled Activate Screensaver

When Session Is Idle. Check this box if you want to completely disable the screensaver. Keep in mind that Blank Screen is actually a screensaver, a quiet alternative to the various flying objects.

Figure 5–4   *Selecting a screensaver.*

To preview a screensaver, click any of the screensavers in the left-hand list and it appears in the display area to the right. For instance, my example in Figure 5-4 shows the FlipFlop screensaver, a brightly colored, 3D surface of tiles that constantly flip back and forth (while exchanging positions with other tiles) as the display rotates.

Let's move on. Directly below the list of screensavers and the preview window is a slider labeled Set Session to Idle After:. It is set to a default of 10 minutes. Stop working for 10 minutes and your screensaver kicks in. Feel free to slide that down to 2 minutes or even 1 if you are a particularly hard worker. Should you want to skip the whole screensaver thing entirely (even the blank screen), make sure you check the box labeled Activate Screensaver When Session Idle.

In an office environment (or a busy household), you probably want to password-protect your screen when you walk away. To do this, click the Lock

Screen When Screensaver Is Active check box. Always remember that your password is case-sensitive.

Moving Things Around

On a fresh Ubuntu install, your desktop is clear of any icons. You probably still have that folder icon from the previous chapter sitting there somewhere, but if you don't, create a folder icon now. Click this icon (hold the click) and drag it to some other spot on the desktop. Easy, isn't it? When you log out from your GNOME session later on, make sure that you click Save Current Setup for future logins so that any changes you make here will follow you into the next session.

The top (or bottom) panel is something else you may want to move. Just drag the panel and drop it to one of the four positions on the desktop (top, bottom, left, or right side). The location, by the way, can also be changed by right-clicking the panel and selecting Properties. On the card that appears (see Figure 5-5), you can select the location, labeled Orientation, off the panel from a drop-down list.

 Semantics Technically, the taskbar is that portion of the bottom *panel* that shows your open programs, letting you quickly click from one to the other. You may find that people speak of the taskbar and the panel interchangeably. That said, the program switcher on the bottom panel is more appropriately called the window list because this is the term used by GNOME.

The top and bottom panels can be quite dynamic things. For instance, deselect the Expand check box and the panel shrinks to only show the space that is used up, leaving you with a small panel in the top or bottom center of your screen. Click Expand again and it fills the entire width. The height of the panel, labeled Size, can also be changed here. Click the Autohide check box and the panel drops out of sight when you move the mouse away. If, like me, you don't like the whole disappearing panel thing but you do, from time to time, want to quickly banish it, click the Show Hide Buttons check box. Buttons with arrows appear at each end of the panel. Click the arrow and the panel vanishes out off to the side.

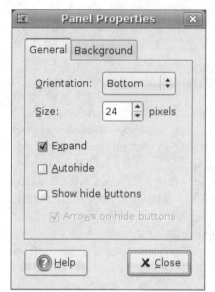

Figure 5–5
The Panel Properties dialog lets you change the location of the panel as well as the size.

All of these things apply to the bottom panel as well, but as I mentioned, most people tend to think of the bottom panel as the taskbar (once again, because GNOME refers to this as the window list, I will use this term instead). That's because you see small rectangular boxes identifying each running program, task, or window. Click those buttons and the program either minimizes or maximizes. To modify the taskbar, right-click the vertical bar directly to the left of the Show Desktop button and select Preferences from the pop-up menu (see Figure 5-6).

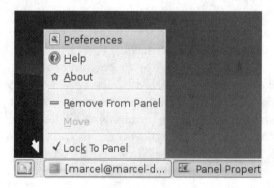

Figure 5–6
To change the window list properties, right-click the small vertical bar directly to the right of the Show Desktop icon (identified here with a small arrow).

When the Window List Preferences dialog appears (see Figure 5-7), you'll see two tabs labeled Behaviour and Size. Let's start with the Behaviour tab. As you can see, tasks can be organized based on the workspace they occupy and how they are grouped. The top portion of the dialog defines which tasks (or windows) are represented in the bottom panel. The default is to only show windows from the current workspace. If you decide to override this, just be aware that the window list can get very full, very quickly.

Figure 5–7
By default, only those tasks in the current workspace are displayed.

To understand window grouping, consider this example. Let's say that you have a terminal window, a Web browser, and a game of AisleRiot open. Regardless of the setting you choose, all of these tasks will be listed. If you had two terminals instead of the one, then things start to get interesting. Choose the Group Windows When Space Is Limited radio button and both terminals are grouped together under one window list item, but only when you are running a lot of tasks and the window list is starting to get overly busy. To choose between the two, you could click the item which would then pop up the list of running terminals. Choose Always Group Windows and you'll get the same result, but your two terminal sessions are grouped under one item even if they are the only items on the window list.

Is That a Theme or a Motif?

Not a musical theme, but a desktop theme. A theme is a collection of buttons, decorations, colors, backgrounds, and so on preselected and packaged to give your desktop a finished and coherent look. Some themes even incorporate sounds (for startup, shutdown, opening and closing program windows, and so on) into the whole package. It can be a lot of fun. Your Ubuntu system comes with several themes. That default brown theme you are looking at right now is called Human.

Let's jump right in and play with themes a little bit. Click System on the top panel, navigate to the Preferences menu and select Theme. When the Theme Preferences dialog appears (see Figure 5-8), you'll see the Human

Figure 5–8   The default Ubuntu theme is called Human, but several others are included as well.

theme displayed at the top. Each theme includes a small screenshot to the left of the title and description. Changing from one theme to another is as easy as clicking the name in the list.

You can obviously tell what your system looks like, but it's interesting to see what elements make up a theme. Knowing about the various elements is also a great first step to creating a desktop environment that is truly your own. For those reasons, click the Theme Details button. A three-tabbed window appears with the labels Controls, Window Border, and Icons (see Figure 5-9). Each of these tabs represents one of the major theme elements and each can be modified individually from the theme it represents, according to your tastes.

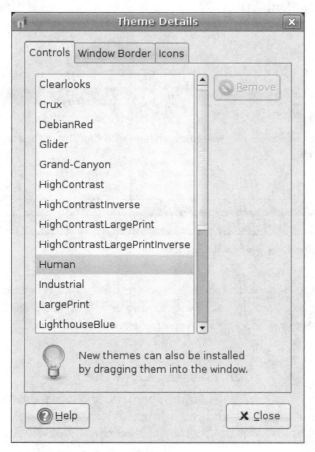

Figure 5–9 The Theme Details dialog lets you fine tune the various elements that go toward making a theme.

Let's look at each individually, starting with controls. These represent most of what you see when you are looking at a theme. The colors, style of sliders, shape of buttons, and tabs . . . all these are elements that fall under this category. I think of it as the look and feel of the GNOME interface.

Window border is just that—the frame and the layout of the buttons that go at the top of the window title. Changing the window border can also define whether frames have square or rounded corners. Figures 5-10 through 5-12 give you a little sample of how changing this one item impacts the look of your system.

Figure 5–10   Human is the classic Ubuntu theme. Notice that the window title is centered.

Figure 5–11   Sandy colors give way to ocean hues with the Ocean Dreams theme. Can you hear the surf?

Figure 5–12   The Crux window decoration.

The last tab deals with icons. These are the icons you see on your desktop, on your panel, and in your Nautilus file browser. You should probably be aware that not every icon theme replaces every type of icon.

Defining Your Own Theme

While you are busy changing controls, borders, and icons, take a look at your Theme Preferences dialog and you'll notice that something very interesting is happening. At the top of the theme list is something new: Custom Theme.

Next to this title is a small thumbnail of how this theme of yours is shaping up. You should also notice that the Save Theme button is no longer grayed out (see Figure 5-13).

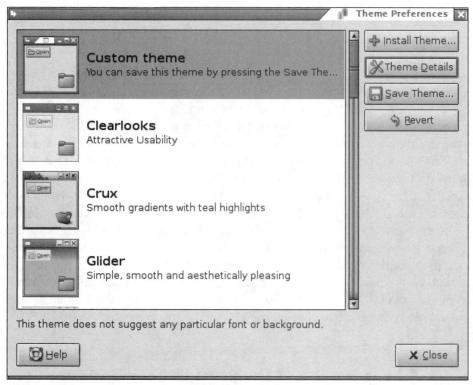

Figure 5–13   When you start changing settings, the theme manager offers you the opportunity to save your new theme.

If you like the new look you have created, it's time to save it. Click the Save Theme button and a dialog appears asking you for a theme name and a short description. Click the Save button and your new theme will be part of the list.

To go back to the system default, either choose Human from the list or click the Revert button.

Adding New Themes

The fashion slaves among you will quickly grow tired of the themes and styles your system comes with—there are quite a few but not nearly enough for those surfing the edges of what's hot today. That's why you should keep the following Web sites in mind:

```
http://www.gnome-look.org
http://art.gnome.org
```

You'll find tons of themes, alternative wallpapers, and icons—enough to keep you busy for a long, long time. Installing a new theme is as easy as finding something you like, saving it in a folder or on your desktop, and then dragging the theme bundle onto the Theme Preferences dialog. A small dialog appears asking you to confirm the installation, and that's all there is to it. Keep in mind, however, that some of the listed themes may just affect the Controls tab. As such, they don't appear in the theme list, but do show up when you click Theme Details.

Icons work the same way. Just download them and drag them onto the Theme Preferences dialog, confirm that you do indeed want to install this icon theme, and then look for it under the Icons tab.

I know we haven't talked about getting on the Net yet; we still have a few things to cover. If you just can't wait, you can jump over to Chapter 7. Just make sure you come back here. You wouldn't want to miss anything.

Adding Icons and Shortcuts to Your Desktop

I covered this topic somewhat in the last chapter, but it is time to look at this in detail. While working with Nautilus, you might recall that you had a directory called Desktop and that this directory actually *was* your desktop. If you want to get a file onto your desktop, you can just drag and drop (copy or link) a file there. A good reason for doing this is that it puts things you use on a regular basis (a business spreadsheet perhaps or a contact list) right where you can quickly get to them.

The single most useful icon you will likely want to add to your desktop is a link to a program on your system, what GNOME calls a Launcher. This is something you might have called a *shortcut* in the Windows world. Maybe you need to have your word processor or your CD player handy. Whatever it is, you would like it there in front of you.

Tip This is jumping ahead a bit because we don't cover surfing the Web until Chapter 9, but I do need to mention it here. Another useful icon is a link to a Web site. Let's say that you routinely visit the Google News site and that you would like to have that come up just by clicking an icon on your desktop. It's easy. Use Firefox to get to the site, then drag the link onto your desktop. An icon is created for you. You can even drag a link from a Web page you are viewing onto your desktop.

You need to understand that you aren't really putting the program there, but rather a link to it. Right-click the desktop and move your mouse cursor over Create Launcher. The dialog or card that opens has two tabs (see Figure 5-14).

Figure 5–14 When you select Create Launcher, a two-tabbed window appears. The default is to create an application as in this example.

The first tab, Basic, is where most of the action takes place. Start by choosing a Name for the program. This doesn't have to be the program name, but what you want to see on the desktop. Generic Name is more to identify the category or program, and whatever you enter under Comment appears in a tooltip when you pause your mouse over the icon. You don't have to enter anything in the Generic Name or the Comment fields. The Command section includes a Browse button so you can use the file browser to locate your program; however, if you know the command name, you can just enter it manually. For example, if you want a link to the OpenOffice.org Writer, you enter `/usr/bin/oowriter`.

Notice the Type field with Application selected from the drop-down list. As it turns out, an application (or a program, if you prefer) just happens to be the default type of launcher you can create. Click the list and you see that you can also create a link to a file, a folder, and several other file types.

Directly below the type entry, there is a button labeled No Icon. This is something you probably want to change. Clicking this button brings up a large collection of icons from which you can select whatever happens to take your fancy (see Figure 5-15).

Figure 5–15   Selecting an icon for your new launcher.

When you are happy with your changes, click OK. Your new program link (which you can launch with a double-click) should appear on your desktop.

Shell Out To create a shortcut icon for a command, you first have to know what the command is and where it is. To be honest, a command or program (such as the GNOME calculator, gnome-calculator) could be almost anywhere on the disk. For the most part, programs tend to be in one of the bin directories— /bin, /usr/bin, or /usr/local/bin. You can also use the whereis command to tell you exactly. For instance, to know where the gnome-calculator program is, I would type the following at the Terminal shell prompt (the dollar sign ($)).

```
sh-3.1$ whereis -b gnome-calculator
gnome-calculator: /usr/bin/gnome-calculator
/usr/bin/X11/gnome-calculator
```

In some cases, you may see more than one file associated with a program's name, but the actual executable to use is in /usr/ bin. The bin, in this case, stands for binary—in short, a program.

To get an even shorter return on your search, use the which command:

```
sh-3.1$ which gnome-calculator
/usr/bin/gnome-calculator
```

Tip If the application you want on your desktop appears in the menu, you can just click the item and drag it onto your desktop. When you release the mouse button, the icon appears.

Applets Galore:
Back to the Panel!

Sounds a lot like the title for a new Hollywood blockbuster, doesn't it?

Applets are, as you might have gathered from the name, small applications. You'll find a few of them embedded in the panel at the top and bottom of your graphical desktop. These little programs are engineered to fit nicely into your panel and window list, while still providing useful functionality. The window list is just one of many applications embedded in that panel. Other embedded applications include the workspace switcher, the menu, the clock, and even the notification area (sometimes called the system tray).

Although we could work with either (or both) of the GNOME panels, I'm going to concentrate on the bottom one for now.

The default look and size of the bottom panel is roughly 24 pixels by default. Depending on the nature of the program, applets embedded in a panel of this size tend to be a little hard to look at. Luckily, this is easily resolved by changing the size of the panel as described earlier in this chapter. To make some of these applets useful, you will most likely want to increase the default panel size. In my experience, and on my monitor, 48 pixels is pretty much ideal.

Now that you've prepped your panel, it's time to find and add some of those applets. Right-click the panel and a small menu appears. Click Add to Panel and a list of all the available applets appears (see Figure 5-16). This list may be one single list with a short description of the applet in question, or it may be organized into categories. Scroll down and find something you like, then click the Add button. For my first applet, I chose the one labeled Fish, an animated swimming fish that pops up random bits of cleverness using the `fortune` (or fortune cookie) command. And, yes, the fish's name is Wanda. And, no, I did not make this up.

In a few seconds, your applet appears in the panel. When an applet starts, it rarely starts in the position I want. Luckily, moving it is an easy process. Simply right-click the applet and a small menu appears (see Figure 5-17). One of the options is Move. Click here and a small hand icon appears that allows you to drag the applet to wherever you want it to live. You can even move it to another panel (more on that in a moment).

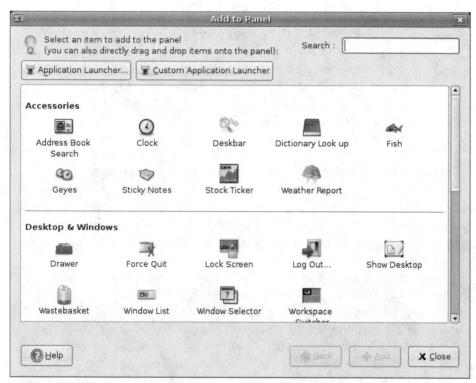

Figure 5–16 Adding an applet to the GNOME panel.

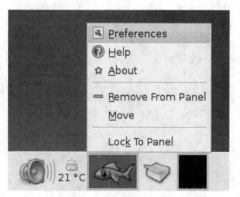

Figure 5–17 Each applet can then be configured, moved, or removed.

Tip People with a three-button mouse can click the applet using the middle button and drag it to wherever they want. Scroll-wheel mice offer similar functionality because most wheels are actually a third button (try clicking your mouse wheel). It's not unusual for applications in the Linux world to take advantage of the middle mouse button, but its use is often overlooked.

Have another look at that menu and you'll see that there are some other useful options. For instance, each application may have its own set of configurations. The fish applet I had you install comes with a small handful of additional graphics—you may not like fish. Just click the Preferences menu to make your changes. Finally, should you decide that the program you chose is just taking up space, there's a Remove option.

When the applet mania has taken hold, you may find yourself out of space. Yes, it is time to add another panel. Right-click somewhere in your panel's empty space. From the pop-up menu, select New Panel. A blank, gray panel appears; you can drag it to any location that you see fit. As with the original panel, selecting the properties dialog allows you to change the size to fit the applets you have in mind.

I'm going to share some of my favorites with you, although they are not all entirely useful in terms of work. The Dictionary Lookup applet is a must, as is the Weather Report program. The fortune Fish (mentioned earlier) is fun, as are the eyes that follow your mouse pointer around the screen. The Take Screenshot applet is particularly useful when you are doing documentation. Because I work on a variety of systems, I'm also rather fond of the Terminal Server Client and the Connect to Server applets. (I briefly mentioned this last one in Chapter 4, but via Nautilus.)

I'm going to leave the discussion of applets here, but I invite you to try others and discover your own favorites. Go ahead. Explore!

Miscellaneous Changes

Let me give you one final *treat* before I close this chapter. Click System on the top panel, and then select Keyboard Shortcuts from the Preferences menu. You'll discover lots of interesting keyboard shortcuts to do things such as switching from one application to the other, switching from one workspace to the other, opening and closing windows, getting help, taking a desktop screenshot (in case you want to share your fashion sense with others), and so on.

Resources

GNOME-Look.org
    http://www.gnome-look.org

Art.GNOME.org
    http://art.gnome.org

Chapter

6

Printers and Other Hardware

Ah, hardware . . . "I hate hardware!"

Part of the personal computer experience seems destined to be an eternal battle in getting your current system to talk to the latest and greatest devices. There's always a new, hyper-fantastic, 3D video card; mind-blowing stereo sound system; or hair-trigger game controller out there. Then there are everyday devices, such as modems, scanners, and printers. Getting all these devices to work with your system is something that has caused us all grief over time, regardless of what operating system we were running.

We are used to assuming that anything works with Windows, but even that isn't true. From time to time, even Windows users must visit hardware vendors' Web sites to download a driver. One of the things that sets Ubuntu Linux apart is its intelligent and accurate hardware detection and support. Most things will be automatically configured without a fuss. In this chapter, I'm going to give you the tools you need to deal with common issues and give you some tips on avoiding problems in the first place.

Yes, It Runs with Linux!

Device support under Linux is excellent. The sheer number of things that will work "out of the box" without you having to search for and install drivers is impressive and, quite frankly, beats your old OS. That doesn't mean all is rosy, however. Let me be *brutally* honest here. Some devices have been written to work with Windows and only Windows . . . or so it seems. One of the great things about this open source world is that developers are constantly working to write drivers to make it possible to run that faster-than-light communications card.

If you haven't already bought that new gadget, there are a couple of things that you should do. For starters, if you are in the store looking at that new printer, pull the salesperson aside and *ask* whether it runs with Linux. If the person doesn't know (which is sometimes a problem, but less so as time goes on), take a few minutes to check out the excellent Hardware HOWTO document. You can always find the latest version by surfing on over to the LDP's Linux Hardware Compatibility HOWTO page:

```
http://www.tldp.org/HOWTO/Hardware-HOWTO/index.html
```

If you don't find what you are looking for there, check out the hardware compatibility guide on your Linux vendor's site. In the case of Ubuntu Linux, that means paying a visit to the Ubuntu Wiki and checking out the hardware support pages:

```
https://wiki.ubuntu.com/HardwareSupport
```

 Quick Tip Red Hat's hardware catalog is also worth the visit, regardless of what version of Linux you are running. The URL follows. However, keep in mind that URLs do change on Web sites. If you don't find it there, just go to the main Red Hat site at `http://www.redhat.com` and look for *hardware*.

```
http://bugzilla.redhat.com/hwcert
```

Although Ubuntu Linux is Linux, different releases of different vendors' products may be at different levels of development. Consequently, at one time or another, Red Hat may have slightly more extensive support for hardware than the others, and a month later SUSE may have the widest range of support.

As Linux gains in popularity, you'll find that hardware vendors are increasingly interested in tapping into this ever-growing market. I've had the experience of being on site, adding hardware to a customer's system (Ethernet cards come immediately to mind), and finding that the system did not have the drivers. I quickly visited the Ethernet card manufacturer's Web site and found precompiled drivers ready and waiting for me.

Plug and Play

For the most part, adding a device to your Ubuntu Linux system is simply a matter of plugging it in. If the device doesn't just appear and you don't want to configure it manually, a reboot forces hardware detection, and the device should be recognized by the system and configured. *Universal Serial Bus (USB)* devices tend to be even easier because of their hot-plug nature. In other words, you don't need to reboot the system in order to have a USB device recognized, and you can unplug it while the system is running. For instance, plug in a USB key or USB pen drive and it simply appears in your Places menu (see Figure 6-1).

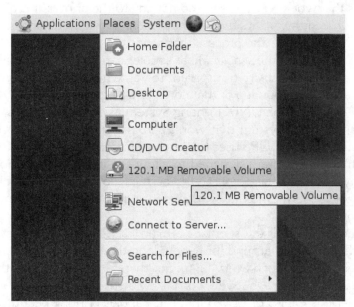

Figure 6–1   A 128MB USB drive appears in the Places menu (note that the formatted size of the drive is only 120.1MB).

Getting a device recognized is only part of it, though. Just because your system knows about the device doesn't necessarily mean that it is configured for your applications. Although you generally don't have to find and install drivers, it does happen, just as it does in the Windows world. It wouldn't be fair to you if I simply ignored this little tidbit, so I won't.

Let's take a look at the most popular, and sometimes the most frustrating, piece of hardware computer users are faced with. That's right, I'm talking about printers.

Printers and Printing

This might seem like a silly thing to mention, particularly if your printer was automatically detected, configured, and tested at boot time. Nevertheless, there are things that you might want to do with your printer, and we should probably cover some of these now. Furthermore, *printing is one of the most important functions* a personal computer can perform. It's good to get it right. On that note, I'm going to spend a little bit of time talking about printers and printing. *Trust me*, it's going to be lots of fun.

Printing under Linux works on the basis of *print queues*. At its simplest, this means that whenever you send something to the printer, it is queued in a directory where it awaits its turn at the printer. This de-queuing is known as *spooling*. Consequently, the process that sends the print jobs from the queue to the printer is called the *spooler*. That spooler can be one of a small handful of programs, all of which are transparent to you when you print from applications. Here's a quick roundup of the more popular spoolers.

CUPS, the Common UNIX Printing System, is designed to be a platform-independent printing system that works across a great number of UNIX flavors, including Linux. CUPS uses the Internet Printing Protocol (IPP), a next-generation printing system designed to allow the printing of any job to any printer, anywhere. At this point, CUPS certainly looks like the spooler of the future. Most modern Linux distributions include CUPS, and Ubuntu uses it transparently.

The second most likely spooler you run into is LPD, the classic UNIX spooler. LPD has been around for a long, long time and continues to be distributed with pretty much every Linux out there. I mention it mostly for historical reasons. It's there, but you won't likely be using it.

Whether it is CUPS or LPD, GNOME handles printing beautifully. Adding, configuring, or removing a printer is done through the system printing manager. Click System on the top panel, then select Printing from the Administration submenu. A window labeled Printers appears with an icon labeled New Printer (see Figure 6-2).

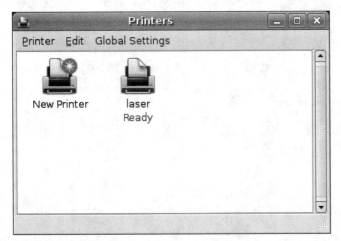

Figure 6–2 When the printing manager starts up, you will likely see nothing more than a New Printer icon. However, your Ubuntu system automatically picks up other configured printers.

Tip If you are on a network with shared printers, click Global Settings on the menu bar and select Detect LAN Printers.

Notice that in my case, there is already a printer listed (laser). That's because I already have a network accessible printer available on my network. In all likelihood, you will only see the New Printer icon, and that's a great place to start. To add a printer, start by making sure your printer is plugged in and online. Next, click Printer on the menu bar and select Add Printer. You can also just double-click the New Printer icon. Assuming you have a supported printer and that it is connected and online, Ubuntu should autodetect your printer (see Figure 6-3).

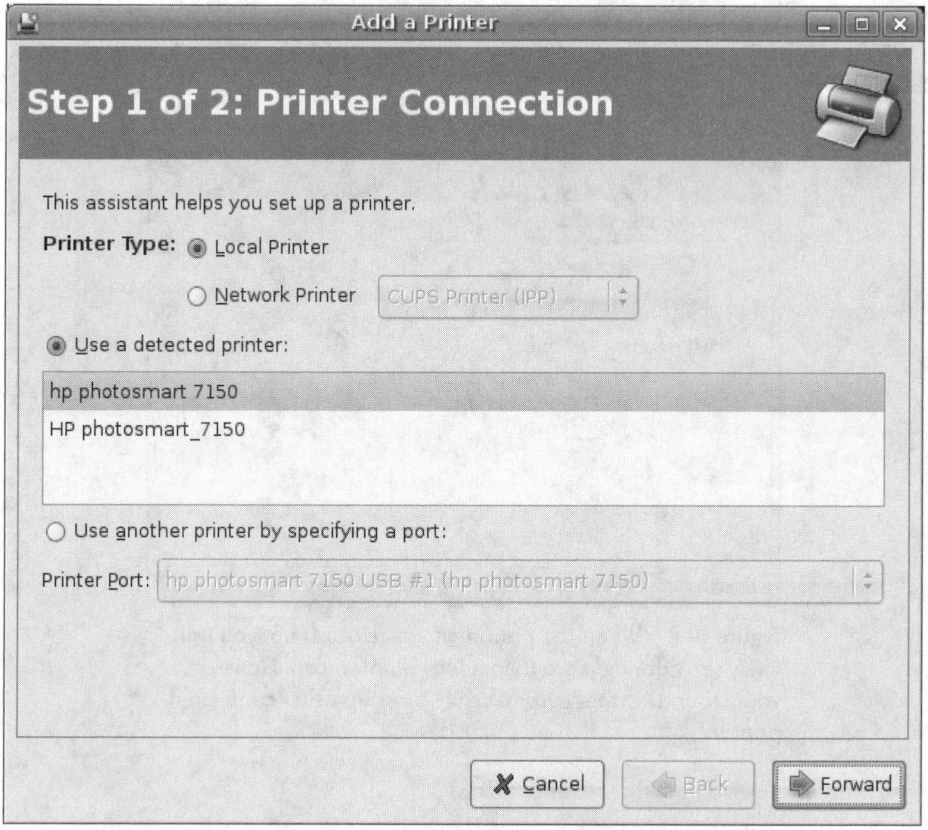

Figure 6–3   If your printer is supported, it should be automatically detected.

In my example, the system handily noticed my HP printer and all was well from the start. Click Forward and we get to the driver selection screen. Because the printer in this case was properly identified, the system also offers a driver for that printer (see Figure 6-4).

If you don't think this is the right driver or the system hasn't properly autodetected your printer, you can select a different manufacturer and model on this screen. Both options provide a drop-down list with a number of choices. With most printers, there is one recommended driver and it is listed next to the Driver label. You can see that the driver listed here is actually the first item in a drop-down box, which means there can be more than one printer. Generally speaking, the selected driver is the recommended driver and is identified as such.

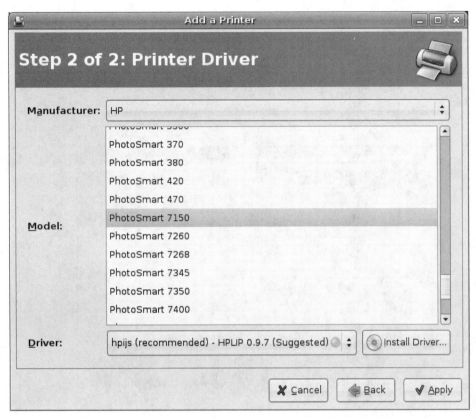

Figure 6–4   The second screen is the driver selection screen. You can also specify a different manufacturer and model here.

Notice the button labeled Install Driver. On many printers, you can find PPD (printer definition) files either on the printer manufacturer's Web site or via the Linux printing site (linuxprinting.org), even if that driver isn't included with your Ubuntu Linux system. If you have such a printer file downloaded, and your printer's driver is not in the list, click this button and the standard GNOME file selector appears. Navigate to the driver's location and install it. When you are happy with your choice, click Apply to have your changes take effect. The new printer appears in the Printers dialog (see Figure 6-5).

Note I've mentioned how some companies aren't very forthcoming with drivers for Linux systems. This is changing, however, and some printer manufacturers offer excellent support for Linux. These include HP and Brother, among others.

Figure 6–5   As new printers are configured, they appear in the Printers dialog.

Now that there are two printers configured, take a look at the laser printer, the one that was automagically detected on the network. Notice the check mark icon on its top left. That indicates that this is the system's default printer. To change the default output to another printer, right-click the printer and select Make Default from the pop-up menu.

Network Printers

The example I gave you is for a locally connected printer, one that was auto-detected by your system. What if the printer make and model isn't detected or you need to use a network-based printer, perhaps one hanging off a Windows network? Let's look at a more complex installation. Once again, double-click New Printer to bring up the Add a Printer dialog.

The radio button for Local Printer is selected by default. Click the radio button for Network Printer for a network connected printer. To the right, there is a drop-down box with options for a CUPS printer (IPP), a Windows printer (SMB), a UNIX printer (LPD), and an HP JetDirect network adapter. For this example, I choose a Windows printer because this is be a common scenario for home users. As soon as you select SMB, your Ubuntu system scans your local network for Windows machines and Windows workgroups. If it finds one, an Authentication Required dialog appears (see Figure 6-6).

Figure 6–6 As Ubuntu identifies Windows machines on your network, it asks you for a username and password to access those machines.

Enter the information and click Connect. The Add a Printer dialog you saw earlier changes to display options specific to the type of network printer you are trying to configure (see Figure 6-7). In the case of a Windows network printer, there are fields for the Host name of the Windows machines on your network and for the shared printer.

Tip It's not unusual for Samba (Windows file sharing on Linux) servers to be part of a modern network. Printers shared on these machines look identical to the way they do on any other Windows system on the network. As such, Samba servers and their printers are listed as well.

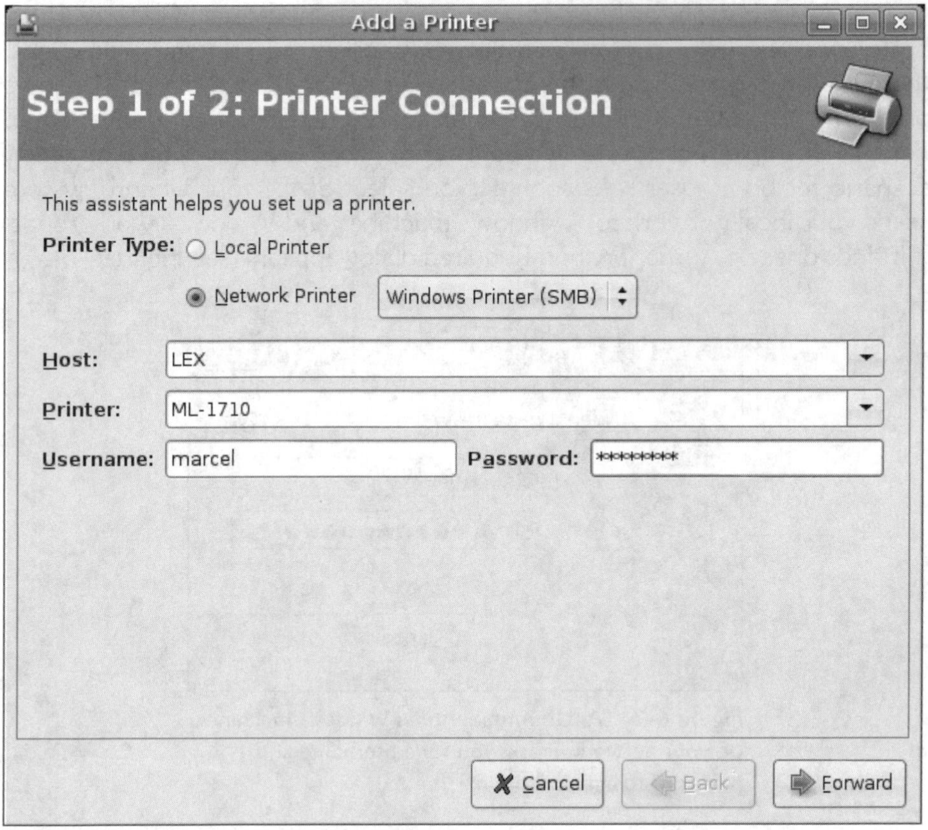

Figure 6–7   Configuring Ubuntu to access a Windows network printer.

Select a Windows host, then select a printer from the list below it. If you had multiple machines on your network, it is possible that the Username and Password filled in here doesn't match those you entered earlier. Confirm that the information is correct, then click Forward. Once again, you'll find yourself at the printer driver selection screen (see Figure 6-8).

Click Apply and your printer is added.

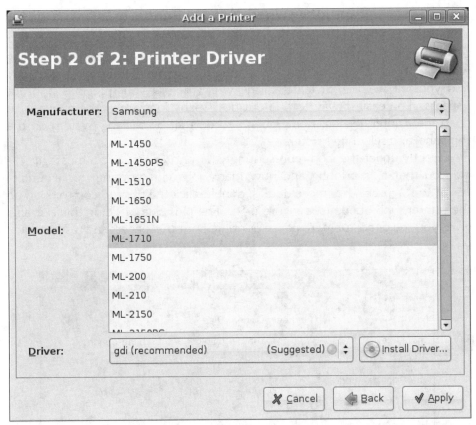

Figure 6–8 Your next step is to select the manufacturer and model for your printer. The driver should be autoselected but note that there can be others besides the suggested option.

Tip For more information on printing from different machines and different operating systems, check out the following URLs:

```
https://wiki.ubuntu.com/NetworkPrintingFromWin2000

https://wiki.ubuntu.com/NetworkPrintingFromWinXP

https://wiki.ubuntu.com/NetworkPrintingFromMacOSX
```

Print Jobs—Where Are My Print Jobs?

When you send something to the printer, you generally expect action quickly. Something better start coming out of that printer soon. If there is something wrong with the printer or you are sharing that printer with others, you may find yourself waiting, at least a little while, before your precious printout appears. The easiest way to find out how many jobs are in the queue is to open the Printers dialog. Remember, you do that by clicking System on the top panel and selecting Printers.

Directly under the icon representing your printer, you see a message telling you that it is printing and how many jobs it is printing (for example, `Printing 2 jobs`). For more details, double-click the printer icon to open up the printer's job queue (see Figure 6-9). The plus side of doing this is it also gives you the opportunity to pause printing, print test pages, and resume jobs.

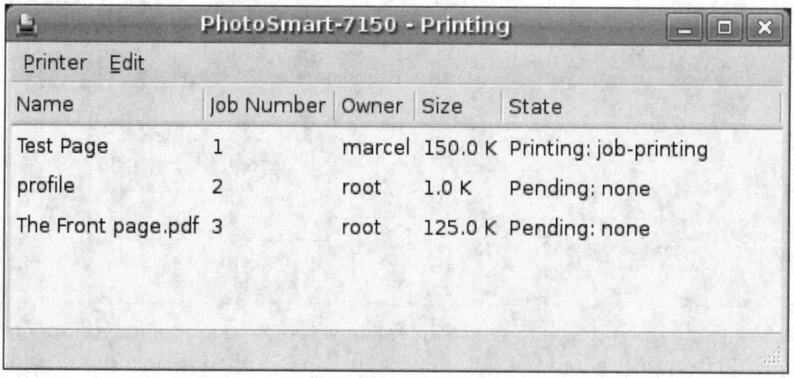

PhotoSmart-7150 - Printing				
Printer Edit				
Name	Job Number	Owner	Size	State
Test Page	1	marcel	150.0 K	Printing: job-printing
profile	2	root	1.0 K	Pending: none
The Front page.pdf	3	root	125.0 K	Pending: none

Figure 6–9   Double-click the printer icon to bring up the print queue information.

Let's face it. From time to time, we all end up sending something to the printer we wished we hadn't. *"No, I only meant to print the first 5 pages, not 500!"* Luckily, you can also cancel a job. Just click the line to highlight it, and then click Edit on the menu bar, followed by Cancel Jobs.

See, printers aren't so scary after all.

Getting Familiar with Your Other Hardware

Meeting new people isn't always easy. Sociologists tell us that there is a complex interplay that takes place whenever we meet someone new, much of it subconscious. Although it is possible to meet someone and instantly like him or her, it is more likely that you become comfortable enough to develop a friendship only after having been around a person for some time—in other words, after you've gotten to know a person better.

Now, what the heck does this have to do with hardware and your Linux system?

Well, it's like this . . . . For most, the computer we use is a black (or beige) box with a few things plugged into it and some magic happening inside that makes it possible to surf the Internet. Anything that falls outside the small subset of applications we use makes us uneasy. That's why the notion of trying something new may be intimidating. The best way to get over that is to become comfortable with what you have.

Ubuntu's Device Manager is a great place to start for getting to know what makes up your system (see Figure 6-10). You can find it by clicking the System menu on the top panel and selecting Device Manager from the Administration submenu. Or, you can bring it up by pressing <Alt+F2> and typing in **hal-device-manager**, its program name.

As soon as the Hal Device Manager loads up, you'll notice that the program window is broken into two main panes. The left side lists all the various device classes and subclasses that make up your system. Beside each major item, there's a small arrow that collapses or expands that particular device or device class' components. Click any item and details about that item are displayed in the right pane.

Why don't we take a few minutes to explore this hardware landscape? Let's start with PCI devices.

PCI Devices

Adding a PCI device definitely requires a reboot because we are talking about internal devices, though your system likely has PCI devices already installed. These are cards that fit into the slots inside your computer. When you reboot the machine, Linux should be able to scan for these cards and identify them without any problem. When you click a PCI device, you'll see that a third tab appears in the right pane. Click the tab to get more vendor-specific information on the device (see Figure 6-11). This is particularly useful if there is a configuration issue and you need to identify your device's make and model number.

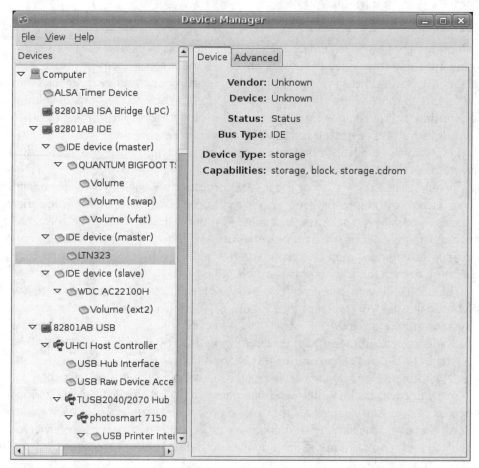

Figure 6–10   GNOME's Hal Device Manager.

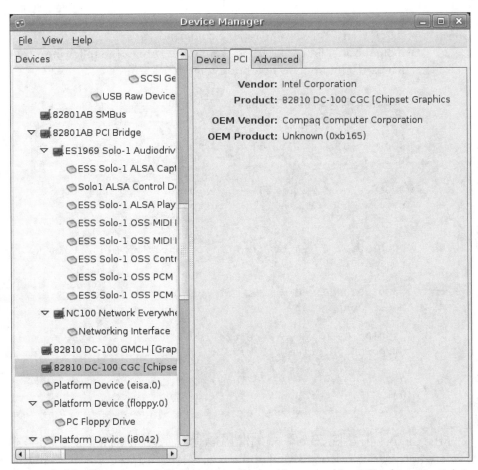

Figure 6–11 When listing PCI devices, the Device Manager adds a PCI information tab in the right pane.

Shell Out You can also run the command /sbin/lspci for a more succinct list of all PCI devices on the system. The following is a partial list from my notebook computer:

```
0000:00:00.0 Host bridge: ATI Technologies Inc
RS200/RS200M AGP Bridge [IGP 340M] (rev 02)

0000:00:01.0 PCI bridge: ATI Technologies Inc PCI
Bridge [IGP 340M]

0000:00:06.0 Multimedia audio controller: ALi Corpo-
ration M5451 PCI AC-Link Controller Audio Device
(rev 02)

0000:00:07.0 ISA bridge: ALi Corporation M1533 PCI
to ISA Bridge [Aladdin IV]

0000:00:08.0 Modem: ALi Corporation M5457 AC'97
Modem Controller

0000:00:09.0 Network controller: Intersil
Corporation Prism 2.5 Wavelan chipset (rev 01)

0000:00:0a.0 CardBus bridge: O2 Micro, Inc. OZ601/
6912/711E0 CardBus/SmartCardBus Controller
```

If the Linux kernel has the appropriate device drivers available as modules, they are automatically loaded, and nothing else needs to be done to make the device available. The reason that this information is useful has to do with those times when you do not have a driver handy or directly available. Being able to get the details on the troublesome device in this way is the first step toward getting it working.

A classic example of this is the Winmodem, so called because it was designed to work specifically with Windows. If you have one of these modems and it was not automatically configured by the system, never fear. I'll talk about Winmodems in more detail later in the chapter. For the moment, let's talk USB.

USB Devices

The whole idea behind USB was eventually to replace all those different connectors on the back of a computer. That includes serial ports, parallel ports, and mouse and keyboard connectors. The acronym stands for *Universal Serial Bus*. On any USB system, there is at least one USB hub and whatever devices are attached. If you look at Figure 6-12, you can see information displayed on two USB controllers (one is a USB 2.0 port, the other USB 1.1), a Labtec webcam, a mini USB wheel mouse, and my Palm Zire 72 (selected), all connected to my system.

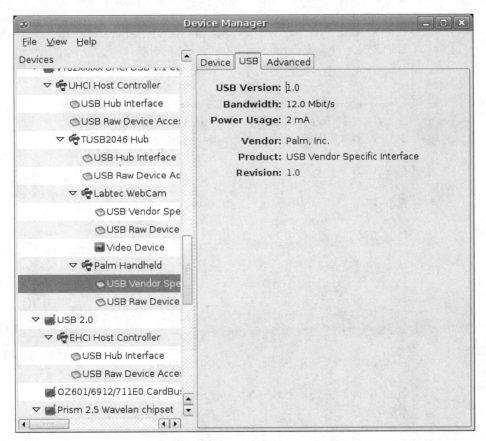

Figure 6–12   The Hal Device Manager displaying USB information on a connected Palm device.

Notice that in the case of a USB device, like my Palm Zire 72, a third tab appears on the right pane. It is labeled USB and clicking it displays additional information specific to the USB device currently selected.

Trivia Time I casually mentioned that my notebook computer had both USB and USB 2.0 ports. It's worth noting because not all systems have both and there is a difference between the two. The new USB 2.0 uses an identical connector to the original USB 1 port but the hardware supports a much faster rate of information exchange. This is particularly useful for devices that must transmit a large amount of information, such as a digital video camera. USB 1 has a speed of 12Mb per second, whereas the new USB 2.0 can transmit data at 480Mb per second.

Shell Out To get a list of USB devices, try the command `lsusb`. The following output is from my notebook:

```
$ lsusb

Bus 003 Device 001: ID 0000:0000

Bus 001 Device 004: ID 0830:0061 Palm, Inc.

Bus 001 Device 003: ID 0c45:6029 Microdia
Triplex i-mini PC Camera

Bus 001 Device 002: ID 0451:2046 Texas Instru-
ments, Inc. TUSB2046 Hub

Bus 001 Device 001: ID 0000:0000

Bus 002 Device 002: ID 04fc:0013 Sunplus Tech-
nology Co., Ltd

Bus 002 Device 001: ID 0000:0000
```

The sheer number of USB devices available is phenomenal, to say the least, and the list is growing. Many of these devices use a standard set of drivers, which means that a number of things can literally be plugged in and used—no need to mess with loading drivers because it is all being done for you.

You noticed the word *many* in that last sentence, right? Keeping track of what works (*and what doesn't*) and providing access to drivers that aren't included in current distributions is the *raison d'être* of the *Linux USB Device Overview* Web site. If you find yourself looking at a new webcam, and you aren't sure whether it is supported under Linux, look there first:

```
http://www.qbik.ch/usb/devices/
```

The site is organized into sections, depending on the device type (audio, video, mass storage, and so on). Each device is assigned a status identifying just how well a device is supported, from *works perfectly* to *works somewhat* to *don't bother*.

Modems versus Winmodems

Well, here's something scary. . . .

Way back when, in the introductory chapter, I mentioned Winmodems as one of the few minuses of running Linux. You'll recall that a Winmodem is a modem designed to work only with Windows. They are sometimes referred to as *software* or *controllerless* modems and tend to be less expensive than controller-based modems.

If you are running a Winmodem, all is not lost. The Linux community is nothing if not resourceful. Even when manufacturers are slow to notice Linux users, the same isn't true the other way around. As more and more people run Linux, this becomes less and less of a problem. In time, hardware manufacturers may be building for Linux first and Windows second. In the meantime, check out the *Linmodems.Org* Web site at `http://www.linmodems.org` and you should be up and running shortly.

So just how do you transform a Winmodem into a Linmodem? Well, let me give you an example.

Among the more common Winmodems out there are those based on the Conexant chipset; these are starting to be very well supported. For the latest driver, just head on over to Linuxant's Web site (not related to Conexant) at http://www.linuxant.com. Not only can you get source drivers, but pre-compiled packages are available for a number of popular Linux distributions.

Identifying the Winmodem is your first step. You can use the GNOME device manager to browser through your PCI hardware, where you will get a lot of detail. You can also *shell out* and use the `lspci` command for a quick list of all the PCI devices found on your system. Here's what it looks like:

```
$ lspci
00:00.0 Host bridge: VIA Technologies, Inc. VT8367 [KT266]
00:01.0 PCI bridge: VIA Technologies, Inc. VT8367 [KT266 AGP]
00:06.0 Communication controller: Conexant HSF 56k Data/Fax/
Voice/Spkp    (w/Handset) Modem (WorldW SmartDAA) (rev 01)
00:08.0 Ethernet controller: Realtek Semiconductor Co., Ltd.
RTL-8139/8139C (rev 10)
00:11.0 ISA bridge: VIA Technologies, Inc. VT8233 PCI to ISA
Bridge
00:11.1 IDE interface: VIA Technologies, Inc. Bus Master IDE
(rev 06)
00:11.2 USB Controller: VIA Technologies, Inc. USB (rev 18)
00:11.5 Multimedia audio controller: VIA Technologies, Inc.
VT8233 AC97    Audio Controller (rev 10)
01:00.0 VGA compatible controller: nVidia Corporation NV11
[GeForce2 MX DDR] (rev b2)
```

In some cases, you will find precompiled driver packages. Some are specific to your release, and others are generic. In the case of my Conexant-based Winmodem, the site provides a generic installer that should detect your system and install itself accordingly.

As per the instructions that followed the install, I typed the following command:

```
/usr/sbin/hsfconfig
```

A short dialog followed, asking me for the country (Canada, in my case), after which the program compiled and installed my driver for me. It even linked the newly created device, `/dev/ttySHSF0`, to `/dev/modem`. I was ready to use my modem without a care.

Shell Out From the shell prompt, I can verify the location of my modem with this command:

```
$ ls -l /dev/modem
```

The system then responds with this information:

```
lr-xr-xr-x   1  root   root   8 Sep  9   11:23
/dev/modem  -> /dev/ttySHSF0
```

The preceding listing is all one unbroken line.

The Winmodem/Linmodem Roundup

Clearly, none of this whole Winmodem problem applies if you are using an *external* modem or happen to be among the lucky ones using a cable modem connection or high-speed DSL access from your local phone company. For others out there, it can be a bit more complicated. I've already given you the address of the Conexant Web site, and I will give you more right here.

Remember, *many of these modems* can be made into useful and productive members of Linux society with a visit to the right Web site. On that note, here's my roundup:

Conexant Modems (HCF and HSF)

```
http://www.linuxant.com
```

Smart Link Modems

```
http://www.smlink.com
```

Lucent Modems

```
http://www.physcip.uni-stuttgart.de/heby/ltmodem/
```

PCTel Modems

```
http://linmodems.technion.ac.il/pctel-linux/
```

What? More Devices?

We've covered a lot of ground here, but we are by no means finished. Those things we attach to our PCs aren't much good if we don't put them in context with the tools and applications we use them with. Those tools tend to require a somewhat more in-depth examination. For instance, burning CDs isn't just about creating collections of your favorite songs. People use them for back-ups, as well, or to make collections of digital photos for sharing with the family. I'll tell you all about CD burning in Chapter 18. Most CD and DVD burners are automatically recognized under Linux.

The same is true of scanners. These gizmos are incredibly handy devices for the home or office. Aside from converting nondigital pictures to place on your Web site, you can use your scanner as a photocopier and as a way to send faxes when the pages require your signature (you can fax from a word processor, after all). For the most part, your scanning application autodetects your scanner and configures it for you (see Figure 6-13). You'll find XSane under your Graphics submenu.

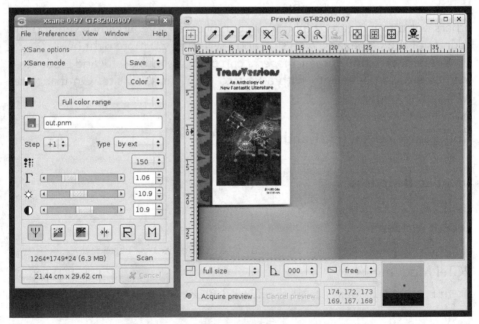

Figure 6–13   XSane, the image scanning application included with Ubuntu, autodetects and automatically configures many popular scanners.

By the way, XSane is also a great program for sending images in an email, faxing documents, or making photocopies.

To help you in choosing a scanner that is well supported under Linux, check out the SANE (Scanner Access Now Easy) page of supported devices.

```
http://www.sane-project.org/sane-supported-devices.html
```

There's also a scanner search engine on that page to make locating your devices that much easier.

Resources

Linux Hardware Compatibility HOWTO

```
http://www.tldp.org/HOWTO/Hardware-HOWTO/index.html
```

Hardware Catalog at Red Hat

```
http://bugzilla.redhat.com/hwcert
```

Linmodems.org (Winmodems under Linux)

```
http://www.linmodem.org
```

LinuxPrinting.org (Linux Printer Database)

```
http://www.linuxprinting.org
```

Linux USB Device Overview

```
http://www.qbik.ch/usb/devices/
```

SANE Project, Supported Devices

```
http://www.sane-project.org/sane-supported-devices.html
```

Ubuntu Hardware Support Wiki

```
https://wiki.ubuntu.com/HardwareSupport
```

Chapter

7

Connecting to the Internet

I'm going to start this chapter with a little Networking 101. It will be *fun*—really. For those of you who already know everything about TCP/IP and how IP networks operate, you can skip ahead a few paragraphs.

Communication over the Internet takes place using something called the *TCP/IP protocol suite*. TCP/IP actually stands for *Transmission Control Protocol/Internet Protocol*, and it is the basic underlying means by which all this magic communication takes place. Everything you do on the Net, whether it is surfing your favorite sites, sending and receiving emails, chatting via some instant messaging client, or listening to an audio broadcast—all these things ride on TCP/IP's virtual back.

TCP/IP is often referred to as a *protocol suite*, a collection of protocols that speak the same language. Essentially, this comes down to the transmission and reception of IP packets. Those packets have to get from place to place, and that means they need to know how to get there. IP packets do this in exactly the same way that you get from your house to someone else's house. They have a home address from which they go to a remote address.

Each and every computer connected to the Internet has a unique address called an *IP address*, four sets of numbers separated by dots (for example, 192.168.22.55). Some systems that are always online (banks, Web sites, companies, and so on) have a *static* address. Dial-up connections for home users tend to be shared—when you aren't connected, someone else may be using the same address—which is referred to as a *dynamic* IP address.

You may be wondering how a symbolic Web site address such as `www.marcelgagne.com` translates to the dotted foursome I mentioned previously, and that would be an excellent question.

Think of the real world again. We don't think of our friends as 136 Mulberry Tree Lane or 1575 Natika Court; we think of them by their names. To find out where our friends live, we check the phone book (or ask them). The same holds true in the digital world, but that phone book is called a *domain name server* (DNS). When I type a symbolic (that is, human readable) address into my Web browser, it contacts a DNS (assigned by my Internet service provider (ISP)) and asks for the IP address. With that IP address, my packets almost know how to get to their destinations.

Almost?

To reach an address in the real world, you get out of your driveway and enter some road to which all other roads are connected. If you drive long enough, presumably you get to Rome (having often been told that *all roads lead to Rome*). Before you can get to Rome, you enter your default route, namely, the street in front of your house. The same principle exists in the virtual world. For your IP packages (an email to your mother, for instance) to get to its destination, it must take a particular route, called a *default route*. This will be the IP address of a device that knows all the other routes. Your ISP provides that route.

That concludes Networking 101. Not particularly complicated, is it?

Before You Begin

Connecting to the Internet is one if those things you set up once, then forget about. Still, you need to get some information from your ISP up front. The basics are as follows:

- Your username and password
- The phone number your modem will be dialing to connect (if using a dial-up modem connection)

- The IP address of the DNS (name servers, described earlier)
- The IP or symbolic address of your SMTP and POP3 email hosts
- The IP or symbolic address of your news server (optional)

All of this information likely came with your contract when you first signed up with your ISP. Armed with this information, you are ready to begin.

Getting on the Net

As I write this, there are three very popular methods of connecting to the Internet, notwithstanding your own connection at the office. These are cable modem, DSL service from the phone company, or good old-fashioned dial-up modem. The first two are usually referred to as *high-speed* or *broadband* connections, and dial-up access is usually made fun of because it feels very slow when compared to the higher speed methods.

With all the press and hype about high-speed service, you would think that this is all people run. Think again. As I write this, the vast majority of people in North America, and indeed the world, is still connecting through a dial-up connection. Make no mistake—as Mark Twain might have remarked, the rumors of dial-up access's demise are greatly exaggerated. You may be among the majority who are still using dial-up; I'll cover that in detail.

If you are ready, let's begin.

Connecting to the Net with a Modem

Most ISPs provide dial-up access through the Point-to-Point Protocol, or PPP. To set up a network connection or pretty much any type, just run the Network Settings program. Click System on the top panel, then Administration, and finally, Networking. You can also use your <Alt+F2> Run Application shortcut and type in **network-admin** in the dialog box. If you are starting to like the feel of the command line, enter "**network-admin &**" in a terminal window. Since this is an administration function, you'll be asked for your password (see Figure 7-1).

Figure 7–1   Administrative functions like this require that you enter your password.

Tip You may have noticed in the preceding paragraph that I added an ampersand (&) to the end of the `network-admin` command. When you start a command from a shell prompt, it normally runs in the foreground. This means you can't start another process at the shell until the current one finishes (you could, of course, open up another shell). The ampersand tells the shell to put the process in the background so that you can run other commands.

When the Network Settings tool comes up for the first time, it lists, at minimum, a modem connection that is currently not configured (see Figure 7-2). Even if you don't have a modem built in to your machine, an option for configuring one is still available. In your list of connections, you may also see an Ethernet connection. Most modern machines usually have an Ethernet card built in, so this is likely. We'll use my test machine as an example, which, as you can see, has both a network card and a dial-up modem attached.

Before you jump in and configure your modem connection, look at the drop-down box labeled Location near the top of this window. The idea here is that you can have multiple dial-up (or network) accounts. Most people probably use just one, but you can also use it to set up multiple profiles of the same account. If you happen to be a road warrior or globe trotter with a notebook, you can create location profiles for the various cities you visit.

Figure 7–2 The Network Settings application is used for all network connections, including dial-up.

By default, there are no locations defined. If you go ahead and configure a network connection without creating a location, those settings are your default. To add a new location, click the drop-down box (it is empty at this point) and click Create Location. A small dialog appears (see Figure 7-3), in which you enter the name of this location (for example, `London office`). When you have entered the name, click OK.

Figure 7–3
Your network configuration can have multiple locations defined.

Because you are probably doing this to deal with traveling profiles, you may want to add at least two entries here, one for home and one for away.

Configuring Your Dial-up Connection

A dial-up connection generally implies a PPP, or Point-to-Point, connection. Click Modem Connection to highlight that selection, then click the Properties tab. The Interface Properties dialog appears. It consists of three tabbed windows labeled General, Modem, and Options. If the General tab isn't selected by default, click it now. Look for and check the box labeled Enable This Connection. You'll find it on the General tab under the Connection heading for device ppp0 (see Figure 7-4). The additional fields in this window should no longer be grayed out.

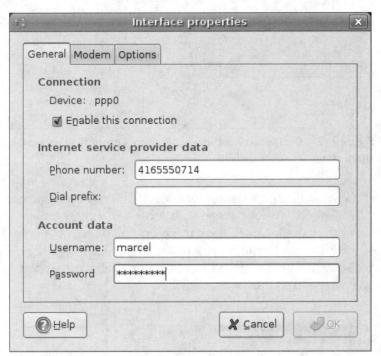

Figure 7–4   Your first step is to enable the connection, then enter your ISP's connection information.

Enter your ISP's dial-up phone number and, if need be, a dialing prefix. Below that, enter the username and password that was supplied to you when you set up the account. Now, click the Modem tab.

I covered devices in the previous chapter, specifically the issue of modems, and it is particularly relevant here. If you click the Modems tab, you'll notice that the modem port is not set. Click the drop-down list and you'll see several possibilities including /dev/modem, which is a symbolic link to the actual port for the modem. That might be /dev/ttyS0, but it could be many other things, as well. You have the option of specifying the modem port yourself, but the easiest way to discover the modem is to click the Autodetect button (see Figure 7-5).

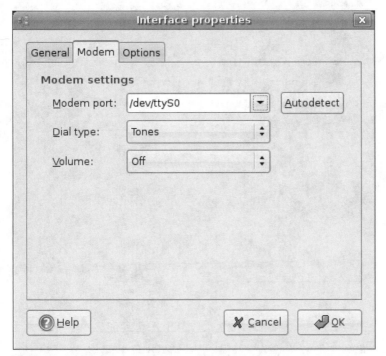

Figure 7–5 If you don't already know where your modem is connected, click the Autodetect button.

The Dial Type setting lets you choose between tone and pulse dialing. I can't personally remember encountering a pulse service for many years now, but if yours still uses it, click the drop-down box and select Pulses instead of Tones. Finally, there's a Volume setting (Off, Low, Medium, and Loud) so you can listen to your modem dial out and make that cool screeching noise.

The third and final tab is labeled Options (see Figure 7-6). You'll find Set Modem as Default Route to the Internet and Use the Internet Service Provider Nameservers check boxes selected. Unless you have good reason to change these settings (that is, as instructed by your ISP), leave them alone. You may, however, select the last check box, Retry If the Connection Breaks or Fails to Start to automatically reconnect should anything interrupt your Internet connection.

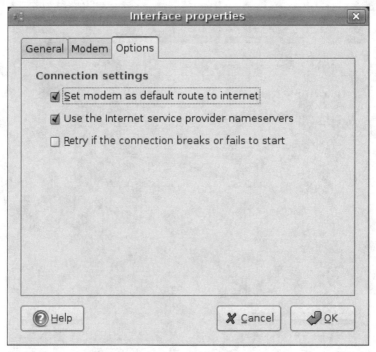

Figure 7–6   You may want to configure your modem to automatically redial if the connection drops.

Click OK and you return to the main Network Settings screen with Modem Connection still selected (refer to Figure 7-2). The difference here is that the Activate button is no longer grayed out. Click the button to dial out to the Internet.

Cable Modems and High-Speed DSL

For the most part, if you installed your Linux system with the cable modem connected, this is probably already working, and you have nothing left to do. If, however, you are already up and running and you are just now getting a cable modem, it is probably time for a few pointers. Quite frankly, these days (with a modern Linux distribution), there isn't much to it.

To begin with, cable modems aren't modems in the classic sense. The so-called modem is connected to your cable TV service on one side and to an Ethernet card inside your PC on the other. High-speed access through your phone company's DSL service is similar in that they provide you with an external, modem-like device (in many cases, it is really a router) that also connects to an Ethernet card.

The Ethernet card (which should be automatically detected by your system) gets an IP address from the cable modem via the Dynamic Host Configuration Protocol (DHCP). Although this address may appear permanent in that it rarely (if ever) changes, it is nevertheless dynamic, because your actual Ethernet card gets its address whenever it connects.

The process of getting your system configured varies a bit from distribution to distribution, but only cosmetically. When you install your new Ethernet card (for access through the cable modem), it should be autodetected by the system on reboot. As part of that process, the system asks you whether you want to configure the card. The answer is yes, of course. Next, the system asks whether you want to supply an IP address or have it autoconfigure via DHCP. With a cable modem, as with DSL, autoconfiguring is what you want.

Now that I've told you how incredibly *easy* it is to do this, I'm going to mention that there are many different providers of high-speed cable and DSL access. This means that if your system doesn't autorecognize and configure your connection, you may need to do one of these things. For cable modems, the answers vary, but start by checking out the Cable Modem HOWTO at http://www.tldp.org for details on your particular geographic location.

If you are on a phone company DSL service, you want to use the pppo-econf package (already installed as part of your Ubuntu setup). Open a shell (Terminal) and run the command with administrator permissions. Do this by typing this command:

```
sudo pppoeconf
```

This is a text-only utility and basically a fill-in-the-blanks session. The first screen checks for your Ethernet card and asks you to confirm its location. Because most people only have one Ethernet card, this is usually a fairly simple choice to make. You want to make sure that your DSL modem is plugged in and turned on because the next screen scans for the existence of your DSL modem to continue with setup. Then, you are asked for the username and password provided by your Internet service provider for this connection.

The last step in this configuration dialog is a question about whether you want the connection to come up automatically. This is generally a good idea. After you have completed this setup, you likely don't need to run this utility again (unless you switch ISPs, of course).

Going Wireless

Notebook computers used to be the exception rather than the rule, but falling prices have made these little portable powerhouses increasingly attainable. Sit in any airport waiting room and it seems as though every other person is sitting, typing at a notebook. Furthermore, they are running wireless. The open notebook isn't an unusual sight at coffee shops either. In fact, these days, wireless networks are everywhere, quite possibly in your home. Now all you need to do is get connected.

Linux has excellent hardware support and that includes wireless support. Unfortunately, there are still drivers that are written for Windows only or in the case of my own notebook, the Linux driver may lack functionality. My own notebook's wireless card works fine on my home network, but it only works so well. For instance, the standard Linux driver that supports the card doesn't allow for things like scanning.

The Windows-only Driver Dilemma

As sometimes happens, manufacturers aren't 100 percent forthcoming with information or specifications to make full Linux support easy. I truly admire the incredible talent and energy of Linux developers who provide Linux with excellent drivers while working in a vendor black hole. Nevertheless, this lack of information was the impetus for the NdisWrapper project, which makes it possible to use Windows NDIS drivers via a loadable Linux kernel module. Luckily, your Ubuntu Linux system makes this extremely easy and I'll show you how.

Click System on the top panel and navigate to the Administration sub-menu. There, click the Windows Wireless Drivers menu option (command name ndisgtk). Because this is an administrative function, you are asked for your password to confirm. After you enter it, the Wireless Network Drivers dialog appears (see Figure 7-7).

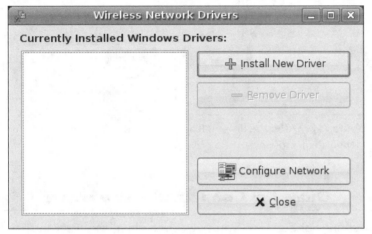

Figure 7–7 At first, you don't see any installed Windows drivers.

To install a Windows NDIS driver, click the Install New Driver button. A small dialog appears asking you to select an INF file. Below that is a button labeled Location. Click the button to bring up the GNOME file manager and navigate to the location of the Windows INF file that corresponds to your particular wireless card. When you have chosen your driver and returned to the dialog, click the Install button to install the driver. If you have chosen the right driver and everything has gone well, you should be back at the main window; but it now shows an installed driver and lists the hardware as present (see Figure 7-8).

Now that your driver is installed and your hardware is recognized, you can go ahead and configure your network settings by clicking the Configure Network button. The Network Settings dialog you used earlier appears (refer to Figure 7-2).

See, it was easy, wasn't it?

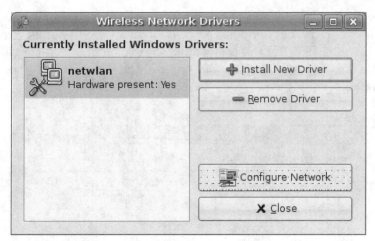

Figure 7–8   After the driver is loaded, your network card should identify itself as present.

Okay, I'm Connected—Now What?

Good question. For starters, you have everything the Internet has to offer. You can surf the Web (which I cover in Chapter 10), send email (Chapter 11), download and install software, and find and download music and videos. The Internet is a vast cornucopia of news, information, conversation, sights, sounds, and a thousand other things. When looking at all of its offerings, it is easy to forget that it really all comes down one thing—*communication*.

The Internet was born on communication; email specifically was the tool that drove its development into the globe-spanning network that it is today. That means electronic mail, Web browsing, and the increasingly popular instant message.

I'll tell you all about instant messaging with Ubuntu shortly, but first, it's time to discuss software. Not the software you have installed, but the amazing, free software that is still out there, waiting for you, on the Internet. In the next chapter, you will learn how easy it is to install software packages and keep your system up-to-date with Ubuntu.

Resources

Ubuntu Information on Wifi and Ndiswrapper

`https://wiki.ubuntu.com/WifiDocs`

Ubuntu Wiki Page on pppoeconf

`https://wiki.ubuntu.com/ADSLPPPoE`

8

Installing New Applications

Your Ubuntu Linux system arrived with a collection of great software, with packages to handle everything from word processing to email, surfing the Web, instant messaging, even games to help you unwind. As you take the time to experiment and learn about your system and everything it has to offer, eventually you'll want more than what you have. That's why I'm going to show you how to install that software, easily and without fuss. I will also tell you about updates and how to make sure that your system is patched and secure. You'll be amazed at how easy it is to search for the software you need and how fast you can have it up and running.

Before we get into finding and installing software, I'd like to address a little myth. You have no doubt heard that installing software on Linux is difficult and that it is inferior to what you are used to in the Windows world. Nothing could be further from the truth. In fact, software installation under Linux is actually superior to what you are leaving behind in your old OS.

Security Note When you install software and software pack-ages, you must often do so as an administrative user, also known as root. As root, you are all powerful. Linux tends to be more secure and much safer than your old OS, but that doesn't mean disasters can't strike. Know where your software comes from and take the time to understand what it does. That's why sticking with the Ubuntu repositories, which give you access to several thou-sand packages through Synaptic, is the best approach. Synaptic? Don't worry. I'll explain.

Linux and Security

When it comes to installing software, security is something we should talk about. I've already said that you should know where your software is coming from, but that is only part of the consideration. That's why I'm going to clear up some bad press Linux gets when it comes to installing software.

In the Windows world, it is frighteningly easy to infect your PC with a virus or a worm. All you have to do is click on an email attachment, and you could be in trouble. With some email packages under Windows, it "helps" you by automatically opening your email attachments, or connecting you to Internet links, which can cause trouble. You won't find many Linux packages provided as simple executables (.EXE files and so on). *Security is the reason.* To install most packages, you also need root privileges. Again, for security reasons, Linux demands that you be conscious of the fact that you might be doing something that could hurt your system. If an email attachment wants to install itself into the system, it must consult the root user first.

Package managers, such as `rpm` (the RPM Package Manager) or Ubuntu and Debian's `dpkg/apt-get`, perform checks to make sure that certain dependencies are met or that software doesn't accidentally overwrite other software. Those dependency checks take many things into consideration, such as what software already exists and how the new package will coexist. Many of you are probably familiar with what has been called *DLL hell*, where one piece of software just goes ahead and overwrites some other piece of code. It may even have happened to you. Blindly installing without these checks can be disastrous. At best, the result can be an unstable machine—at worst, it can be unusable.

Installing software under Linux may take a step or two, but it is for your own good.

Identifying Software Packages

Most major Linux distributions have in common the concept of a package—a prebuilt bundle of software ready to be installed on your system. Despite the numerous distributions out there, most use the same package management systems. They often have different ways of dealing with them, but the packaging system remains pretty consistent. Most distributions these days use either the RPM format of packages or DEB. Because it is based on Debian, Ubuntu Linux uses DEB format packages.

Assume that I am talking about a hypothetical package called ftl_transport. If I were looking for this package to install on my Ubuntu system, I would find it in this type of format:

```
ftl-transport_2.1-1_i386.deb
```

The first part is the package name itself. The numbers just after the underscore (and just before the hyphen) indicate the software version number. The number following the hyphen is the package release number. Following that is the architecture for which the package was compiled (i386, in this case). The final prefix, .deb, is a dead giveaway that this is a Debian package, sometimes referred to as a DEB.

The Simplest Way to Add Applications

In the next section, I'm going to show you a detailed way to find, install, update, and maintain software for your Ubuntu Linux system. Before I do that, however, I want to show you a simple, easy-to-use tool for installing packages on your system. You've no doubt seen this entry in the menu several times as you have worked through the various chapters of this book. It's time to look at the Add Applications program.

To get started, click Applications on the top panel and select Add/ Remove. It's the last item on the list. Installing software requires system privileges, so you are asked for the password first. Enter it and a few seconds later, the Add/Remove Applications dialog appears (see Figure 8-1). There is a short delay as the program reads the database of available and installed applications. The command name for this program is gnome-app-install.

Figure 8–1   The Add Application dialog can be used to remove programs as well. It's the easy way to add and remove packages.

To the left, in a vertical sidebar, is a list of categories into which all of the available applications are sorted. These categories include Games, Graphics, Office, System Tools, and others. Click on a category and the list of applications that exist in that category appear in the top right window. Below the top right-hand pane is another window. This is the description window. Click on an application above and a description appears below.

Let's just jump right in and see how easy this is to use. Then, we'll investigate it in a bit more detail. At the top right of the screen, you'll see a little box with a Search label to the right of it. Type **game** in the text box. In seconds, the install program locates every package it knows of that that has the word *game* somewhere in either the title or the description. The results appear in the left pane (see Figure 8-2).

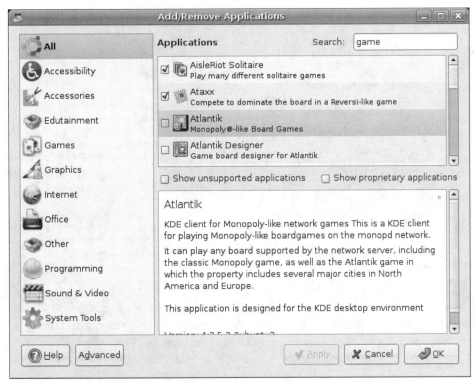

Figure 8-2 By searching the word *game,* the program returns all of the applications it knows about with the word *game* in the title or description.

Select a game from the list and read its accompanying description. If this sounds like a good choice, click the check box next to the program's name, then click the Apply button at the bottom of the main window. Before things get rolling, you are asked to confirm your list of packages. If you are happy with the choices, click Apply. A dialog appears informing you of the installer's progress as it downloads, unpacks, and installs the packages you have selected (see Figure 8-3).

Note The Ubuntu DVD included with this book includes all of the supported Ubuntu packages, whether installed or not. What this means is that for many packages, you don't need to download from the Internet if you installed Ubuntu from the DVD. Just have the disk ready when the system asks you for it. This is a boon for those of you who may not have access to a broadband connection.

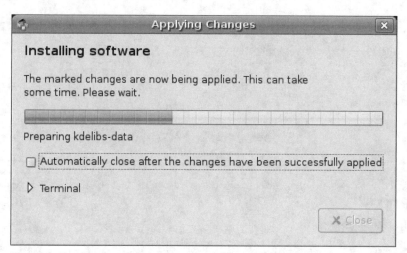

Figure 8–3 A progress dialog displays information about the download and the installation.

When the installation is complete, you get a nice message alerting you to that fact along with a list of the major packages you have selected. Then, the package and dependency list are rebuilt and you are ready to start again.

Removing Installed Packages

Should you decide that you want to remove a package—not a bad idea if you aren't using the software—go back to the Add/Remove Applications dialog and search for the package. That's the quickest way to find it. You could also browse down the applications list to find it. To actually remove the package in question, uncheck the box next to the program name and click Apply. A confirmation dialog appears asking you to confirm that you do indeed want to remove this package. If this all sounds familiar, that's because it is essentially the reverse of installing software.

But Wait, There's More!

Before we move on, let me direct your attention to those two check boxes below the list of applications (see Figure 8-4). If you pause your mouse cursor over the "Show unsupported applications" or "Show proprietary applications" check boxes, you'll find literally hundreds of applications that aren't part of the official Ubuntu release.

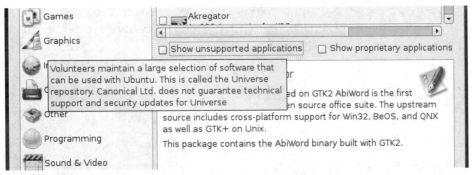

Figure 8–4 The packages you see listed are by no means everything. There are hundreds of additional, unsupported packages available. Just click the check boxes to show unsupported and proprietary applications.

Occasionally, packages rely on other packages and removing packages becomes a somewhat more complex issue. A message appears suggesting that you use Advanced mode. This Advanced mode is the Synaptic package manager and despite the word *Advanced*, it is still very easy to use. Let me tell you about it.

The Synaptic Package Manager

Before we get started, I want to tell you about package repositories, sites where Ubuntu Linux packages are stored and available for download. By default, Ubuntu comes preconfigured with standard and security update repositories. To get access to certain packages, like the MP3 software I tell you about in Chapter 18, you will want to enable the extra Universe and Multiverse package repositories. It's easy. Really.

Let's start by firing up Synaptic. Click System on the top panel and select Synaptic Package Manager from the Administration submenu. Because installing software requires administrator privileges, you are asked to enter your password for confirmation. A few seconds later, you are looking at the Synaptic window (see Figure 8-5).

The Synaptic window is broken up into three major areas, or panes. The left-hand bar lets you identify software based on its category. Below the category listing are four buttons labeled Sections, Status, Search, and Custom. The main portion of the window is divided horizontally on the right. To the top, packages are listed. Clicking one of these packages shows a description of the software in the lower pane. Along the top, you'll find the classic menu bar, and directly below, an icon bar with buttons that provide access to some of the most common functions.

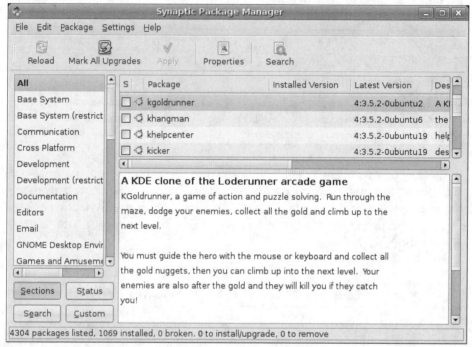

Figure 8–5 The Synaptic package manager with the kgoldrunner package selected. The bottom part of the main window displays information about the selected software.

Adding Repositories

Because I made such a big deal of it, let's start by adding those other repositories. From the Synaptic main window, click Settings on the menu bar, and then select Repositories. A Software Preferences dialog appears (see Figure 8-6). You'll see three tabs, one labeled Installation Media, another labeled Internet Updates, and the other, Authentication. By default, the Installation Media tab should be selected.

We'll get to those repositories in just a second, but first click on the Internet Updates tab. Look for a check box labeled "Check for updates automatically." It should be checked on by default. There's a combo box next to the label with Daily selected. A little later in this chapter, I will cover the subject of system updates. This is how you define whether and how often the system checks for updates. I find that daily is an ideal choice for me, but you can change that to every two days, weekly, or every two weeks.

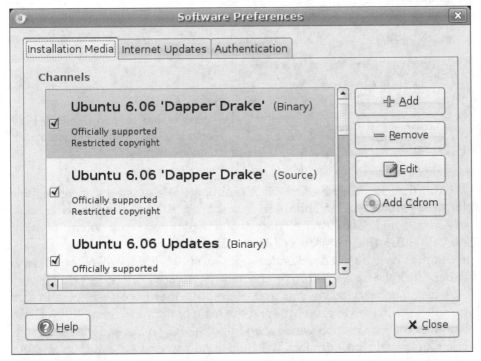

Figure 8–6   The Software Preferences dialog is where you define what repositories Ubuntu has access to. It's also where you can set your system to watch for automatic updates.

Now, on to those extra repositories: Click back to the Installation Media tab. If you scroll down the list of Sources in that Installation Media window, you see the repositories that your system already knows about and uses. Some things are listed as officially supported; some possibly with restricted copyright. The Universe and Multiverse repositories don't fit neatly into these categories, partly because they aren't officially supported. Click the Add button to show and select these other options. The Add Repository dialog appears (see Figure 8-7).

Figure 8–7
Adding repositories means defining the constraints you are willing to accept on those repositories.

Click the check boxes next to Community Maintained (Universe) and Non-free (Multiverse) to add these repositories. All four check boxes should now be selected. Click Add to close the dialog. If you scroll down the list of Sources under the Installation Media tab, you'll notice that these binary repositories have been added under a Ubuntu 6.04 "Dapper Drake" (Binary) header. Click the Close button on the main Software Preferences dialog.

A dialog appears telling you that the repositories have changed and that you should click the Reload button on the main Synaptic window. Click Close to dismiss the information window and that takes you back to the main Synaptic window. It's time to click the Reload button and let Synaptic find out about all those new packages you told it about.

Installing Software with Synaptic

Using Synaptic to install an application isn't all that different from what I showed you earlier, but Synaptic is quite a bit more flexible and more powerful than the basic GNOME package installer.

To search for a package, click the Search button on the icon bar. A small Find window appears with an empty field, into which you can enter your search terms (see Figure 8-8). Below the Search field is a combo box that lets you define where the search takes place. The default is to look in the package name and the description for the package. For most, this will satisfy 99 percent of the time. You can, however, also search for a particular version number, the package maintainer's name, dependencies, and provided packages. Let's enter instant messaging in the search field, and click the Search button.

Figure 8–8
The easiest way to locate packages with Synaptic is to click the Search button and type in what you are looking for.

The result is a list of packages that have the words *instant messaging* somewhere in their description. Click each package individually to get a description of that package. Should you decide you want to install a particular package, right-click the package name and select Mark for Installation (see Figure 8-9).

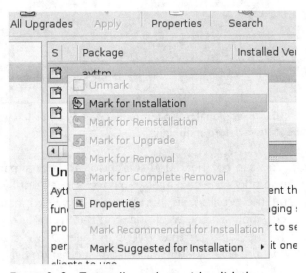

Figure 8–9   To install a package, right-click the package name and then select Mark for Installation from the drop-down menu.

Part of what makes Synaptic such a joy is that it takes all the work out of having to know what other packages might be needed when you choose to install something. If the software you want needs three additional packages, Synaptic knows and lets you know as well (see Figure 8-10). In my example, there are six additional packages required. Synaptic wants to know if I want to have them automagically marked for installation as well. If you accept— and generally speaking, you always do—click the Mark button to continue.

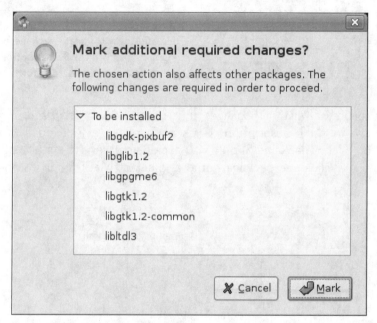

Figure 8–10   If additional packages are required, Synaptic lets you know about them before continuing.

At this point, you can go ahead and search for additional packages if you want. Synaptic remembers the packages you have chosen until you choose to install them or quit the program. When you are ready to install what you have selected, click Apply on the Synaptic icon bar. You get a final window telling you about all the packages that will be installed, how much space will be used, and how big the download itself will be (see Figure 8-11).

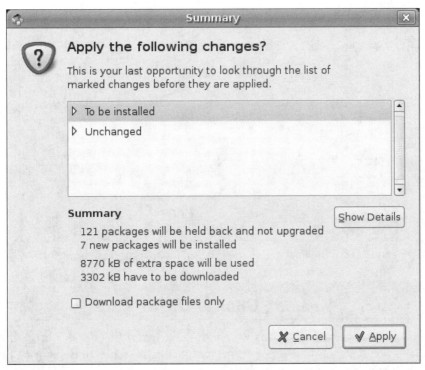

Figure 8–11 As a final step before installing your packages, Synaptic provides a summary of what it will do.

The install begins, first with the packages being downloaded over the Internet. This is followed by the system preparing the packages for upgrade and ends with the installation of the packages themselves. Throughout the process, a dialog alerts you to the various steps and provides a status bar (see Figure 8-12) so you have some idea of how long the whole thing will take.

Depending on the speed of your machine or the number of packages, this could take from several seconds to several minutes or more. The process bar gives you some clues as to how much time this will all take. When the process is done, you get a final dialog letting you know that all changes (installations, upgrades, package replacements) are done. Click Close and you go back at the main Synaptic window.

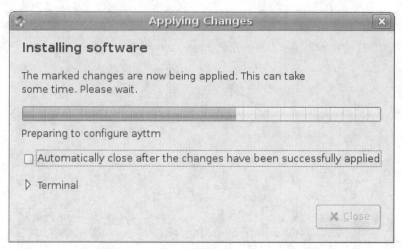

Figure 8–12   The final step in the process: Your packages are being installed.

Keeping Ubuntu Up-to-Date

If your system is connected to an always up, Internet connection, Ubuntu regularly scans its update repositories for general patches and security fixes. When something becomes available, you see a message pop up at the top of your screen (see Figure 8-13). These updates may be anything from patches and fixes to security updates. The latter is a particularly good reason to stay on top of the latest updates.

Figure 8–13   From time to time, you may see a pop-up similar to this one, alerting you to software updates.

It is possible that you do not see the preceding pop-up. Depending on whether you've already seen the message, banished it earlier, or whether you've been busy installing packages, the red icon itself is a giveaway. If you pause your mouse cursor over it, you see a tooltip alerting you to the number of updates available (see Figure 8-14).

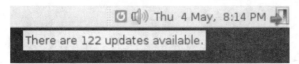

Figure 8–14 Watch for the update icon in the top panel. Pausing your mouse over the icon generates a tooltip with additional information.

There are a couple of things you can do here. The first is to just click the icon. This starts the update manager. Right-click the icon and a pop-up menu appears with a number of options. You can choose to view the available updates, update the package list now, or go ahead and install the updates. There's also an option here to change the update manager preferences.

Regardless of whether an update icon is present in the top panel, you can also start the update manager by clicking System on the top panel and selecting Update Manager from the Administration submenu. Remember that the system only checks for updates according to the schedule you selected earlier in the chapter. It is possible that there are updates you need to check on before the scheduled time (for example, you've heard about a security update and you want to check on it now). Either way, because this is an administrative function, you are asked for your password before continuing. Enter it and the Software Updates window appears (see Figure 8-15).

At the bottom of this window, there's a Show Details label with a small arrow to the side. If you want to find out what a particular update does or what changes come with an update, click the arrow. The window splits into a top and bottom pane with an information pane at the bottom. Click a package name up top and the description of changes appears below.

Unless you have good reason not to, you can usually accept the changes. Click the Install Updates button and the packages start to download. If you have followed along up to this point, what happens next will be familiar to you. The installation of those packages follows the same approach you saw with Synaptic and the basic GNOME package installer.

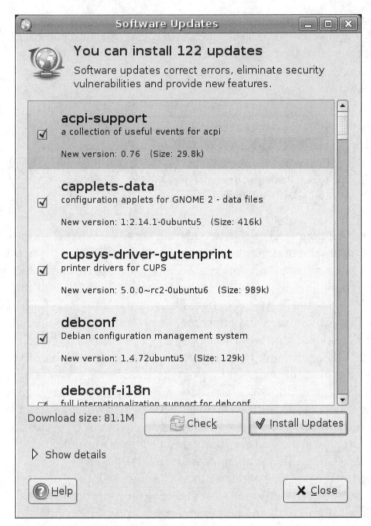

Figure 8–15   The Software Updates window lists all of the current packages available for update.

DEBs, the Shell Way

For most, using Synaptic, or the simple package installer I told you about earlier, is definitely the way to go. However, as with many things, there is another way to do it and this way involves working down at the shell. If you are interested in finding out what goes on beneath Synaptic's slick exterior, take a look at this short introduction to package administration using the Linux shell.

In the Debian world, of which Ubuntu is a part, there are two useful commands for dealing with packages at the command line: dpkg and apt-get. The most basic method of installing a package is with this format of the dpkg command:

```
sudo dpkg --install ftl-transport_2.1-1ubuntu1.deb
```

dpkg is the basic package installation tool for Debian and Debian-based systems such as Ubuntu. The previous command installs the package. This one removes it:

```
sudo dpkg --remove ftl-transport
```

Note If it looks like I am saving keystrokes here, there is a reason. I only indicate the package release number and subsequent extensions at installation time. To remove a package, you only need the package name itself.

You should be aware that there is another step to consider when removing a package. Although the program is now gone from your system, its configuration files remain (which can be a good idea). To get rid of those as well, you need to purge the package:

```
sudo dpkg --purge ftl-transport
```

Now that I have had you do it the long way, you could start with a purge to both *remove* the package and *purge* the configuration files in one step.

Great, but Can You Tell Me What Is Already There?

Sure thing. If you want to get a list of every package on your system, use the --list option to dpkg. You might want to pipe that output to the more command:

```
dpkg --list | more
```

If something in that list should prove interesting and you would like to know more about the package, try the `--print-avail` flag. In this example, I try to discover something about the mysterious `mtools` package:

```
dpkg --print-avail mtools
Package: mtools
Priority: standard
Section: otherosfs
Installed-Size: 468
Maintainer: Luis Bustamante <luferbu@fluidsignal.com>
Architecture: i386
Version: 3.9.9-2.1ubuntu1
Depends: libc6 (>= 2.3.2.ds1-4)
Suggests: floppyd
Size: 195994
Description: Tools for manipulating MSDOS files
```

The preceding information only prints information about an installed package. As with many things in the Linux world (and life in general), there is more than one way to do this. You could also use the other indispensable command-line tool, `apt-get`—to be specific, `apt-cache`, one of `apt-get`'s related utilities:

```
apt-cache show mtools
```

The results of this command are identical to those of the preceding `dpkg` example.

Finding out a Package's Current Release Level

To find out the version of a package that is already installed on your system, use the `-l` flag. In the following example, I query the system to find out what version of `bash` (the Bourne Again Shell) I am working with:

```
dpkg -l bash
Desired=Unknown/Install/Remove/Purge/Hold
| Status=Not/Installed/Config-files/Unpacked/Failed-config/
  Half-installed
|/ Err?=(none)/Hold/Reinst-required/X=both-problems
  (Status,Err: uppercase=bad)
```

```
||/ Name              Version          Description
+++-==============-===============-===========================
ii  bash             3.1-2ubuntu6    The GNU Bourne Again SHell
```

What Is That Strange File?

Let's say that you are wondering what some file is doing on your system. For instance, there is something called pinwrapper in my /usr/bin directory and I don't remember installing it. Furthermore, if I try to look it up in the man pages, I am told that there is no information on this file. Using the -S flag, I can have dpkg identify what package this file was a part of:

```
dpkg -S /usr/bin/pinwrapper
bluez-utils: /usr/bin/pinwrapper
```

Even though I don't remember installing this bluez-utils software, I can now use apt-cache show bluez-utils to tell me what this package is for. As it turns out, they are tools for using Bluetooth devices.

Using apt-get to Install or Update Software

People who use Debian distributions on a regular basis sometimes point to this wonderful little program as the reason why Debian is so great. Well, I certainly won't be the one to deny that apt-get is wonderful.

If you want to install a package called tuxtype (a great typing tutor for kids, by the way), this is how to do it:

```
sudo apt-get install tuxtype
Reading package lists... Done
Building dependency tree... Done
The following extra packages will be installed:
  libsdl-image1.2 libsdl-mixer1.2
The following NEW packages will be installed
  libsdl-image1.2 libsdl-mixer1.2 tuxtype
0 upgraded, 3 newly installed, 0 to remove and 1 not
  upgraded.
Need to get 4341kB of archives.
After unpacking 6038kB of additional disk space will be
  used.
Do you want to continue [Y/n]?
```

The great thing here is that you do not have to go to a variety of sites to hunt down and identify appropriate software. You call `apt-get` with the install parameter and off you go. Notice as well that `apt-get` automatically picks up dependencies for a given package and installs them when needed. If you want to update to the latest version of `tuxtype`, substitute the `install` parameter with `upgrade`.

I don't want to confuse things here but speaking of updates, one of the most important things an administrator must do is keep packages up-to-date. You can install upgrades to all installed packages with this version of the `apt-get`:

```
sudo apt-get upgrade
```

Perhaps the most famous example of Debian's prowess is symbolized by the following command:

```
sudo apt-get dist-upgrade
```

This is, by no means, something that is used on a regular basis. It is used to upgrade from one major release of a distribution to another (say Breezy to Dapper).

Graphical or Nongraphical?

That is the question, or at least one of them. I routinely work with the command line and with the graphical desktop. Despite my comfort at the command line, I still use Synaptic and find it an invaluable tool.

What should you use? Synaptic is certainly easier for a new user, but the point of showing you these things is two-fold. First, I'd like you to realize that there is more than one way to do it. That applies to graphical tools (as you saw earlier in this chapter) and command-line tools. Second, I want you to see that the shell isn't that scary, even for dealing with things like software installation. In Chapter 21, the final chapter of this book, I'll give you a great introduction to working with the Linux shell.

9

Instant Messaging, and IRC, Too!

Words, words, words . . . and then a whole lot more words, all of them flowing from one person to another. Whatever cool content exists on the world's Web sites, the Internet is still all about communication.

These days, a new kind of communication has evolved—I call it mini-email. The one-liner. The short and sweet message. The instant message. The Net-connected society has grown to love those quick, always-on means of sending each other information. My own parents (who live in another province) send me a daily one-line weather report via their Jabber instant messaging client. If you are coming from the Windows world, there's a good chance you already have one of these accounts, either with Yahoo!, AOL, MSN, or Jabber.

Why Jabber?

Because Jabber is an open protocol, it doesn't belong to anyone in particular, so there is no single company driving its destiny (although there are companies using Jabber). Jabber uses a decentralized approach, so the system is more robust. In fact, anyone can run a Jabber server if he wants to. This is a boon to companies that may want to run a *private*, *secure* instant messaging network.

 Trivia Time Google Talk, an increasingly popular instant messaging service, uses the Jabber protocol.

Whether you choose to run Jabber, Yahoo!, MSN, or something else, the ideal instant messaging client is a multiprotocol client, one that lets you talk to all these services without having to run a client for Jabber, one for AOL, one for Yahoo!, one for . . . well, you get the idea. In this chapter, I'm going to cover two superb Linux instant messaging clients. One is a great multiprotocol client that handles all your favorite chat services. The second is a powerful IRC client.

What's IRC, you ask? IRC is Internet Relay Chat, and next to your telephone, it is possibly the greatest real-time communication system in the world. I'll tell you all about it shortly.

Instant Messaging with Gaim

Gaim is one of the best multiprotocol instant messaging systems out there, period. Furthermore, this is one you can share with the people you know who are still running that other operating system. This is one favor they will thank you for. With Gaim, they no longer need a client for Yahoo!, another for MSN, and *yet another* for AOL because Gaim (`gaim.sourceforge.net`) is available for Windows as well. It even looks and works the same under both operating systems.

To start Gaim, look under the Applications menu, and then select Internet. You'll see an entry there for Gaim Internet Messenger. The actual command name is `gaim`, in case you would rather start it from the shell or via the <Alt+F2> run program dialog.

The first time you start up Gaim, you get a simple window with text fields for Account (sometimes known as a *Screen Name*) and Password (see Figure 9-1). The Account field is blank, letting you know that you don't have any accounts set up. Obviously, before we start using instant messaging through Gaim, we are going to need at least one account.

Figure 9–1   First time out with Gaim.

Look below the text fields and you see three buttons labeled Accounts, Preferences, and Sign on. Click the Accounts button and the Accounts window appears (see Figure 9-2). At this stage of the game, there is nothing in it.

Click Add, and the Add Account window appears. At the top of that window, you should see a drop-down list labeled Protocol. By default, it says AIM/ICQ. Click the button labeled Protocol and you see a number of possibilities including AIM/ICQ, Gadu-Gadu, GroupWise, IRC, Jabber, MSN, Napster, and Yahoo (see Figure 9-3).

Figure 9–2   The Accounts management screen.

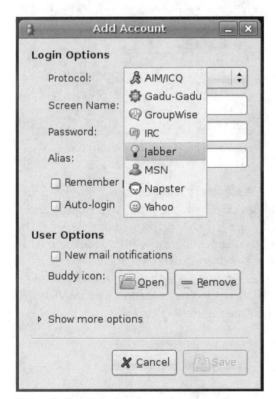

Figure 9–3   Gaim supports a number of different IM protocols.

Select Jabber from the list and watch as the window changes from AIM/ICQ to reflect the requirements of setting up a Jabber account (see Figure 9-4).

Figure 9–4   Creating a Jabber account.

Enter your Screen Name (this doesn't have to be your real name), Password (don't use an important password), and Alias. To get a free account with jabber.org, you can leave the Server name as is. The Resource name can also be safely left as Gaim. Unless you want to be asked for your password each time you log in, click the Remember Password check box. In much the same way, if you would like your Gaim client to log in to Jabber automatically every time you start up the client, click the Auto-login check box as well.

When you are happy with the information you have entered, click the Register button. The Jabber.org server should respond with a Register New Jabber Account confirmation window, which gives you the opportunity to add some information like an email address. Just click the Register button to confirm and you are good to go. Your Accounts window now shows your new account (see Figure 9-5).

Tip   The jabber.org server provides space and resources for people to get free instant messaging accounts and you can choose to take advantage of this service. However, some companies use their own instant messaging server for security and audit reasons. In this case, you change the Server field to be something other than jabber.org, such as chat.yourcompany.dom.

Figure 9–5   The Accounts dialog now reflects the newly added account.

You can either sign on here (by clicking the Online check box) or click Close and sign on from the main Gaim window. With your first time in, you get a welcome message from the Jabber.org server. You can close this window or visit the site (as indicated in the message) for additional information.

Now that you have your very own Jabber instant messaging account, you need some people to talk to. There are online chats that you can join by clicking Buddies on the menu bar and selecting Join a Chat. You can also use the keyboard shortcut by pressing <Ctrl+C> instead. You can add friends to your Buddy List by selecting Add a Buddy from the menu. Your friends have to give you their screen names, of course.

After you have added your buddies to the list, they get messages letting them know that you want to add them. When they see the pop-up window shown in Figure 9-6, they click Accept, at which point, you can begin conversations with them.

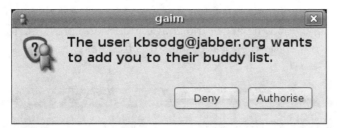

Figure 9–6   Do you accept your new buddy?

This accepting of buddies has to happen at both sides of the connection. They accept you, after which you accept them. Think of it as saying, "I do," but to a more casual, dare I say, *virtual* relationship.

After all this acceptance has taken place, your buddies appear in your Buddy List (see Figure 9-7). The icons beside their names in your Buddy List indicate whether your friends are on.

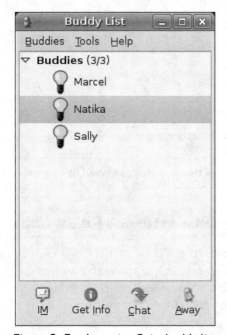

Figure 9–7   An active Gaim buddy list.

If a friend is on, double-click her name and start chatting (see Figure 9-8). Enter text in the bottom part of the chat window and press <Enter> (or click the Send button) to send your message. It is that easy.

Figure 9–8   Now that you are connected, it's time for a little chat.

IRC: Internet Relay Chat

Internet Relay Chat, better known as IRC, is a distributed client-server system in which users can communicate with any number of other users in real time. IRC servers host channels that are dedicated to discussion forums on specific topics. These topics aren't fixed other than by convention and the whims of the IRC operators. If you are old enough to remember CB radio (that is, those of you in your mid-30s and up), you pretty much understand IRC—at least in the human sense of the experience.

A number of IRC servers exist around the world, some with thousands of channels. IRC servers can also peer with other servers. IRC channels cover a plethora of topics, from purely social to politics to business or to high technology. In the Linux world, there are channels devoted to programming in most of the popular languages, as well as your favorite Linux distribution, office applications, games, and so on. IRC channels are great places to meet and exchange information, ask questions, answer questions, or just plain chat. All this chatting takes place via an IRC client such as XChat, which I will now discuss.

Note It's true that the majority of IRC servers tend to be vast collections of topics linked to other servers around the world. There are private IRC servers as well for more focused discussions. I run one of these servers myself to provide a meeting place for my readers on a channel called #wftlchat (more on this later in this chapter). Users on #wftlchat can ask questions, help each other out, or just plain chat.

XChat

To start XChat, click the Applications launcher on the top panel, navigate to Internet and click XChat IRC (program name, xchat). When the program starts for the first time, you see a window with your username listed as a nickname (see Figure 9-9). There are also alternative nicknames listed on the off chance that someone else might be using that name already. Even though this defaults to your username, or your login name, you can choose whatever you like here. In fact, most people on IRC have some nickname other than their own names. On IRC, you'll see me logged in as wftl. That is my nickname.

If you know which network the channel you want to connect to is on (or if you just want to see what channels are available), click one of the choices in the list of Networks and click the Connect button. One that you might find interesting right off the bat is the Ubuntu Servers entry, which automagically logs you into the #ubuntu discussion channel, a great place to ask Ubuntu Linux specific questions. However, I do want to show you how to add other networks. Let's add my own IRC server here so you can see how it's done.

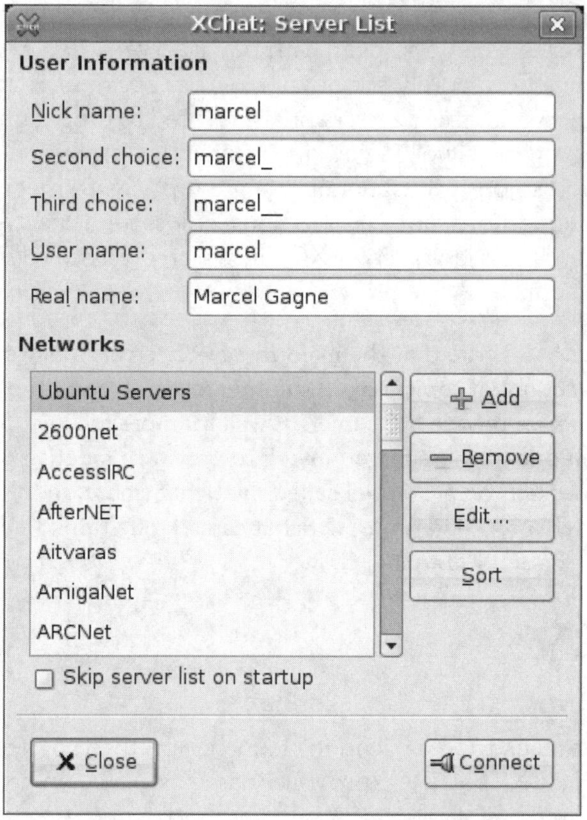

Figure 9–9 Even when running XChat for the first time, a large number of networks is already configured.

First, click the Add button to the right of the Networks list. The words *New Network* are highlighted at the top of the Networks list. Change that to something that makes sense. In my case, I entered *WFTL IRC Server*. Now, this entry is just that—a placeholder for a list of servers within a network (there can be one or many). Click Edit and the Edit Server dialog appears (see Figure 9-10). At the top, there is one host listed, `newserver/6667`. This is just a sample entry and needs to be changed to something real. On my IRC server, that's `chat.marcelgagne.com/6667`. You don't generally need to worry about this, but 6667 is the TCP port that IRC operates on.

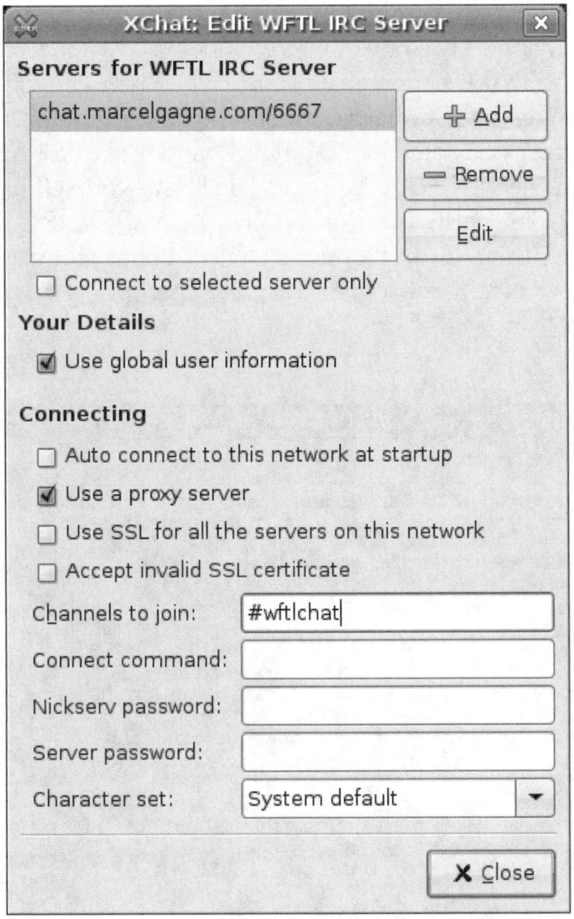

XChat: Edit WFTL IRC Server ☒

Servers for WFTL IRC Server

chat.marcelgagne.com/6667

   ➕ Add

   ➖ Remove

   Edit

☐ Connect to selected server only

Your Details

☑ Use global user information

Connecting

☐ Auto connect to this network at startup

☑ Use a proxy server

☐ Use SSL for all the servers on this network

☐ Accept invalid SSL certificate

Channels to join: #wftlchat

Connect command:

Nickserv password:

Server password:

Character set: System default   ▼

   ✖ Close

Figure 9–10 Each network can contain one or more servers. Furthermore, you can choose to have XChat log you into a channel when you connect.

Tip It's easy to find out which servers are part of which network. For instance, if you click the Ubuntu Servers entry and click Edit, you'll see a server entry for `irc.freenode.net`, the host on which the Ubuntu discussion groups reside.

Each IRC server can have potentially hundreds of channels or it can have just one. If you happen to know what channel you want to connect to, you can add it here so that it happens automagically when you log in. Look a little further down under the Connecting section to the Channels to Join field. As that label indicates, you could join multiple channels, but for my server, #wftl-chat is what you need. Click Close and you'll find yourself back to the main XChat window Networks list. Make sure the WFTL IRC Server entry is highlighted, and then click Connect. The XChat conversation window appears with your nick name logged in to the appropriate channel (see Figure 9-11).

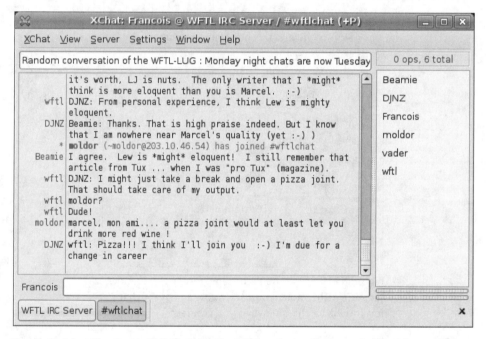

Figure 9-11   Chatting in IRC. To the right is a list of people currently logged in to the channel.

To ask a question or talk to the group, just type your message in the text field to the right of your nick name at the bottom, then press <Enter>. Notice the network name and channel name on the buttons at the bottom of the window. It is possible to join multiple channels at the same time when chatting on IRC.

Learning More About IRC

IRC has some interesting commands that you might want to know about. IRC commands are fronted by a slash character (/) followed by the command name. Some commands can be used by all users, whereas others are for channel administrators only. To find out what commands are available to you, type **/help** in the text field and press <Enter>. The list of commands appears in the chat window itself. Here are a few of the more common and useful commands:

`/help`	Lists IRC commands.
`/help command_name`	Gets help on a particular command.
`/nick new_name`	Changes your nickname.
`/join #channel`	Joins a specified channel.
`/part`	Leaves the channel.
`/list`	Lists the available channels.
`/me Some_action`	Prints your nickname followed by text of your action and highlights the message in a different color. Try it. It's fun.

Tip Beware of the `/list` command. On some servers, this can return a massive list of channels.

IRC is a fantastic resource and one I recommend highly, but with a cautionary suggestion. This vast, distributed network of real-time discussion groups has evolved a culture all its own, with its own rules of etiquette, rules that should be respected. Channels have operators who monitor traffic and requests from users. Operators can also send you packing if you don't behave. There may also be *bots*, small programs designed to handle simple administrative requests, so not every user you see is necessarily human.

It's easy to get hooked on IRC when there is so much at your disposal, but it's also good to take some time and read a little primer on what it's all about. Check out the IRC primer in the Resources section for a great introduction to the world of IRC.

Another great resource is the netsplit.de IRC information site where you'll find a search engine for channels and topics, as well as a comprehensive list of IRC servers and networks.

I'll see you online.

Resources

Gaim Instant Messaging

```
http://gaim.sourceforge.net
```

Google Talk

```
http://talk.google.com
```

Jabber Software Foundation

```
http://www.jabber.org
```

A Short IRC Primer

```
http://www.irchelp.org/irchelp/ircprimer.html
```

Netsplit.de IRC Information Site

```
http://irc.netsplit.de
```

Chapter

10

Surfing the Net with Firefox

When it comes to Web browsers on the desktop, Linux users are faced with an embarrassment of riches with plenty of alternatives to choose from. For those who are looking for a screaming fast browsing experience and can do without the graphics, Linux offers a number of text-based browsers. (I'll mention these briefly at the end of the chapter.)

In the graphical world where most people spend their browsing time, the hottest and coolest browser of the day is Firefox, and it just happens to be the default browser found in Ubuntu Linux. Before Firefox made its appearance a short while ago, everyone assumed that the browser world belonged to the browser from Redmond, the security-problem-plagued Internet Explorer. As I write this, Internet Explorer has dipped to below 90 percent of the browser market share in North America and below 80 percent in Europe. This is quite the feat considering that Internet Explorer commanded something around 95 percent of the market before Firefox. Better security and advanced features have drawn millions of users away from Microsoft's browser. Firefox is an exciting program and I'll show you how it works in this chapter.

Mozilla versus Firefox

Firefox is distributed by the same people who distribute the Mozilla browser. In fact, Firefox is a Mozilla product.

What's the difference between Mozilla and Firefox? The actual Mozilla browser is more like the Swiss Army knife of browsers. It includes an email package and IRC client, is ideal for reading newsgroups, and comes with an HTML editor. Firefox, on the other hand, is strictly a Web browser (see Figure 10-1). It's smaller, faster, and more geared to its primary job, providing you with a superior surfing experience. To get the equivalent standalone email package, you would download Thunderbird (mentioned in Chapter 11). Right now, I'd like to concentrate on Firefox, so let's get started.

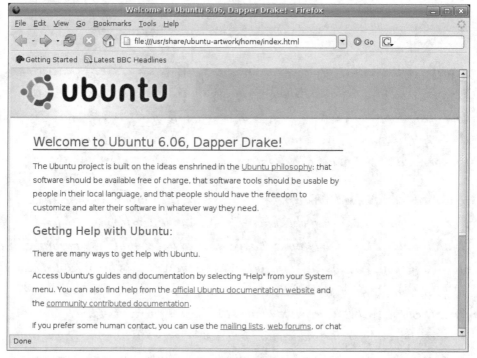

Figure 10–1   Firefox is an excellent and capable browser that is setting the world on fire.

To start Firefox, click the Application menu in the top panel, navigate to the Internet submenu, and then select Firefox Web Browser. There's also a quick access icon for Firefox in the top panel. Directly to the right of the

System menu, there's a blue globe. Pause your mouse cursor over the icon and it identifies itself as Firefox.

Working from Home

When you first start Firefox, it takes you to its home, currently a Welcome to Ubuntu page, locally installed on your system. The location is identified in the URL/location bar directly below the menu bar. Getting to a Web site and navigating Firefox is much the same as it is in any other browser you have used, particularly if you were using Mozilla (or Firefox) with your old OS. All you do is type the URL of the Web site you want to visit into the location bar, and away you go. If you would like to start each time on a personal home page, this is easily done.

 Tip Take the time to check out and visit the links on the Ubuntu welcome page. They point to some valuable resources, some of which you may want to bookmark.

Click Edit in Firefox's menu bar and select Preferences. The Preferences window opens up with a number of icons running along the top, directly under the title bar, from which you select what part of Firefox you want to modify. By default, it opens up to the General category (see Figure 10-2). Directly below, in the Home Page section, there are three buttons. The first button, Use Current Page, enters whatever URL (or page) you are currently visiting into the Location field as your home page. The middle button, Use Bookmark, brings up a dialog with your current bookmarks. Clicking the Use Blank Page button starts Firefox on a blank page. Of course, you could just type the URL into the Location field, click OK, and be done.

 Quick Tip Before closing the Preferences dialog, did you notice that the Location field actually says Location(s)? That's right, it could be plural. If you have multiple tabs open (which I'll cover next), the Use Current Page button becomes Use Current Pages. When you click the Home icon, Firefox opens tabs to all your favorite pages. If you want to manually enter a list of pages into the location bar, just separate each page with the pipe symbol, | (usually found above the backslash key on your keyboard).

Figure 10–2   Setting your home page in Firefox's Preferences menu.

Keeping Tabs on the Web, Firefox Style

Firefox sports a great feature called *tabbed browsing*. Here's how it works.

Sometimes when you are viewing Web sites, you want to keep a particular site open while moving to another place on the Web. Normally, you click File and select New Window. This is fine, except that if you keep doing this, you'll wind up with many versions of a browser open on your desktop. Switching from one to the other involves doing a little digital juggling. Tabs make it possible to bring a nice, clean air of sanity to what could otherwise become a very cluttered taskbar (or desktop). With tabbed browsing, you open additional Web sites in the same browser window, and then move from one to the other by clicking the open site's appropriate tab.

Here's how you do it. Start by visiting a site of your choice. Now click File, select New, and choose New Tab from the drop-down menu. You can also use the <Ctrl+T> keyboard shortcut to do the same thing. Notice that Firefox identifies your sites with tabs just below the location bar (see Figure 10-3), or if you have it turned on, your Bookmarks toolbar. Add a third or a fourth tab if you like. Switching from site to site is now just a matter of click-ing the tabs on your single copy of Firefox.

Figure 10–3   Firefox showing off its tabs.

Tip   Here's a cool trick. In the Linux world, there's a right mouse button, a left mouse button, and, often, a middle mouse button. Even if you don't have a middle mouse button, you can still mimic the action of the middle button by pressing the left and right buttons at the same time. Many applications, including your desktop environment, can take advantage of this middle button (or phantom middle button).

Why am I telling you this? Click a link using the middle button and that link automagically opens up in a new tab. Cool? Cool.

While in tab mode (as shown in Figure 10-3), you can right-click a tab to bring up the tab menu. From there, you can close or reload the current tab (or all tabs) and even open new tabs. Another way to close the active tab is to click the X at the end of the tab list.

 Tip After you have several tabs open, you might decide that you would like a particular site in another position. Let's say that you are using one site more than another and you would like it in the first position but it is currently at the end. No problem. Just click the tab and drag it to the new position.

Go for the Big Screen

Just as there's no comparison between your old twenty-inch TV and that new fifty-inch flat panel HDTV, nothing beats looking at the virtual world through a big screen. As much as I would like to, I can't increase the size of your monitor, but I can help you with the next best thing. When you are busy surfing the Internet and you want as much screen as possible, why not try Firefox's full-screen mode?

At any time while you are viewing a page, you can click View on the menu bar and select Full Screen. The title bar disappears, as do the top and bottom panels and all other border decorations. Another, quicker way to switch to full-screen mode is to press <F11>. Pay attention to this because this is how you switch back to normal view.

Ban the Pop-up Ads, Forever!

Honestly, I can't think of a single person who likes to visit a Web site, only to have that site throw up annoying pop-up window ads. Firefox lets you stop this easily. Actually, Firefox has pop-ups blocked by default, but you may want to alter that behavior for some sites. Here's how.

Start by bringing up the Preferences menu again (click Edit on the menu bar and choose Preferences). From the category list, choose Content (see Figure 10-4). You'll see a check box labeled Block Popup Windows. Next to that label is a button labeled Allowed Sites. Clicking this button allows you to specify sites where pop-ups may be desirable. When you are satisfied with your configuration, click OK to close the Preferences menu.

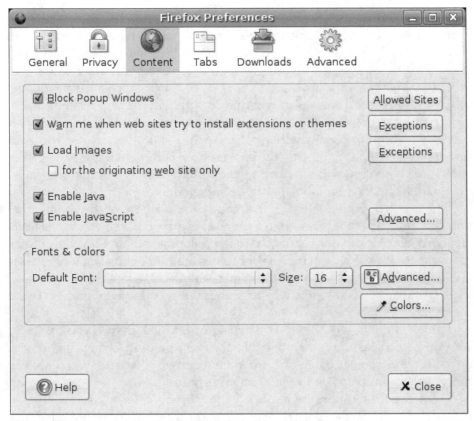

Figure 10–4   Firefox lets you specify sites where pop-ups are okay.

When Firefox intercepts a pop-up, it displays a message like the one in Figure 10-5.

Figure 10–5   Firefox has blocked a pop-up. What would you like to do?

Clicking the Preferences button at the end of the bar offers you three choices. You can allow pop-ups for that particular Web site or edit the pop-up blocker preferences for that particular Web site. You also have the option of choosing never to see the message when pop-ups are blocked.

Yummy . . . Cookies

Not that kind of cookie. Cookies are simply small text files transmitted to your browser (or system) when you visit a Web site. The original idea behind cookies was that a server would give you a cookie as a marker to indicate where you had previously visited. That cookie might store a username and password to access a particular Web site or other information related to your visit, such as an online shopping cart. When you next visit the site, the server would ask your browser whether it had served you any cookies, and your browser would reply by sending the cookies from before. In this way, the Web site would recognize you when you next visited, and certain useful defaults would be set up for you. Cookies can be very good.

The problem with cookies is that they can also be shared within larger domains, such as advertising rings. Using these shared cookies, advertisers can build a profile of your likes and dislikes, tailoring and targeting advertising to you specifically. Many people object to this method of building user profiles and consider the use of cookies to be quite unethical, an invasion of privacy. The dilemma then is to find a way to accept the cookies you want and reject the others.

Firefox is quite versatile in its handling of cookies. Before you excitedly turn off all cookies, do remember that they can be useful, particularly with online services such as banks and e-commerce sites. That said, you may very much want to curb cookie traffic as much as possible.

From the Preferences menu, open the Privacy category submenu (see Figure 10-6). Below the category icons, you see a tabbed list of options. Click the tab labeled Cookies to configure your options.

Unless you want to refuse all cookies, leave the Allow Sites to Set Cookies check box checked. Then, from the Keep Cookies drop-down box, choose Ask Me Every Time. Click Close, and resume your surfing. When you visit a site that tries to set or modify a cookie, an alert pops up, alerting you to the cookie and asking you how to proceed (see Figure 10-7). If you decide to deny a cookie and you never want to see another cookie from that site, check Use My Choice for All Cookies from This Site before clicking Allow for Session or Deny.

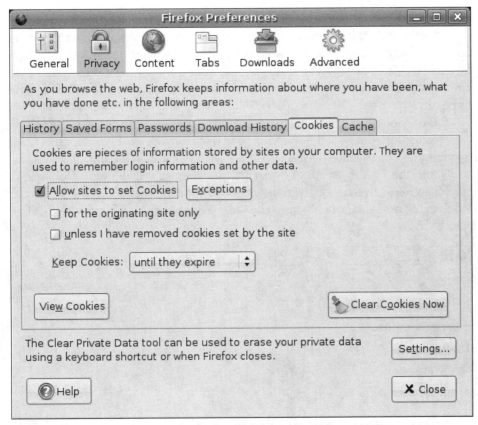

Figure 10–6 Back to Firefox's Preferences menu to configure cookie policies.

Figure 10–7 A pop-up allows you to allow or deny a cookie. This is a good site to allow all cookies from.

The Firefox Sidebar

The Firefox sidebar is a quick way to get to your information, in this case browsing history and bookmarks. You can have one or the other at your side by clicking View on the menu bar and selecting the Sidebar submenu. One quick way to activate the bookmarks sidebar is by pressing <Ctrl+B>. The same keystroke banishes the sidebar.

You may already know that your system keeps a history of Web sites you have visited. By default, that history goes back nine days. The amount of history can be set by clicking Edit on the menu bar and selecting Preferences. You'll find the History settings under Privacy, just as you did with Cookies.

To activate the history sidebar, choose it from the View menu (under Sidebar) or press <Ctrl+H> and the sidebar appears (see Figure 10-8). The

Figure 10–8
The Firefox history sidebar—it's a jump to the past.

history sidebar makes searching for a site you visited in the last few days easy. At the top of the sidebar, you see a Search field. Just type your search keywords in the location bar and press <Enter>. Click any link displayed and you are instantly transported to that site.

Extending Firefox

Firefox is an excellent browser on many counts, but one of its coolest features is its capacity for adding features and capabilities through a system of extensions. Extensions are program enhancements that can dramatically change how you work with your browser. This framework of extensions makes Firefox not just a great browser, but a superior browser.

To experience Firefox extensions, click Tools on the menu bar and select Extensions. A window appears with a list of the extensions already in your system. On a fresh install, there is usually nothing here other than the language pack. Along the bottom of this window is a button labeled Find Updates (see Figure 10-9). This feature keeps the extensions you use up-to-date. Next to it is a Get More Extensions link, which is where we begin our journey.

Figure 10–9 The Firefox extensions window not only gives you access to installed extensions, but provides a link to many others.

When you click that link, a new browser opens to the Firefox Add-ons site. You can also visit the site directly, without going through the extension dialog, by visiting `https://addons.mozilla.org/firefox`. The Extensions tab is selected with some of the latest and most popular extensions front and center. You can also search based on categories from blogging to humor, navigation, search tools, news reading, and more. Some are extremely useful and designed to make your browsing more efficient. Some are just plain silly. Each extension has a description and a link to install it. If this is your first visit, click the We Recommend button for some great suggestions.

Let me show you an example by installing a totally silly extension, Anthony Howe's Bork Bork Bork!, an extension that makes your Web pages look as though they were written by *The Muppet Show's* Swedish Chef. After I click the Install link on the extension's description page, a window appears asking for confirmation before installing the extension (see Figure 10-10). There's also a warning about installing malicious software. To continue, click the Install Now button.

Figure 10–10   Installing your extension is just a click away.

That's it. You must restart Firefox to have the new extensions loaded. Now, when I surf to a site, I can right-click the page and select View Bork Text from the menu and in a few seconds, my page is translated into something only the Swedish Chef could understand (see Figure 10-11).

Figure 10–11 Close-up of my Web site with *Borked* text.

My silly example aside, there are some must-have extensions. Some of the more popular extensions include AdBlock, BugMeNot, ForecastFox, and FoxyTunes. Browse the Firefox extensions page, try a few, and come up with your own favorites. Of course, not all extensions are on the Firefox site. One of my personal favorites is Tab Preview, from *Ted's Mozilla Page* (see the Resources section). This handy little extension provides a thumbnail view of your tabbed pages when you pause your mouse cursor over the tab.

Firefox extensions are hugely popular and numerous programmers have contributed their own. Several sites have also appeared to review and discuss the latest extensions. Enter **favorite Firefox extensions** in your Google search bar and enjoy.

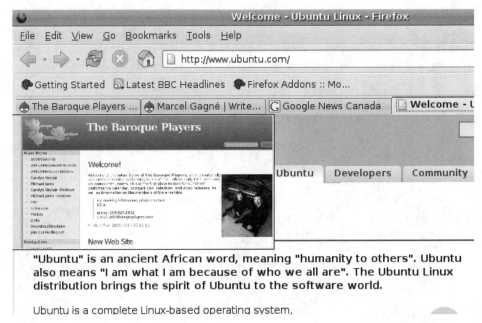

Figure 10–12   Tab Preview provides a handy thumbnail view of your tabbed pages.

Wrapping Up—Other Browsers to Consider

Firefox, as I mentioned, is the default browser that comes with Ubuntu, but it is by no means your only choice. If you like Firefox, you might also want to look at Mozilla (http://www.mozilla.org) as a full-featured browser suite featuring an email client, HTML editor, and more. Konqueror, another excellent browser, comes as part of the KDE desktop but you don't need to install KDE to take advantage of it. Just search for Konqueror with your Synaptic package installer.

We can't stop there. You also have access to some text-only browsers such as Lynx and Links. Neither of these comes pre-installed with Ubuntu, but both are easily added if you are curious.

Shell Out When you feel like seeing the World Wide Web without its clutter of images, why not give lynx or links a try? Where can you get these? That's right, search Synaptic first. Then, open a Terminal shell (look in the Accessories menu under Applications) and try the following:

```
lynx http://www.marcelgagne.com/
links http://www.marcelgagne.com/
```

You may be amazed at the speed and performance of non-flashy Web surfing.

Resources

Firefox

> http://www.mozilla.com/firefox

Firefox Extensions

> https://addons.mozilla.org/firefox

Konqueror Web Site

> http://www.konqueror.org

Links Text Web Browser

> http://links.twibright.com

Lynx Browser

> http://lynx.isc.org/

Mozilla Project Home

> http://www.mozilla.org

Tab Preview Extension

> http://ted.mielczarek.org/code/mozilla/tabpreview/
>   index.html

Chapter

11

Evolution: Email and More!

When we think about the Internet these days, we think about Web browsers first. To those of us who have been on the Net for more years than we care to admit, that always seems a bit strange. The chief medium of information exchange on the Internet has always been electronic mail, or email. Although the perception has changed, email is probably still the number one application in the connected world.

For a powerful, graphical email client, your Ubuntu Linux desktop comes with a powerful email package called *Evolution*. Those of you who are coming from that other OS, and who might be pining for the look and feel (and the integration) of Outlook, are going to be pleasantly surprised. Evolution features powerful email functionality, address books, calendaring, to-do lists, and so on. Keep reading—in just a few keystrokes, I'll have you sending and receiving mail like a Linux pro.

Be Prepared . . .

Before we start, you need to have some information handy. This includes your email username and password, as well as the SMTP and POP3 server addresses for sending and receiving your email. All of this information is provided for you by your Internet service provider (ISP) or your company's system administrator.

Evolution

It's hard for some people moving to Linux to say goodbye to certain familiar applications. One of the most commonly used email packages in the Windows world is Outlook and its cousin, Outlook Express. Those users feel right at home on their new Linux desktops when they fire up Evolution. A look at Figure 11-1 no doubt seems extremely familiar. In fact, Evolution looks and feels like Outlook but with some very important improvements.

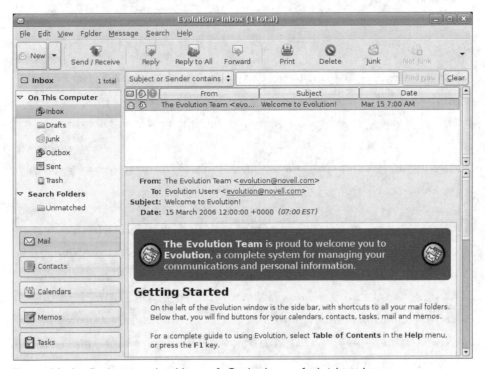

Figure 11–1   Evolution makes Microsoft Outlook users feel right at home.

To start Evolution, click Applications on your top panel and navigate to the Internet menu (see Figure 11-2). Evolution Mail is the menu entry to start this package. One other place to find Evolution is next to the System menu on the same panel. You'll see an icon for Evolution right beside the Firefox icon.

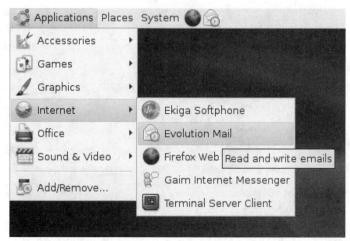

Figure 11–2   *Evolution is found in the Internet application menu but also on the top panel. It's the second icon right of the System menu.*

Upon starting Evolution for the first time, you are presented with the Evolution Setup Assistant to take you through the various preparatory steps. After clicking Forward through the introductory window, you are asked for your default identity. This is where you enter your Full Name and Email Address, along with other options, such as a Reply-to address (see Figure 11-3).

When you are done, click Forward, and then enter information for receiving mail. You start by selecting a Server Type. For most users, this is POP or IMAP. Evolution allows you to set up other servers as well, including Novell GroupWise, Microsoft Exchange, Usenet news, and several others. Now, enter the hostname of the POP3 or IMAP host (as provided by your ISP or system administrator), as well as your username. If you don't want to enter your password each and every time Evolution checks for mail, you should click the Remember Password check box. When you click Forward, you have the opportunity to decide whether Evolution checks for mail automatically (the default is to check every 10 minutes). Don't set this unless you are always connected, otherwise you can choose whatever interval suits you. When you are done, click Forward again, and you can configure your outgoing mail.

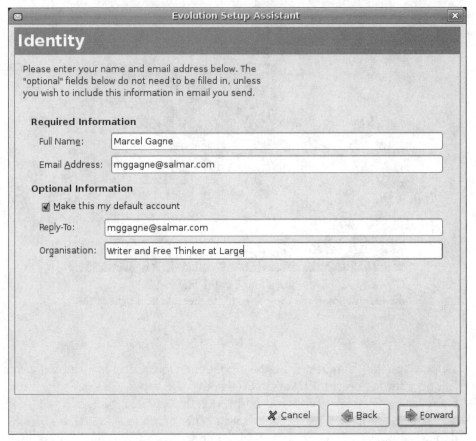

Figure 11–3   Evolution's Setup Assistant.

 Tip Depending on what kind of connection you chose earlier, there can be a number of different options associated with this screen, so take a moment to carefully read the options. Most home users use POP, which has only a couple of options.

The default Server Type for sending is SMTP, and that is almost certainly what you need. Enter the hostname as provided by your ISP (or system administrator), and click Next. The Account Management screen follows with your new email account listed as it is displayed in Evolution. If you prefer, you can change this to be a name rather than an email address. When you are finished, click Forward.

The final step is to select your time zone. Select an area on the map (preferably near to where you live) to narrow down your search. The map zooms in to the area you clicked, allowing you to fine-tune your selection (see Figure 11-4). Make your final selection (you can use the drop-down box to aid in your selection), click Forward again, then click Apply, and you are done.

Figure 11–4   Evolution's Setup Assistant zooms in to help in selecting your time zone.

Evolution starts up with a list of resources called On This Computer, highlighted in the left-hand sidebar. The most notable of these resources is, of course, your email (see Figure 11-5). Evolution comes with a default collection of folders, including your Inbox, a Drafts folder, a folder for Junk mail, a Sent folder, and a Trash folder. For most people using broadband or always on connections, the Outbox spends most of its time empty. Of course, you will create your own additional folders as you use the package.

Figure 11–5   *Closeup of On This Computer.*

Directly below the folders list, a set of rectangular icons runs down the left-hand sidebar. These give you access to your Contacts, Calendars, Memos, and Tasks.

Sending and Receiving Mail

To send a message, start by clicking the Inbox icon (in the left-hand sidebar), then click the New button just below the menu bar. By default, Evolution creates a new mail message, but notice as well that there is a drop-down arrow just beside the word New (refer to Figure 11-5). Click that button and you can create an appointment (more on that in Chapter 12), a contact, a task, and so on.

To create a new mail message, you can also click File on the menu bar and select New, then Mail Message from there. Evolution's compose window appears (see Figure 11-6).

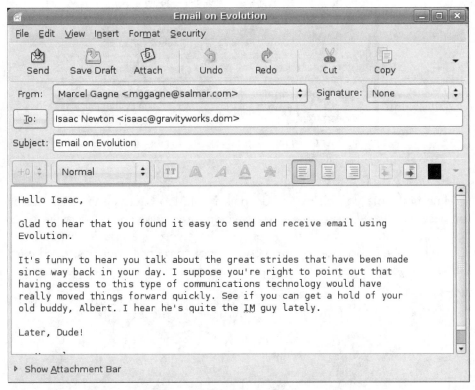

Figure 11–6 Sending a message with Evolution—the compose window.

If you have ever sent an email message, this is pretty standard stuff. Fill in the person's email address in the To field, enter a Subject, and type your message. When you have completed your message, click the Send button on the compose window (or click File on the compose window's menu bar, and then select Send).

To pick up your email, make sure once again that you have the Inbox button selected, then click the Send/Receive button (see Figure 11-7) at the top of Evolution's main window (or click Actions on the menu bar and select Send/Receive).

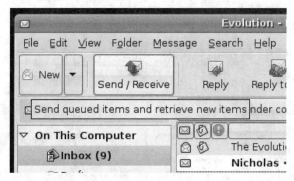

Figure 11–7   Click Send/Receive to check for and send email.

The first time you pick up your mail, Evolution pauses and asks you for the password (see Figure 11-8). You have an interesting choice to make here. To the left of the words Remember This Password is a check box that lets you lock in the information. If you choose not to record your password with Evolution, you have to enter your password each time you check for mail.

Figure 11–8   Would you like Evolution to automatically remember your password?

Your Little Black Book

The ladies and gentlemen reading this book have by now wondered when I was going to talk about address books. After all, email implies some kind of socializing, whether it is business or personal. When composing an email message (as in Figure 11-6), notice the To button to the left of where you enter the email address you are sending to. Clicking this button brings up a list of email addresses from your address book, from which you can select to whom you would like the message to go.

The only problem is that you probably don't have anything in the address book at this moment. Assuming you are starting from scratch, look in the Evolution sidebar on the left side and you see a large button labeled Contacts. When Evolution's address book opens up on the right side, you can click File and select New, and then Contact; or, you can click the New icon directly beneath the File menu. Keyboard wizards can press <Ctrl+N>. The dialog shown in Figure 11-9 appears.

When the Entry Editor appears, add whatever information is appropriate for the contact. The person's name and his email address are sufficient if these are all you need. When you are finished entering information, click OK.

Another way to add names to your address book (and by far the *easiest*) is to take the address from a message that has been sent to you. While you are viewing someone's email to you, right-click the email address in the From field. Select Add to Address Book from the pop-up menu. Click Add to Address Book, and a small Quick-Add window appears (see Figure 11-10). Confirm that the full name and email address are as you expect them to appear, then click OK, and you are done.

Tip The Evolution address book displays your list of contacts in a default, card-like view. Some may prefer a more compact list, or one sorted according to company. Click View on the menu bar, then select Current View to choose an alternative.

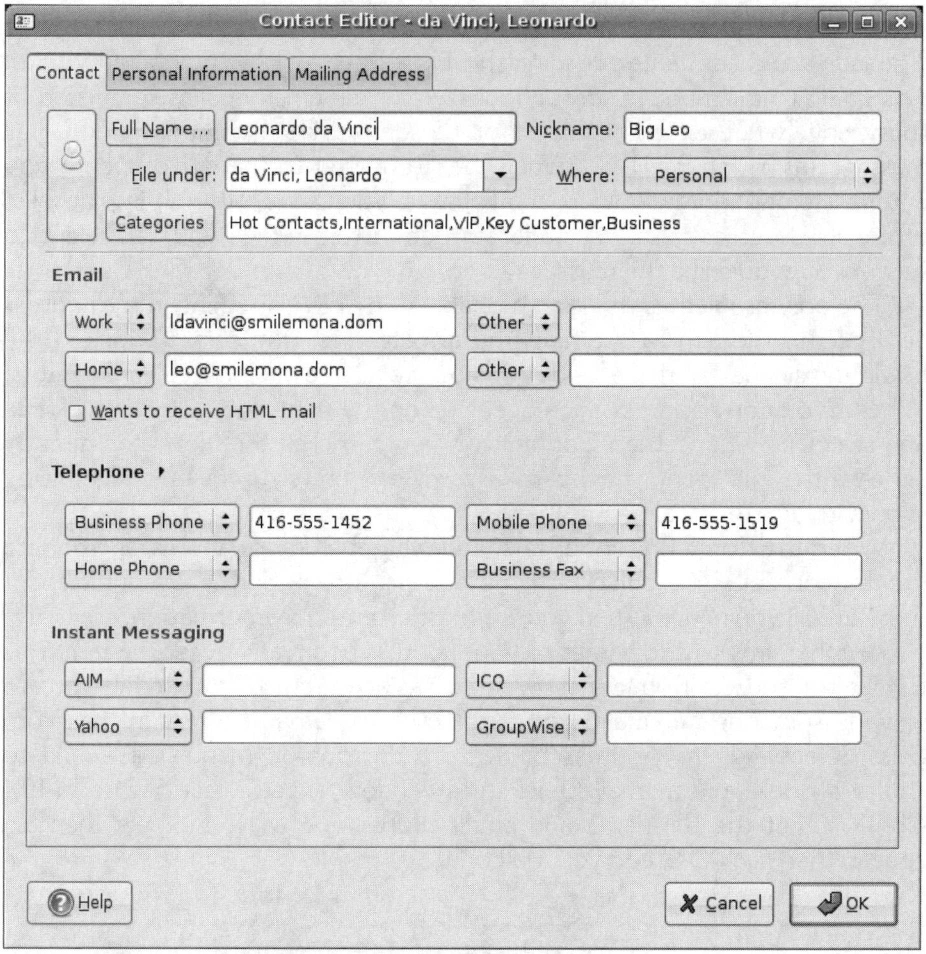

Contact Editor - da Vinci, Leonardo

Contact | Personal Information | Mailing Address

Full Name... | Leonardo da Vinci | Nickname: | Big Leo
File under: | da Vinci, Leonardo | Where: | Personal
Categories | Hot Contacts,International,VIP,Key Customer,Business

Email

Work | ldavinci@smilemona.dom | Other |
Home | leo@smilemona.dom | Other |
☐ Wants to receive HTML mail

Telephone ▸

Business Phone | 416-555-1452 | Mobile Phone | 416-555-1519
Home Phone | | Business Fax |

Instant Messaging

AIM | | ICQ |
Yahoo | | GroupWise |

Help   ✗ Cancel   OK

Figure 11–9   New contact address book information.

Contact Quick-Add

Full name | Isaac Newton
E-mail | isaac@gravityworks.don
Select Address Book | Personal

Edit Full | ✗ Cancel | OK

Figure 11–10
Quickly update your address book
from email headers.

Attached to You . . .

As you sit there writing your letter to your old high-school friend, it occurs to you that it might be fun to include a recent picture of yourself (with your spouse and new baby). After all, you haven't seen each other in 20 years. To attach a file, click the paper clip Attach icon, which is directly below the menu bar. If you have a Nautilus file browser window open, you can also drag an icon from Nautilus into your composer window. In fact, if you have an icon on your desktop, you can drag that into your composer as well, and the images (or documents) are automatically attached.

 Tip Using Nautilus to look for attachments can be handy because you can then take advantage of the preview mode, a real plus with images.

If you prefer the menu bar, click Insert and select Attachment. The Insert Attachment dialog appears, giving you the opportunity to navigate your directories to find the appropriate file. Figure 11-11 shows this dialog in use.

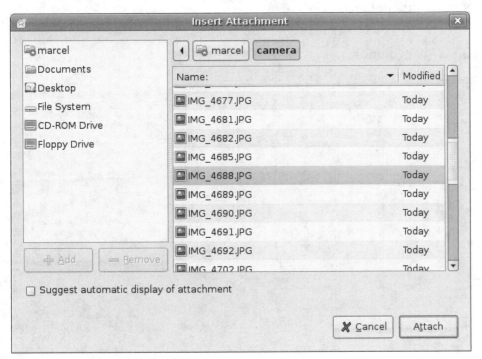

Figure 11–11 Browsing for an email attachment.

After you have attached a file, it shows up in a separate attachments bar that appears at the bottom of your composer window. From there, you can select those attachments and change your mind. Right-click the attachment and select Remove.

Other Options

In this chapter, I've introduced you to Evolution and its features. By no means should you look at these as your only options. If you are accustomed to working with Mozilla mail in the Windows world, these very options are available with Linux, and they work exactly the same. There's also Thunderbird, the mail-only client from the good folks at Mozilla. Thunderbird is an easy-to-use, cross-platform package with great junk mail filtering.

How can you get Thunderbird and install it on your system? Synaptic, and it's yours!

Resources

Mozilla Thunderbird

    http://www.mozilla.com/thunderbird/

GNOME Evolution

    http://gnome.org/projects/evolution/

Chapter
12

Evolution:
Keeping Organized

It is sometimes hard for me to fathom as I look at the piles of papers, books, cables, devices, and toys scattered across my desk, that computers have helped in getting us more organized. No, it's true. Work with me here.

Once upon a time, I used to make appointments, scribble down the information, and hope that I could find it again later. Maybe it wasn't an appointment, but a dinner date or somebody's birthday. Either way, if I got lucky and managed to find my paper planner (or scrap of paper) in time, I might just make it to where I was supposed to be. My friends will tell you that I was always twenty minutes late. These days, I'm only five minutes late. The reason? My personal digital assistant. Currently, it is a Palm Zire 72 but I have had others. There's nothing like an alarm going off to remind you that yes, you do have something planned.

I keep my PDA backed up and synced to my notebook computer, on which I do my writing. My notebook also has a copy of the calendar with all its appointments on it in a great little piece of software called GNOME Pilot. Now, if I happen to leave my PDA in another part of the house, there is a second piece of software ready to warn me when I'm supposed to return a phone call. My life is far from being perfectly organized, but trust me; it has improved dramatically. In time, I'm aiming for being only two minutes late.

Ready? Great. Let's synchronize those watches.

Evolution and Planning

In the last chapter, I mentioned that Evolution was a great email client for those coming from the Windows world, particularly if they are used to working with Outlook. This is equally true when working with Evolution's calendaring applications.

Take a look along the top of the application, just below the menu bar (see Figure 12-1). The icons to the left let you quickly create appointments, send and receive email, print, and so on. To the right, there are a handful of icons providing different calendar views: a day, work week, and so on. There may also be a small down arrow on a button to the far right. If you don't have enough room to show all the calendar views, clicking this arrow shows you the remaining views available.

The main window is broken up into three sections. The main calendar view is located in the center, to the right of the sidebar that lets you select the various Evolution components. To the right of the calendar view, you have one or more small calendars. Clicking a date in that smaller calendar lets you jump right to that date. Below the small calendars, you find a quick summary of your to-do items. Finally, a set of icons runs down the left-hand sidebar, providing you with quick access to Mail, Contacts, Calendar, and Tasks.

Tip To select any number of days (and create your own view), just highlight a sequence of days in the mini-calendars to the right. The main calendar view updates with your selection.

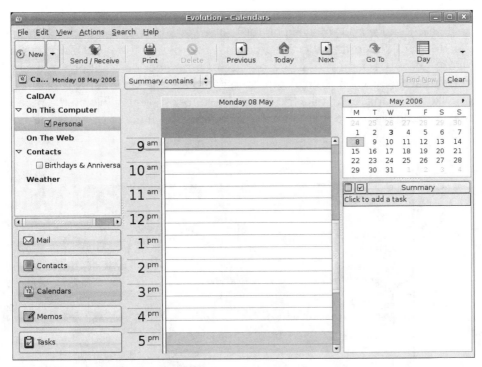

Figure 12–1 Evolution's calendar view.

Creating Appointments

You've got a big get-together coming up and you need all hands on the poker table, er, I mean, *all hands on deck*. Let's take a look at how to set up an appointment, or meeting.

> *Note* Meetings and appointments are, as I used to say in my youth, *the same thing, only different*. Similarities aside, the differences are substantial. An appointment is a personal event blocked on your calendar. A meeting can involve others and require group scheduling functions. In the Add dialog, appointments have only two tabs, Appointment and Recurrence. Meetings add a Scheduling tab and an Invitations tab.

The idea is the same. To create a new appointment in Evolution with a single click, move your mouse pointer to the New button and click (or press <Ctrl+N>). Notice that there is a down arrow beside the New button (see Figure 12-2). Clicking the arrow brings up a number of additional choices from creating a mail message to creating a contact in your address book. If you like, you can always take the multiclick route by clicking File on the menu bar, selecting New, and then selecting Appointment. If you are inviting others to this event, choose Meeting.

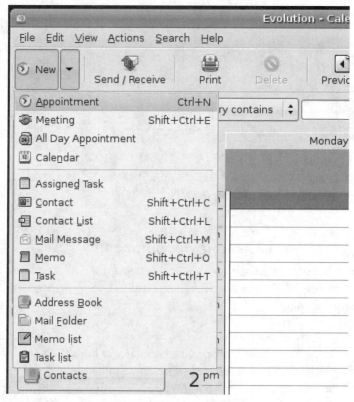

Figure 12-2   The Evolution New submenu.

Another way to do this is to double-click the time slot you want in the main calendar view. As soon as you do this, the new Appointment dialog appears (see Figure 12-3). Start by entering your Summary information (for example, Poker night), and a Location (for example, Jake and Michelle's house). A Start time has been entered as well as an End time but you may have to fine-tune those. Clicking the down arrow beside the date pops up a small calendar from which you can quickly pick the date. The drop-down list associated with the time is broken up in half-hour intervals. Next to the time is another drop-down box, this one labeled For by default. To the right of it is a duration time for the meeting. If you would rather specify an end time, click the For list and select Until instead. The display changes to allow you to enter an end time.

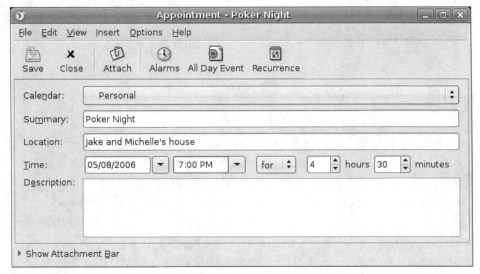

Figure 12–3   Creating an appointment in Evolution.

 Quick Tip Take a look along the top at the icons. You see one labeled All Day Event. Clicking here removes the start and end times and brings up a second little drop-down calendar. At this point, and this might be a bit scary depending on the nature of the event, you can change the second date to reflect a meeting (or appointment) that lasts more than one day.

If this is an important appointment, you likely want to be reminded of it. Click the Alarms icon. A simple Alarms window appears with a default of None selected as the alarm time. To activate an alarm—for example, 15 minutes before appointment (see Figure 12-4)—click the combo box and select a time. Clicking that combo box also allows you to select from three additional settings. The other settings are 1 hour before appointment, 1 day before appointment, and customize.

Figure 12–4 The simplest alarm defaults to 15 minutes before your appointment.

If you choose Customize for your alarm setting, the bottom part of the dialog appears. Your default alarm is still 15 minutes (as shown in the Action/Trigger pane), but you can now Edit this alarm, Remove it, or add modifications by clicking the Add button. A highly customizable Add Alarm dialog appears (see Figure 12-5).

To create a different type of alarm, click the combo box directly below the Alarm label at the top left. The default is Pop up an Alert but you may decide to change it to Play a Sound or Run a Program. You can set a custom pop-up message and even specify a repeat for the alarm. Another way to look at it is *how often do you want to be nagged?* I've got mine set to remind me three additional times every five minutes.

When you are done with the new alarm, click OK. To add more alarms, all you have to do is click the Add button once. Now you get the idea.

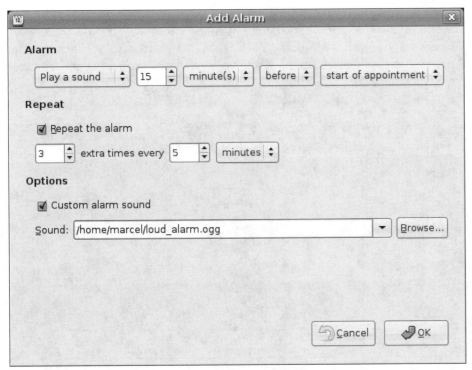

Figure 12–5 Evolution can remind you of your appointments in many different ways.

Let's Do That Again: Evolution Recurrence

Before we move on to making this more than a one-person appointment, let's look at recurrence. If the gang meets for that poker game every week or every month at the same place and time, it just makes sense to enter the appointment once and have the system do the rest for you. Click the Recurrence icon at the top of the Appointment window and the Recurrence dialog appears (see Figure 12-6).

Activate recurrence by clicking the This Appointment Recurs check box. Choose how often you want this appointment to occur and with what frequency (for example, every 2 weeks on Thursday). Directly below is the Exceptions dialog. Click the Add button and a small dialog appears where you can enter the date. There's a small arrow to the right of the date field that brings up a small calendar from which you can make your selection. Select those days that don't apply to the standard recurrence (for example, your holidays) and click OK. You can specify as many exceptions as you like. When you are happy with everything, click the Close button to go back to your Appointment window. Click Save and your new appointment appears in your main calendar view.

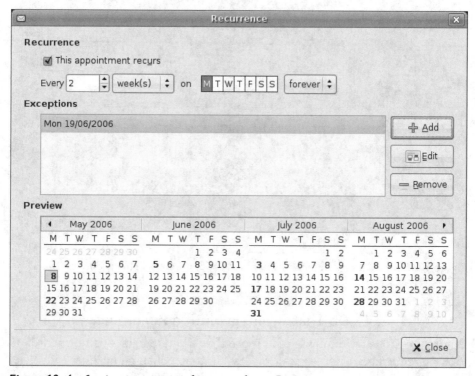

Figure 12–6 Setting recurrence information for an Evolution appointment.

The Makings of a Meeting

What really sets a meeting apart from an appointment, other than a menu option, is that you need to organize and invite people other than yourself. Creating a meeting in Evolution is similar in many ways to an appointment, but the focus is on people.

Click File on the menu bar, navigate to the New submenu, and click Meeting. Another way is to click the arrow to the right of the big New button on the top left and select Meeting from the list. For those who prefer the keyboard for such things, press <Shift+Ctrl+E>. The Meeting dialog appears, ready for you to add details and, of course, people (see Figure 12-7).

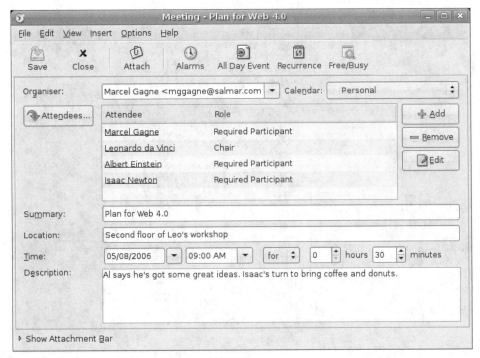

Figure 12–7 Setting up a new meeting.

Along the top, just below the icons, you should see yourself listed as the Organizer of the meeting (assuming you created the entry). Directly below that is a list of attendees. At this point, only you are listed. To the left is a button labeled Attendees. Click that button and a browser for your address book pops up, making it easy to add those who are attending the meeting. With each person you add, you can define that person's role in the meeting. Add them based on whether the individual acts as chair, a participant (required or not), an optional participant (that is, an observer), or Resources.

Below the attendee information, things start to look more like the appointment dialog of earlier. Add summary information, start and end times, and a description. You could just close the dialog at this point but Evolution offers a handy tool for those of you in an office environment. Possibly the toughest thing about getting a whole lot of people together is finding a time when everyone (or nearly everyone) is free. Look along the icon bar at the top of the Meeting window and click the Free/Busy button. The Free/Busy dialog appears with a list of attendees and their available times (see Figure 12-8).

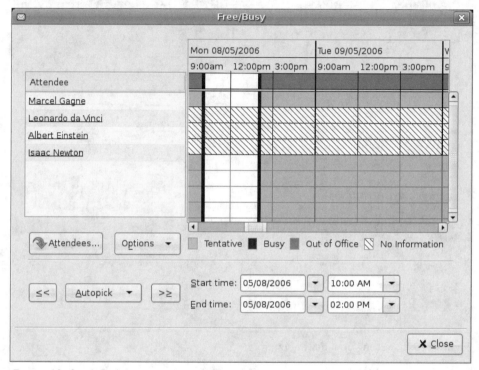

Figure 12–8   Scheduling a meeting with Free/Busy information.

Aside from being able to check other users' free time, you can also use this screen to add further attendees. Just click the Contacts button. Near the bottom of this window, you see the word Autopick in a drop-down box. To the right and left are buttons with double arrows on them. Click these and Evolution automatically selects the next block of time (either before or after your initial attempt) in which all invitees are free based on their published Free/Busy information.

When everyone is added and you finally click OK, Evolution prompts you with a request to send an email invitation to all of your participants (see Figure 12-9). Click Send and your attendees are sent a message in which they can choose to accept or decline the invitation to attend.

Figure 12–9   After you have entered all of the information pertaining to a meeting, Evolution asks whether you want to alert your attendees.

Tip   Eventually, your calendar becomes packed with old appointments and meetings, information that serves no purpose but to slow you down. A purge of old data is healthy from time to time. Click Actions on the menu bar and select Purge. A pop-up dialog appears asking you to select the age of appointments you want deleted—the default is to delete anything older than 60 days.

Tasks and Other To-Dos

When using Evolution, your to-do items are called tasks. Looking at Evolution's main calendar display, you see a summary task list in the lower right pane. Adding a new task is as easy as clicking the Click to Add a Task field. Type a brief description of your task, and then press <Enter>. For a task-only list, click the Tasks button in the left-hand sidebar. That provides you with a much larger view and another quick-entry field.

The click to create method I describe here is for simple tasks. To add more constraints such as a due date, status information, or a detailed description, you can right-click one of your tasks and select Open. To create a detailed task from the beginning, click the New button or select New Task from the File menu. A Task dialog appears offering you a much more detailed view of task creation (see Figure 12-10). The new window allows you to enter a description of the task, assign a start date and time, as well as a completion date and time.

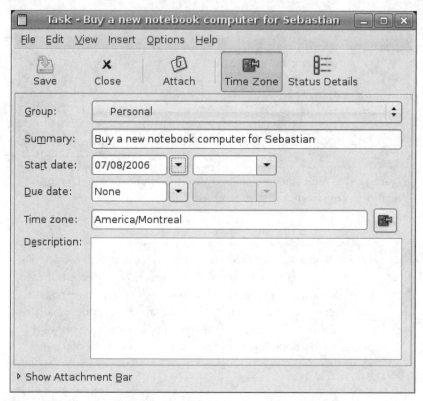

Figure 12–10   A more complete task dialog.

Click the Status Details button to assign priority and status information, such as whether the task has been started, and its percentage of completion (see Figure 12-11). You can also add attachments to the task or refer to a Web page. When you are finished entering your information, close the Task Details window, then click Save to close the new task dialog.

One last, and fairly important, feature is the ability to delegate this task to someone else. Right-click the item you want in the task list and select Assign Task from the drop-down menu. The Task Edit dialog appears showing you as the organizer of the task but with you as the one required participant (it looks very much like the dialog used to add attendees to a meeting). To assign another user to the task, remove yourself from the attendees list, then add a new individual. You can click the Attendees button to enter your address book. When you have entered the information, click Save to update your task. A window pops up asking you whether the assigned task should be sent. The correct answer is, of course, Send.

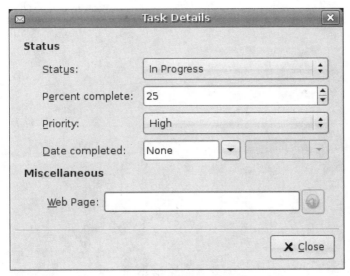

Figure 12–11   Adding status information to a task.

Resources

GNOME Evolution

http://gnome.org/projects/evolution/

13

OpenOffice.org Writer (It Was a Dark and Stormy Night . . .)

I just love using this infamous opening from Edward George Bulwer-Lytton's Paul Clifford (written in 1830) to introduce a chapter on word processing. Those famous words, "It was a dark and stormy night," were made even more famous (infamous?) by Charles M. Schulz's Snoopy, that barnstorming, literary beagle. It just seems fitting considering this chapter's topic— word processors.

Word processors run the gamut in terms of complexity, from simple programs that aren't much more than text editors to full-blown desktop publishing systems. Users coming from the Microsoft world are most likely to use OpenOffice Writer, part of the OpenOffice.org suite.

OpenOffice.org is actually the free sibling of the commercial StarOffice suite. When Sun Microsystems decided to open the source to StarOffice, it became another boon for the open source community, not to mention the average user. OpenOffice became the free version of this powerful word processor, spreadsheet, and presentation graphics package, and StarOffice became the corporate choice. Both of these are full-featured office suites, and users familiar with Microsoft Office will feel right at home with the similarities.

You might well be wondering what differences exist between these two sibling suites. The great difference is the price. For anyone with a reasonably fast Internet connection (or a helpful friend), OpenOffice is *free*. StarOffice, on the other hand, costs something for the boxed set. Included with StarOffice are documentation and support, as well as additional fonts and clipart. That said, you'll find that it is still *far less expensive* than the Windows alternative.

There are other word processor choices at your disposal. They aren't installed, but that's easily resolved with Synaptic (refer to Chapter 8). I'll tell you about some of those choices and why you might want to look into them at the end of this chapter.

Trivia Time It may interest you to know that this book was written using OpenOffice.org Writer 2.0.

Getting Started with OpenOffice.org Writer

Start OpenOffice.org Writer by clicking the Applications menu on the top panel, navigating to the Office submenu, and selecting OpenOffice.org2 Writer (see Figure 13-1).

Shell Out To run OpenOffice.org Writer from the command line (or via your <Alt+F2> shortcut), use the command `oowriter` (think *OpenOffice.org Writer*).

OpenOffice.org Writer starts up with a blank page, ready for you to release that inner creative genius (see Figure 13-2). At the top of the screen, you find a menu bar where commands are organized based on their categories, including the friendly sounding Help submenu (more on that shortly).

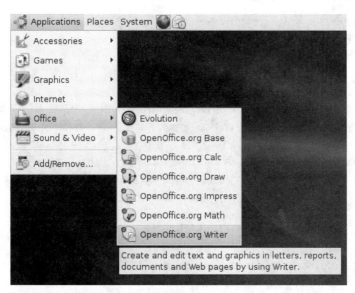

Figure 13–1 OpenOffice.org Writer and its components are in the Office submenu.

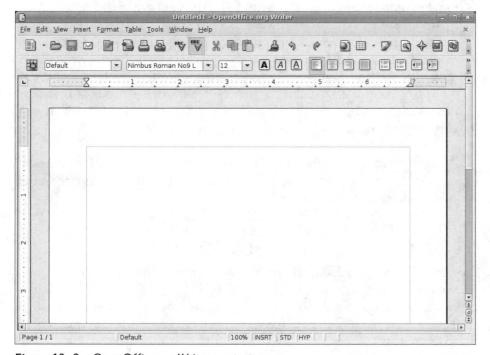

Figure 13–2 OpenOffice.org Writer on startup.

At this point, Writer is open, and you are looking at a blank screen. Let's write something.

Write Now!

As any writer will tell you, nothing is more *intimidating* than a blank page. Because I opened this chapter with a reference to the famous phrase, "It was a dark and stormy night," why don't we continue along that theme? That phrase is often pointed to as an example of bad writing, but the phrase in itself is only so bad. The paragraph that follows is even worse. Type this into your blank Writer page, as shown in Figure 13-3.

Paul Clifford, by Edward George Bulwer-Lytton

It was a dark and stormy night; the rain fell in torrents—except at occasional intervals, when it was checked by a violent gust of wind which swept up the streets (for it is in London that our scene lies), rattling along the house-tops, and fiercely agitating the scanty flame of the lamps that struggled against the darkness. Through one of the obscurest quarters of London, and among haunts little loved by the gentlemen of the police, a man, evidently of the lowest orders, was wending his solitary way. He stopped twice or thrice at different shops and houses of a description correspondent with the appearance of the quarter in which they were situated—and tended inquiry for some article or another which did not seem easily to be met with. All the answers he received were couched in the negative; and as he turned from each door he muttered to himself, in no very elegant phraseology, his disappointment and discontent.

Okay, you can stop there. Isn't that wonderful stuff? If you feel the need to read more, I've got links to the story and the famous Bulwer-Lytton fiction contest at the end of this chapter.

The Hunt for Typos

For years, I've been including the following tag line in the signature section of my emails: "This massagee wos nat speel or gramer-checkered." Given that I continue to use this line, I am obviously amused by it, but never running a spell check is far from good practice when your intention is to turn in a professional document.

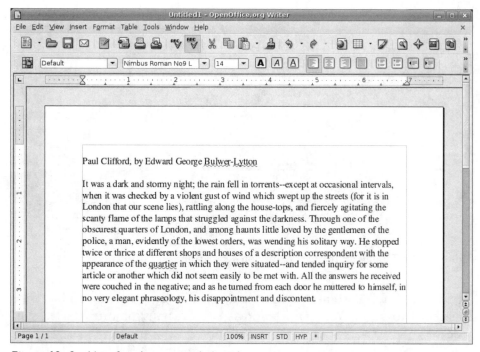

Figure 13–3 Your first document, dark and stormy.

OpenOffice.org Writer can do a spell check as you type without actually correcting errors. With this feature, words that don't appear in the dictionary show up with a squiggly red line underneath them, which you can then correct. Many people find this a useful feature, but some, like me, prefer to just check the whole document at the end of writing. This feature is activated by default but you can deactivate it if you prefer. Here's how.

Click Tools on the menu bar, and then select Options. This is a multipurpose dialog that allows you to configure many of OpenOffice.org's features (see Figure 13-4). For the moment, we concentrate on the auto spell check. To the left of the dialog is a sidebar with many categories. Click the plus sign beside Language Settings. This drops down a submenu from which you choose Writing Aids. Look to the right and you see a section called Options, at the top of which is the check box Check Spelling as You Type. To turn off the auto spell check feature, un-check this box, and then click OK to close the dialog.

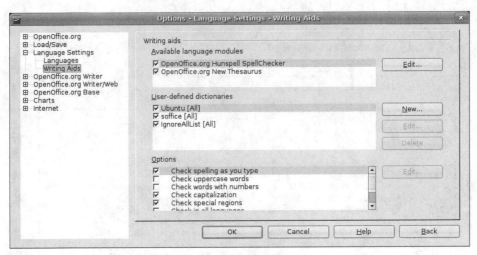

Figure 13–4   Turning off the spelling-as-you-type feature.

To start a full document spell check, click Tools on the menu bar, then Spellcheck to begin. You can also press <F7> at any time to start a spell check.

What Language Is That?

OpenOffice.org supports many different languages, and depending on where you picked up your copy, it may be set for a different language than your own. To change the default language, click Tools on the menu bar, then click Options, Language Settings, and Writing Aids. Look familiar?

The dialog that appears should have OpenOffice.org MySpell Spell-Checker checked (refer to Figure 13-4). You can then click the Edit button next to it and select your language of choice under the Default Languages for Documents drop-down box. When you have made your choice, click OK to exit the various dialogs.

Saving Your Work

Now that you have created a document, it is time to save it. Click File on the menu bar and select Save (or Save As). When the Save As window appears, select a folder, type in a filename, and click Save (see Figure 13-5). When you save, you can also specify the File type to be OpenOffice.org's default Open-

Document Text format (.odt), RTF, straight text, Microsoft Word format, and a number of others. You can even save in Palm doc format so you can take it with you on your Palm device.

If you want to create a new directory under your home directory, you can do it here as well. Click the icon that looks like a folder with a star or globe in front of it (the middle icon near the righthand corner), and then enter your new directory name in the Create New Folder pop-up window.

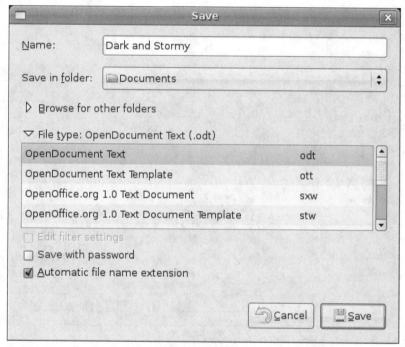

Figure 13–5   It is always good to save your work.

Should you decide to close OpenOffice.org Writer at this point, you can always return to your document at a later time by clicking File on the menu bar and selecting Open. The Open File dialog appears, and you can browse your directories to select the file you want. You can specify a file type via a fairly substantial drop-down list of available formats. This gives you a chance to narrow the search to include only text documents, spreadsheets, or presentations. You can also specify a particular document extension (for example, only *.doc files) or a particular pattern.

Printing Your Document

Invariably, the whole point of typing something in a word processor might be to produce a printed document. When you are through with your document, click File on the menu bar and select Print.

The Print dialog has several options (see Figure 13-6). The easiest thing to do after selecting your printer is just to click OK. The print job is directed to your printer of choice and, in a few seconds, you have a nice, crisp version of your document. You can select a page range, increase the number of copies (one to all your friends), or modify the printer properties (paper size, landscape print, and so on).

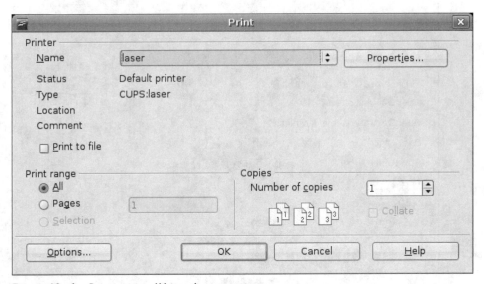

Figure 13–6   Printing your Writer document.

You can also print to a file. By default, this generates a PostScript document, a kind of universal printer language. A number of tools can view Post-Script documents including the Evince PS/PDF viewer included with Ubuntu Linux. Just navigate to any PostScript document with Nautilus, double-click the document, and Evince opens the document for viewing.

You can also save to PDF, something I'll cover a little later in the chapter.

Toolbars of Every Kind . . .

Now that you are feeling comfortable with your new word processor, let's take a quick tour of the various toolbars, icons, and menus in Writer.

The icon bar directly below the menu bar is called the *Standard bar*, and it contains icons for opening and creating documents, cutting and pasting, printing, and other tasks. The Standard bar is common to all the OpenOffice.org applications (Writer, Calc, Impress, and so on).

Below the Standard bar is the *Formatting bar*. It provides common editing options, such as font selection, bolding, italics, centering, and so on. Select words or phrases in your document with the mouse (hold, click, and drag across the desired text), then click *B* for bold or *I* for italic. This bar changes from application to application, depending on what type of formatting is most needed.

At the bottom of the editing screen is the *Status bar*. There, you see the current page number, current template, zoom percentage, insert (or over-write) mode, selection mode, hyperlink mode, and the current save status of the document. (If the document has been modified and not saved, an asterisk appears.)

In all cases, pausing over each of the icons with your mouse cursor makes a tooltip appear, describing the functions of the individual icons.

Help!

Under the Help heading on the menu bar, you find plenty of information. By default, tooltips are activated so that when you pause your mouse cursor over an item, a small tooltip is shown. These tips are terse, usually no more than a couple of words. It's also possible to get a little more information by turning on *extended tips*. Before I tell you how to do that, have a look at Figure 13-7 for a sample of the difference. The image at the top shows the default tip for the Paste icon, whereas the image on the bottom shows the extended tip for the same function.

For that little extra help, click Tools and select Options. Under the OpenOffice.org menu on the right, you find a subsection labeled General. Click there and then look over on the right. You see a check box for Extended Tips near the top. Turning that on gives you slightly more detailed tooltips.

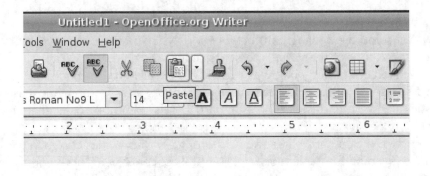

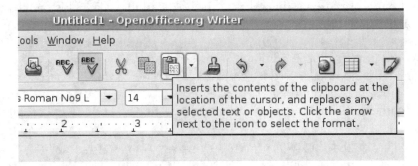

Figure 13–7   What a difference extended tips makes.

If you are looking for help on a specific topic, there's always the included manual. Click Help on the menu bar and select OpenOffice.org Help (you can also press <F1>). The various tabs at the top left of the help screen let you search for topics by application with the Contents tab, alphabetically using the Index tab, and by keyword using the Find tab. You can even set bookmarks under the Bookmarks tab for those topics you regularly access.

To Word or Not to Word?

Ah, that is the question indeed. OpenOffice.org's default document format is the OASIS OpenDocument XML (eXtensible Markup Language) format, an open standard for document formats (it is saved with an .odt extension). As of the beginning of May 2006, the OpenDocument format is an ISO standard. The OpenDocument format is the closest thing to document freedom you can get (short of plain text). The format is vendor and application neutral. You are guaranteed support and portability because it is an open standard. Many organizations such as the European Commission and the State of Massachusetts recommend the OASIS OpenDocument format for the very reasons I've mentioned. In fact, Massachusetts requires the use of open document standards by law. For more on this emerging standard, check the resources section at the end of this chapter.

Alternatively, the main reason for sticking with Word format is, quite frankly, that Word is everywhere. The sheer number of Word installations is the very reason that OpenOffice.org was designed to support Microsoft Office format as thoroughly as it does. That said, if you do want to switch to the OASIS OpenDocument format, Writer provides an easy way to do that. Rather than converting documents one by one, the Document Converter speeds up the process by allowing you to run all the documents in a specific directory in one pass. It also works in both directions, meaning that you can convert from Word to OpenOffice.org format, and vice versa. The conversion creates a new file but leaves the original as it is.

From the menu bar, select File, move your mouse to Wizards, and then select Document Converter from the submenu. To convert your Microsoft Office documents (you can do the Excel and PowerPoint documents at the same time), click Microsoft Office on the menu, and then check off the types of documents you want. The next screen asks whether you want both documents and templates or just one or the other. You then type in the name of the directory you want to import from and save to (this can be the same directory). After you enter your information and go to the next screen, the program confirms your choices and gives you a final chance to change your mind. Click Convert to continue. As the converter does its job, it lists the various files that it encounters and keeps track of the process.

When the job is done, you have a number of files with an .odt extension in your directory. If you change your mind, don't worry. Your original files are still there, so you've lost nothing.

If working with Word documents in Word format is important, then read on. Ah, heck. Even if it isn't, you should read on.

Personalizing Your Environment

Every application you use comes with defaults that may or may not reflect the way you want to work, and this is true with OpenOffice.org Writer, as well.

Click Tools on the menu bar and select Options. There are a lot of options here, including OpenOffice.org, Load/Save, Language Settings, OpenOffice.org Writer (including HTML/Web documents), OpenOffice.org Base (the built in database), Charts, and Internet. Each of these sections has a submenu of further options. Because there are so many options here, I certainly can't cover them all, and besides, I don't want to bore you. Instead, I'll mention a few things that I *think* are important and let you discover the rest.

The main OpenOffice.org dialog covers a lot of general options regarding the look and feel of the applications. Take a moment to look at the *Paths* settings. If you keep your documents in a specific directory, you want to set that here. Under Type, choose My Documents, click Edit, and then enter the new path to your directory of choice.

Let's move on to the very important Load/Save settings menu (see Figure 13-8). If you are constantly going to move documents back and forth between systems running Microsoft Word and your own Linux system running OpenOffice.org Writer, you want to pay special attention here. Click the plus sign to the left of the Load/Save menu item, and then click Microsoft Office.

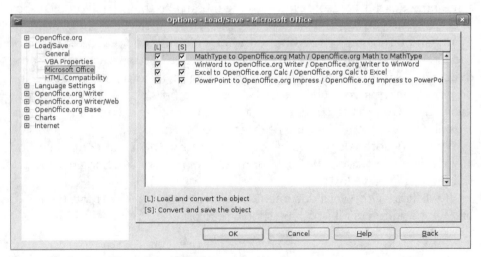

Figure 13–8   Load/Save defaults for Microsoft documents.

Check the Convert on Save (and load) check boxes (labeled [S] and [L] at the top), and your OpenOffice.org Writer documents are saved in Word format by default, whereas your Calc sheets wind up in Excel format. We're almost there. Although the conversion is pretty automatic here, when you try to resave a document that you have been working on, Writer may still disturb you with the occasional pop-up message informing you of the *minuses* of saving in Word format.

You get around this with one other change. In the same menu section, click General. Notice the section Default File Format toward the bottom of the dialog (see Figure 13-9). For the Document type of Text document, select Microsoft Word 97/2000/XP from the Always Save As drop-down list to the right. While you are here (assuming you are making these changes, of course), you probably want to change the Always Save as format for Spreadsheet to be Microsoft Excel, and so on.

Click OK, and you are done.

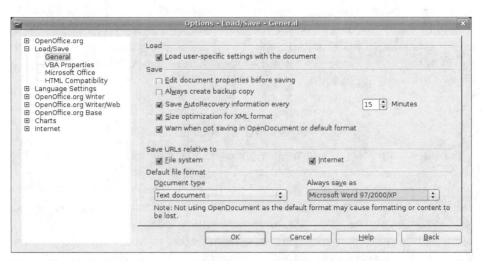

Figure 13–9   Defining the standard file format to be Microsoft Word.

Note I'm not saying that Microsoft's document format is in any way superior. Not only is it not superior, but you are also trapped in a proprietary *standard* that may make it difficult to import your data in the future. It may also be a costly process. Although there's no guarantee that any document format is going to *the standard* in the future, it's nice to know that you can always load and read your old documents. That knowledge and comfort is what the OpenDocument format (again, now an ISO standard)

provides. That said, if you have to move back and forth from the open document format to Microsoft's proprietary format all the time, you don't want to be bothered with doing a save as every time. It just gets tedious.

OpenOffice.org 2.0 can also save in Microsoft's new XML format, which debuted in Microsoft Office 2003.

Let's move on to the OpenOffice.org Writer category (in the left-hand sidebar menu) for changes related specifically to the Writer application. Whenever you start a new document, OpenOffice.org assigns a default font when you start typing. This may not be your ideal choice, and you don't have to accept it. Sure, you can change the font when you are writing, but why do this with every document when you can change it once? Click Basic Fonts, and you have the opportunity to change the default fonts your system uses.

When you are done with the Options menu, click OK to return to the OpenOffice.org application.

A Wizard of Words

OpenOffice.org comes with a number of templates that are available throughout the suite. The document Wizards feature helps you choose and walk through the setup of some basic documents. The easiest way to understand what these wizards can do for you is to dive right in and try one.

On the menu bar, click File, and move your mouse over to Wizards. You see a number of document types here, from letters to faxes to presentations. We use Letter as an example. When the Letter Wizard starts up, it offers you three kinds of letters: business, formal, and personal (see Figure 13-10). Each of these may have different styles depending on the letter type. As you progress through the various steps, you are asked to enter some basic information related to the type of document that you chose. In the case of a letter, this involves an opening and closing greeting, a sender and recipient name and address, and so on. The wizard also lets you save the document as a template so you can use it at a later date.

The wizard also displays a graphical preview of what the document looks like directly behind the design selection window. You shouldn't look at this as a perfect example of what you will wind up with, but it does help in visualizing the final product.

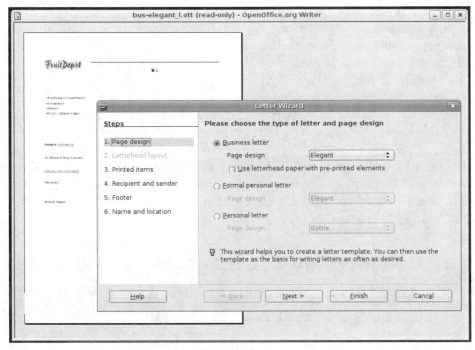

Figure 13–10   Writing using the Letter Wizard.

Navigating Style

With Writer open, click Format on the menu bar, and then select Styles and Formatting. A window labeled Styles and Formatting appears, floating above your document. Pressing <F11> also brings up the stylist. Clicking the X in the corner of the window banishes it. I'd like to give you some idea of how useful this little tool can be in formatting your documents. If you've banished the stylist, bring it back by clicking its icon or pressing <F11>.

 Great Time-Saving Tip   Here's a good trick you might want to keep in mind if you start using styles in a big way. Click the stylist's title bar with your left mouse button and slowly drag the stylist window over to the right edge (or the left) of your Writer window. As the stylist starts to go beyond the edge of the Writer window, you should see a gray vertical outline appear under the stylist. Release the mouse button and the stylist docks into the main writer window (see Figure 13-11).

Whenever you start a new document, it loads with a default style. That style is actually a collection of formatting presets that define how various paragraphs will look. These include headings, lists, text boxes, and so on. All you have to do is select a paragraph, double-click a style, and your paragraph's look—including font style and size—is magically updated. As an example of how to use this, try the following.

Start by reloading your dark and stormy document, and then highlight your title text to select it. The bottom of your stylist shows the text *Automatic*. With your title highlighted, double-click Heading 1. The heading changes to a large, bold, sans serif font. Now click the arrow at the bottom of the list, and change from Automatic to Chapter Styles. Double-click Title, and your title is suddenly centered with the appropriate font applied (see Figure 13-11).

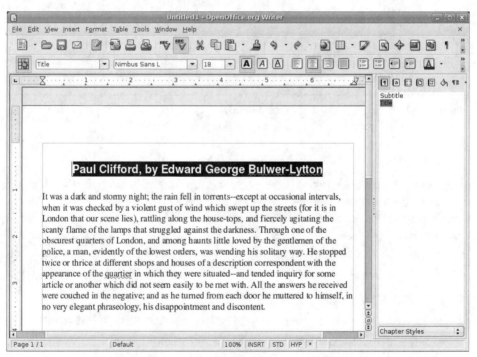

Figure 13–11   *Styles make paragraph formatting easy and consistent. Note that the stylist is docked on the right.*

The stylist is pretty smart. Look to the bottom of the list at those categories—HTML Styles, Custom Styles, List Styles, and so on. Depending on the document type that you are working on, the stylist comes up with a pretty sane list for that Automatic selection. If you call up an HTML document, HTML formatting shows up in the Automatic list.

Quick Undo Tip To remove a docked stylist, drag it out of its dock and drop it above the document itself. It turns back into a floating window. You can also press <F11> and it promptly vanishes from the dock. The great thing about using the function key is that the stylist remembers where it was. If it was docked when you pressed <F11>, it will be when you press it again.

Navigating the Rivers of Text

The second floating window is called the *Navigator.* This is a great tool for the power user or anyone who is creating long, complex documents. When you start up the Navigator by clicking Edit and then Navigator (or by pressing <F5>), you see a window listing the various elements in your document (see Figure 13-12). These are organized in terms of headings, tables, graphics, and so on.

Figure 13–12 The Navigator gives you access to all your document elements.

Quick Tip You guessed it! Just like the stylist, the Navigator can be dragged to either edge of the document and docked into the main writer window. Just make sure you drag it far enough so that it isn't another vertical window next to the stylist, but rather sits above or below it.

What makes this a great tool is that you can use it to navigate a document quickly. Let's say that (as in this chapter) there are a number of section headings. Click the plus sign beside the word *Headings*, and a treed list of all the headings in the document is displayed. Double-click a heading, and you instantly jump to that point in the document. The same goes for graphics, tables, and other such elements in your document.

Speaking of Document Elements . . .

Take a look over at the far right of the Standard bar. See the little icon that looks like a picture hanging on a wall (to the right of the Navigator *star*)? That's the *gallery* of graphics and sounds, decorative elements that can be inserted into your document. When you click the picture (or select Gallery from Tools on the menu bar), the gallery opens up with a sidebar on the left, listing the various themes.

Wander through the collection until you see something that suits your document, and then simply drag it into your document, just as I did with that rather bright ruler below the *Paul Clifford* title in Figure 13-13. To banish the gallery, just click the icon again.

While you were using the gallery, did you notice the words *New Theme* at the top of the category sidebar? Click those words (which is really a button), and you can create a new category of images, clipart, or sounds. If you have a directory of images you've collected, enter the path to that directory, pick a name for this collection, and you are done. Next time you bring up the gallery, you can select from your own custom collection.

Tip How would you like tons and tons of great, license-free, royalty-free, and just plain free, high-quality clipart? Fire up Synaptic, then search for and install `openclipart`.

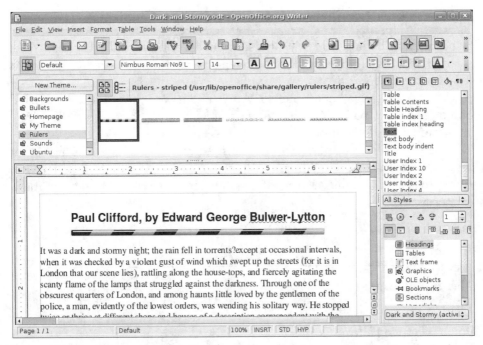

Figure 13–13   Writer with the gallery open above the document, and with a docked stylist and Navigator to the right.

More! Give Me More!

OpenOffice.org comes with a limited number of templates, graphics, and icons. That's one of the advantages of its commercial (nonfree) cousin, StarOffice from Sun Microsystems. However, if you find yourself in need of more templates than you already have or a richer gallery, take careful note of the following Web sites.

The first is called *OO Extras*, and it contains more than two hundred templates for OpenOffice.org Writer, Calc, and Impress. In addition to individual macros, icons, and templates, this Web site (created by Travis Bauer) aims to provide downloadable packages to enhance OpenOffice.org's suite.

You should also pay a visit to the OpenOffice Documentation Project site (run by Scott Carr), which offers much more than extra templates and macros. There are also tutorials, setup guides, user guides, and even some video presentations.

Links for both projects follow in the Resources section.

Alternative Word Processor Choices

Fire up Synaptic and you will find some excellent alternative suites. Make sure you have the Universe and Multiverse repositories before you begin, as described in Chapter 8.

The first package I point out is KWord, and it is part of KOffice, the KDE office suite. KWord is light, fast, and should you choose to run KDE, nicely integrated into the desktop.

The second package I direct you to is Abiword. This one is available for several platforms including Linux, Windows, and even BeOS. Like KWord, Abiword is light and fast, a great alternative for those running on more modest hardware.

Resources

Abiword Web Site

```
http://www.abisource.com
```

Bulwer-Lytton Fiction Contest

```
http://www.bulwer-lytton.com
```

KOffice (for KWord)

```
http://koffice.kde.org
```

OASIS OpenDocument Format

```
http://www.oasis-open.org/committees/office/faq.php
```

OOExtras

```
http://ooextras.sourceforge.net
```

OpenOffice.org Web Site

```
http://www.openoffice.org/
```

OpenOffice.org Documentation Project

```
http://documentation.openoffice.org
```

Sun Microsystems StarOffice

```
http://www.sun.com/software/star/staroffice/
```

14

OpenOffice.org Calc (Tables You Can Count On)

A spreadsheet, for those who might be curious, allows an individual to organize data onto a table comprised of rows and columns. The intersection of a row and a column is called a cell, and each cell can be given specific attributes, such as a value or a formula. In the case of a formula, changes in the data of other cells can automatically update the results. This makes a spreadsheet ideal for financial applications. Take a mortgage payment calculation, for example: change the interest rate in the appropriate cell, and the monthly payment changes without you having to do anything else.

The idea of a computerized spreadsheet probably existed before 1978, but it was that year that Daniel Bricklin, a Harvard Business School student, came up with the first real spreadsheet program. He called his program a visible calculator, then later enlisted Bob Frankston of MIT (Bricklin names him as co-creator) to help him develop the program further. This program came to be known as VisiCalc. Some argue that with VisiCalc, the first so-called killer app was born.

Now that we have the definitions and history out of the way, let's get back to your Linux system and have a look at OpenOffice.org's very own spreadsheet program. It is called *Calc*—an appropriate name, given what spreadsheets tend to be used for.

Starting a New Spreadsheet and Entering Data

There are a few ways to start a new spreadsheet using OpenOffice.org on your Ubuntu Linux system. If you are already working in OpenOffice.org Writer (as I am right now), you can click File on the menu bar, move your mouse to the New submenu, and select Spreadsheet from the drop-down list. Another way is to click the Applications menu on the top panel, navigate to the Office submenu, and select OpenOffice.org2 Calc. When Calc starts up, you see a blank sheet of cells, as in Figure 14-1.

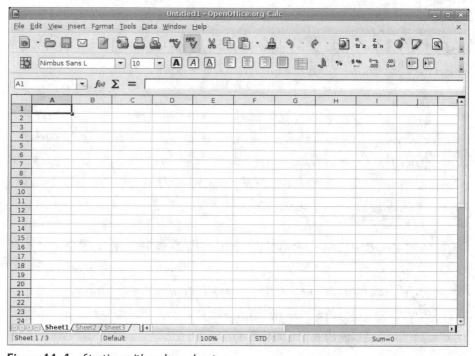

Figure 14–1   Starting with a clean sheet.

Directly below the menu bar is the *Standard bar*. As with Writer, the icons here give you access to the common functions found throughout Open-Office.org, such as cut, paste, open, save, and so on. Below the Standard bar is the *Formatting bar*. Some features here are similar to those in Writer, such as font style and size, but others are specific to formatting content in a spreadsheet (percentage, decimal places, frame border, and so on).

Finally, below the Formatting bar, you find the *Formula bar*. The first field here displays the current cell but you can also enter a cell number to jump to that cell. You can move around from cell to cell by using your cursor keys, using the <Tab> key (and <Shift+Tab>), or simply clicking a particular cell. The current cell you are working on has a bold black outline around it.

Basic Math

Let's try something simple, shall we? If you haven't already done so, open a new spreadsheet. In cell A1, type **Course Average**. Select the text in the field, change the font style or size (by clicking the font selector in the Format-ting bar), and then press <Enter>. As you can see, the text is larger than the field. No problem. Place your mouse cursor on the line between the A and B cells (directly below the Formula bar). Click and hold, then stretch the A cell to fit the text. You can do the same for the height of any given row of cells by clicking the line between the row numbers (over to the left) and stretching these to an appropriate size.

Now move to cell A3 and type in a hypothetical number somewhere in the range of 1 to 100 to represent a course mark. Press <Enter> or cursor down to move to the next cell. Enter seven course marks so that cells A3 through A9 are filled. In my example, I entered 95, 67, 100, 89, 84, 79, and 93. (In my opinion, the 67 score is an aberration.)

Now, we are going to enter a formula in cell A11 to provide an average of all seven course scores. In cell A11, enter the following text:

```
=(A3+A4+A5+A6+A7+A8+A9)/7
```

When you press <Enter>, the text you entered disappears and instead, you see an average for your course scores (see Figure 14-2).

An average of 86.71 isn't a bad score (it is an A, after all), but if that 67 really was an aberration, you can easily go back to that cell, type in a different number, and press <Enter>. When you do so, the average automagically changes for you.

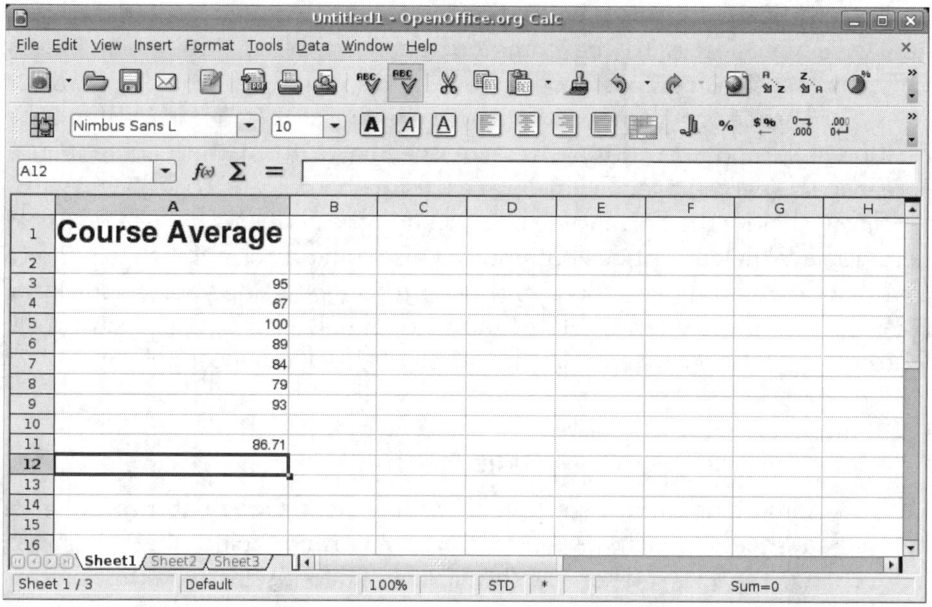

Figure 14–2   Setting up a simple table to determine class averages.

Calculating an average is a simple enough formula but if I were to add seventy rows instead of seven, the resulting formula could get *ugly*. The beauty of spreadsheets is that they include formulas to make this whole process somewhat cleaner. For instance, I can specify a range of cells by putting a colon in between the first and last cells (A3:A9) and using a built-in function to return the average of that range. My new, improved, and cleaner formula looks like this:

```
=AVERAGE(A3:A9)
```

Incidentally, you can also select the cell and enter the information in the input line on the Formula bar. I mention the Formula bar for a couple of reasons. One is that you can obviously enter the information in the field, as well as in the cell itself.

The second reason has to do with those little icons to the left of the input field. If you click that input field, notice that a little green check mark appears (to accept any changes you make to the formula); and to its left, there is a red *X* (to cancel the changes). Now look to the icon furthest on the left. If you hold your mouse over it, a tooltip pops up that says Function Wizard. Try it.

Go back to cell A11, and then click your mouse into the input field on the Formula bar. Now click the Function Wizard icon (you can also click Insert on the menu bar and select Function).

On the left side, you see a list of functions. Click on a function and a description appears to the right. For the function called *AVERAGE*, the description is *Returns the average of a sample*. Because this is what we want, click the Next button at the bottom of the window, after which you see a window much like the one in Figure 14-3. This is where the wizard starts to do its real work.

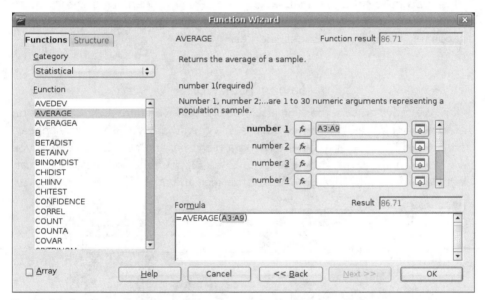

Figure 14–3 Using the Function Wizard to generate a function.

Look at the *Formula* window at the bottom of the screen. You'll see that the formula is starting to be built. At this point, it says =AVERAGE() and nothing else. Near the middle of the screen on the right side are four data fields labeled Number 1 through Number 4. The first field is required, whereas the others are optional. You could enter A3:A9, click Next, and be done. (Notice, while you are here, that the result of the formula is already displayed just above the Formula field.) Alternatively, you could click the button to the right of the number field (the tooltip says Shrink), and the Function Wizard shrinks to a small bar floating above your spreadsheet (see Figure 14-4).

A3:A9

Figure 14–4   The Function Wizard formula bar.

On your spreadsheet, select a group of fields by clicking the first field and dragging the mouse to include all seven fields. When you let go of the mouse, the field range is entered for you. On the left-hand side of the shrunken Function Wizard, there is a maximize button (move your mouse over it to activate the tooltip). Click it, and your wizard returns to its original size. Unless you have an additional set of fields (or you want to create a more complex formula), click OK to complete this operation. The window disappears, and the spreadsheet updates.

Saving Your Work

Before we move on to something else, you should save your work. Click File on the menu bar and select Save (or Save As). When the Save As window appears (see Figure 14-5), select a folder, type in a filename, and click Save. When you save, you can also specify the File Type to be OpenOffice.org's default format, OpenDocument, DIF, DBASE, Microsoft Excel, and other formats.

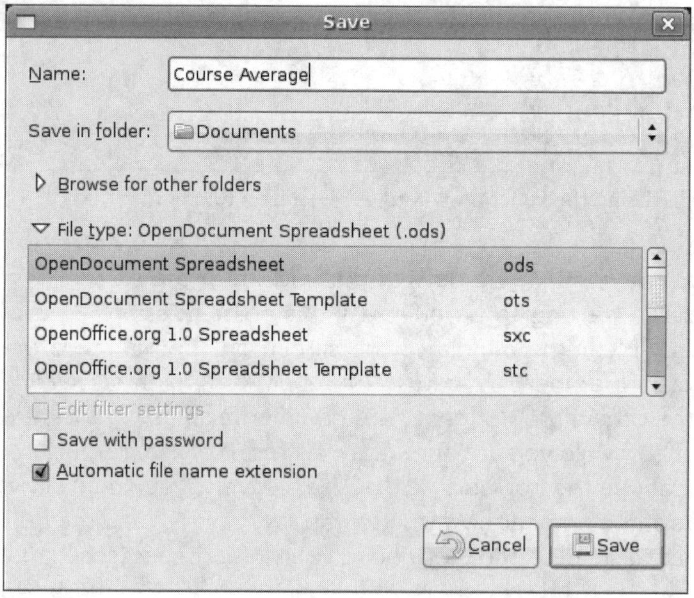

Save		
Name:	Course Average	
Save in folder:	📁 Documents	▲▼
▷ Browse for other folders		
▽ File type: OpenDocument Spreadsheet (.ods)		
OpenDocument Spreadsheet	ods	
OpenDocument Spreadsheet Template	ots	
OpenOffice.org 1.0 Spreadsheet	sxc	
OpenOffice.org 1.0 Spreadsheet Template	stc	

☐ Edit filter settings
☐ Save with password
☑ Automatic file name extension

Cancel   Save

Figure 14–5   Don't forget to save your work.

Should you decide to close OpenOffice.org Calc at this point, you can always go back to the document by clicking File on the menu bar and selecting Open.

Complex Charts and Graphs, Oh My!

This time, I'll show you how you can take the data that you enter into your spreadsheets and transform it into a slick little chart. These charts can be linear, pie, bar, and a number of other choices. They can also be two- or three-dimensional, with various effects applied for that professional look.

To start, create another spreadsheet. We'll call this one Quarterly Sales Reports. With it, we will track the performance of a hypothetical company (see Figure 14-6).

In cell A1, write the title (Quarterly Sales Reports) and in cell A2, write the description of the data (in thousands of dollars). In cell A4, enter the heading **Period**; then enter **Q1** in cell A6, **Q2** in cell A7, **Q3** in cell A8, and **Q4** in cell A9. Finally, enter some headings for the years. In cell B4, enter **2001**, then enter **2002** in cell C4, and continue on through **2005**. You should have five years running across row 4, with four quarters listed.

Time to have some virtual fun. For each period, enter a fictitious sales figure (or a real one if you are serious about this). For example, for the data for 2002, Q2 would be entered in cell C7, and for the sales figure for 2004, Q3 would be in cell E8. If you are still with me, finish entering the data, and we'll do a few things.

Magical Totals

Let's start with a quick and easy total of each column.

If you used the same layout I did, you should have a 2001 column that ends at B9. Click cell B11. Now look at the icon in the middle of the sheet area and the input line on the Formula bar. It looks like the Greek letter Epsilon. Hold your mouse pointer over it, and you see a tooltip that says Sum. Are you excited yet? Click the sum icon, and the formula to sum up the totals of that line, =SUM(B6:B10), automatically appears (see Figure 14-6). All you need to do to finalize the totals is click the green check mark that appears next to the input line (or just press <Enter>).

Because a sum calculation is the most common function used, it is kept handy. You can now do the same thing for each of the other yearly columns to get your totals. Click the sum icon, then click your beginning column and drag the mouse to include the cells you want. Click the green check mark, and move on to the next yearly column.

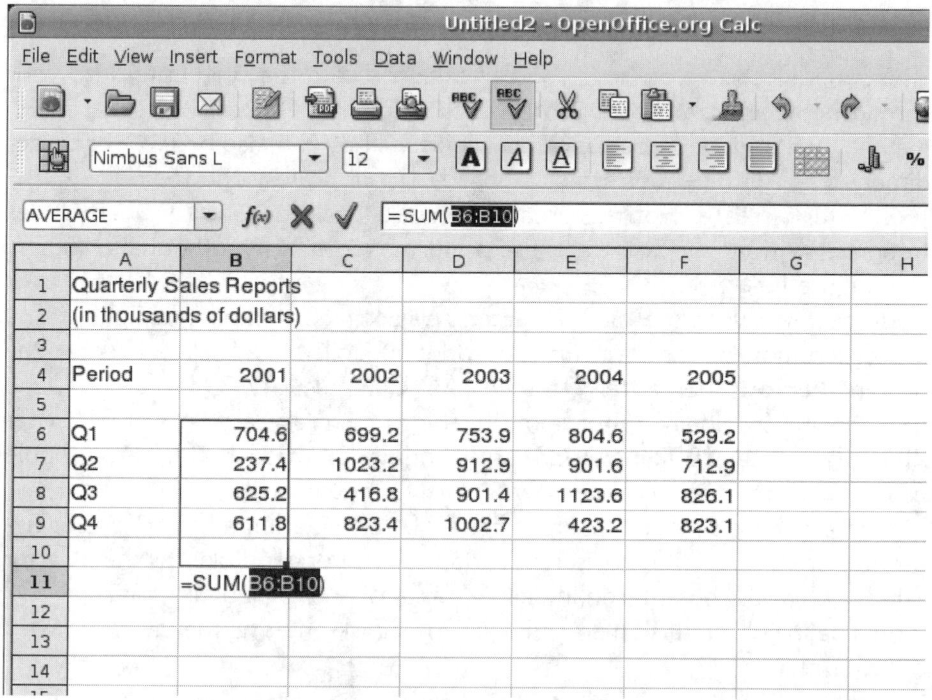

	Untitled2 - OpenOffice.org Calc
File Edit View Insert Format Tools Data Window Help	

AVERAGE   f(x) ✗ ✓   =SUM(B6:B10)

	A	B	C	D	E	F	G	H
1	Quarterly Sales Reports							
2	(in thousands of dollars)							
3								
4	Period	2001	2002	2003	2004	2005		
5								
6	Q1	704.6	699.2	753.9	804.6	529.2		
7	Q2	237.4	1023.2	912.9	901.6	712.9		
8	Q3	625.2	416.8	901.4	1123.6	826.1		
9	Q4	611.8	823.4	1002.7	423.2	823.1		
10								
11		=SUM(B6:B10)						
12								
13								
14								

Figure 14–6   Select a series of cells, and Calc automatically generates totals for you.

Nice, Colorful, Impressive, and Dynamic Graphs

Creating a chart from the data you have just entered is really pretty easy. Start by selecting the cells that represent the information you want to see on your finished chart, including the headings. You can start with one corner of the chart and simply drag your mouse across to select all that you want. Using the spreadsheet we created, select the area that includes cell A4 through to F9. Note that I did not include row 11, the totals line.

Warning If there are some empty cells in your table (in my example, row 5), you need to deselect them. You can do this by holding down the <Ctrl> key and clicking those cells with the mouse.

After you have all the cells you want selected, click Insert on the menu bar, and select Chart. This window gives you the opportunity of assigning certain rows and columns as labels (see Figure 14-7). This is perfect because we have the quarter numbers running down the left side and the year labels running across the top. Check these on.

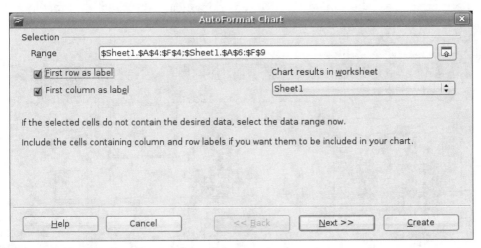

Figure 14–7 The AutoFormat Chart dialog.

Before you move on, notice the Chart Results in Worksheet drop-down list. By default, Calc creates three tabbed pages for every new worksheet, even though you are working on only one at this time. If you leave things as they are, your chart is embedded into your current page, though you can always move it to different locations. At this point, you have a choice to have the chart appear on a separate page (see those tabs at the bottom of your worksheet). For my example, I'm going to leave the chart on the first page. Make your selection, and then click Next.

Note There is also an Insert Chart icon on the Standard bar. If you click that icon (instead of clicking Insert and then Chart from the menu bar), the software automatically assumes that you want the chart in the worksheet. Furthermore, your cursor changes to a small chart icon. Click a location on the document where you want the chart to appear and the AutoFormat Chart dialog appears.

The next window lets you choose from chart types (bar, pie, and so on) and provides a preview window to the left (see Figure 14-8). That way, you can try the various chart options to see what best shows off your data. If you want to see the labels in your preview window, click the check box for Show Text Elements in Preview.

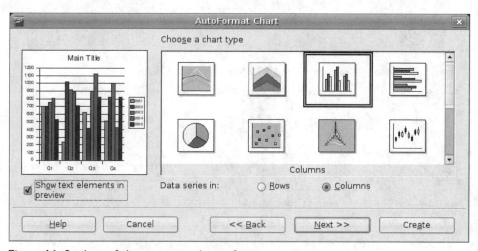

Figure 14–8   Lots of chart types to choose from.

You can continue to click Next for some additional fine-tuning on formatting (the last screen lets you change the title), but this is all the data you need to create your chart. When you are done, click the Create button, and your chart appears on your page (see Figure 14-9).

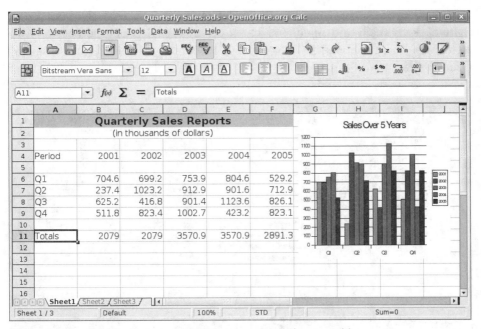

Figure 14–9 Just like that, your chart appears alongside your table.

To lock the chart in place, click anywhere else on the worksheet. You may want to change the chart's title, as well; double-click the chart, then click the title to make your changes. I'm going to call mine Sales Over 5 Years. If the chart is in the wrong place, click it, then drag it to where you want it to be. If it is too big, grab one of the corners and resize it.

What's cool about this chart is that it is dynamically linked to the data on the page. Change the data in a cell, press <Enter>, and the chart automatically updates!

Final Touches

If you select (highlight) the title text in cell A1 and click the Center icon (the one for centering text), the text position doesn't change. That's because A1 is already filled to capacity, and the text is already centered. To get the effect you want, click cell A1, hold the mouse button down, and drag to select all the cells up to F1. Now click Format on the menu bar and select Merge Cells. All six cells merge into one, after which you can select the text and center it.

For more extensive formatting of cells, including borders, color, and so on, right-click the cell, and select Format. (Try this with your title cell.) A Cell Attribute window appears, from which you can add a variety of formatting effects (see Figure 14-10).

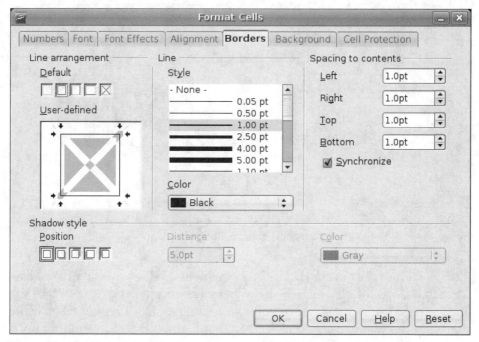

Figure 14–10   The Format Cells dialog allows you to add borders and change the background fill to a cell or group of cells.

A Beautiful Thing!

When you are through with your worksheet, it is time to print. Click File on the menu bar and select Print. Select your printer, click OK, and you have a product to impress even the most jaded bean counter. While you are busy impressing people, keep in mind that you can also export this spreadsheet to PDF with a single click, just as you did with Writer in the last chapter.

Alternatives

Because OpenOffice.org is such an obvious and excellent replacement for Microsoft Office (including Word, Excel, and PowerPoint), it's easy to forget that there are other alternatives. One of the great things I keep coming back to when I talk and write about Linux is the fact that we do have alternatives, some costing no more than the time it takes to download and install them via Synaptic.

When it comes to spreadsheet programs, it's time to fire up Synaptic and do a search using the word *spreadsheet* or one of the following programs. The primary candidates are Gnumeric and KSpread.

Both Gnumeric and KSpread are certainly worth a look, but I've found Gnumeric to be particularly good when it comes to working with Excel spreadsheets.

Resources

Gnumeric

    http://www.gnome.org/projects/gnumeric/

KSpread

    http://www.koffice.org/kspread/

OpenOffice.org's Calc

    http://www.openoffice.org/

Chapter

15

OpenOffice.org Impress (For When You Need to Impress Someone)

Once upon a time, even a simple business presentation could be quite a costly affair. The person putting together a presentation would create her presentation using a word processor (or pen and ink), then transfer it to a business graphics presentation tool. Alternatively, a special design service might be hired to take that next step, but eventually, the whole project would be sent to yet another service that would create 35-mm slides from the finished paper presentation.

On the day of the big meeting, the old carousel slide projector would come out, and the slides would be painstakingly loaded onto the circular slide holder. Then, the lights would dim, and the show would begin. With any luck, the slides would be in the right order, and the projector would not jam.

These days, we use tools that streamline this process, allowing us to create presentations, insert and manipulate graphical elements, and then play the whole thing directly from our notebook computers. The projectors we use simply plug into the video port of our computers. There are many software packages to do the job under Linux. The most popular (and the one I cover here) is part of the OpenOffice.org suite. It is called *Impress*. For those of you coming from the Microsoft world, Impress is very much like PowerPoint. In fact, Impress can easily import and export PowerPoint files.

Getting Ready to Impress

After having worked with OpenOffice.org's Writer and Calc, you should feel right at home when it comes to using Impress. Working with menus, inserting text, spell checking, and customizing your environment all work in exactly the same way. The editing screen is probably more like Calc than Writer in some ways. The Impress work area has tabbed pages so you can easily jump from one part of the presentation to the other. Each page is referred to as a *slide*. Given the history of business presentations—specifically, the making of these 35-mm slides—it's probably no wonder that we still use the same terms when creating presentations with software like Impress.

To start Impress, go to the Application menu on the top panel and select OpenOffice.org Impress from the Office submenu. You can also start a new presentation from any other OpenOffice.org application, such as Writer or Calc. Just click File on the menu bar, select New, and choose Presentation from the submenu.

When you start up Impress for the first time, the Presentation Wizard appears and you are presented with a number of choices. You can start with an empty presentation (see Figure 15-1), work from a template, or open an existing presentation. Incidentally, some earlier versions of OpenOffice.org started with a blank page. You have the opportunity to select this behavior by clicking the Do Not Show This Wizard Again check box.

Figure 15–1 Starting a new presentation with the Presentation Wizard.

Quick Tip At the time of this writing, OpenOffice.org ships with only a couple of Impress templates. As I've mentioned before, one of the differences between OpenOffice.org and StarOffice (its commercial sibling) is that StarOffice comes with a number of templates. That said, you can still download some free templates from `ooextras.sourceforge.net`.

The Presentation Wizard allows you to select from existing presentations, as well as templates. For the moment, I'm going to stick with the very basics. Leave Empty Presentation selected, and click Next. Essentially, this starts us off with a blank slide. Step 2 gives us the opportunity to select a slide design (see Figure 15-2). You may find a few options for slide design here (these would be your templates). Choose <Original>. Before you click Next, pause first and have a look at the options for output medium. By default, Impress creates presentations designed for the screen (or a projector connected to your PC).

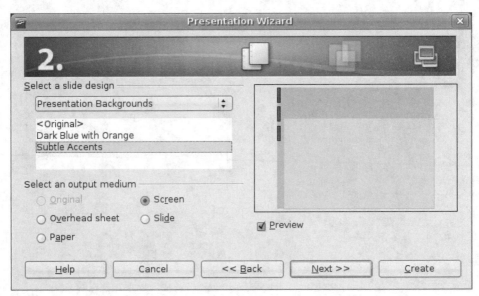

Figure 15–2   Impress defaults to creating presentations designed for the screen.

Step 3 lets you define the default means for slide transition (see Figure 15-3). You've seen these transitions; as someone shows a presentation, slides dissolve to show the next one or fly in from the left or drop like a trap door closing. At this stage of the game, pick one of these effects from the Effect drop-down box , and then choose the Speed of that transition. On the right side, there is a preview window that shows you what the effect looks like when you select it.

Directly below the slide transition selection, you select the presentation type. Your choices are Default and Automatic. By default, transition from slide to slide is done by pressing a key, whether it is <Enter> or the spacebar (you can define this). Presentations can also run without any intervention from the person giving the presentation. By selecting Automatic, you can define the amount of time between slides or between presentations. Accept the default setting here and click Create to start building your presentation.

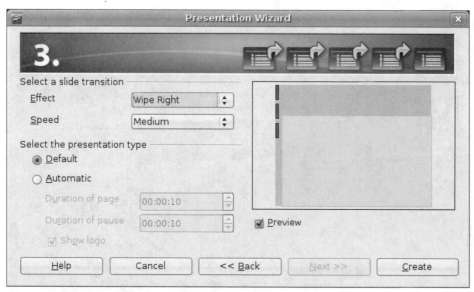

Figure 15–3 *Selecting slide transition effects.*

Now we have everything we need to start working on our presentation. Impress opens to a blank page that is divided into three main panes or frames (see Figure 15-4). On the left, small previews of all your slides are displayed (just a single blank one at this moment). If you chose a background, it is used in the slide previews. As you work, you can quickly move to any slide you want by scrolling down the lists and clicking the slide. Below each preview is the slide's title. By default, the title is Slide, followed by the slide's number in sequence. If you don't like this naming convention, you can easily override it by right-clicking the title and selecting Rename Slide.

To the right, another pane is visible with a number of potential slide layouts having small preview images. This is the Tasks pane and it is further divided into four sections: Master Pages, Layouts, Custom Animation, and Slide Transition. By default, the Layouts section is open. From here, you can decide the appearance of the slide, the number of columns, title locations, and so on. If you pause over one of the images with your mouse cursor, a tooltip appears, telling you a little about the layout format.

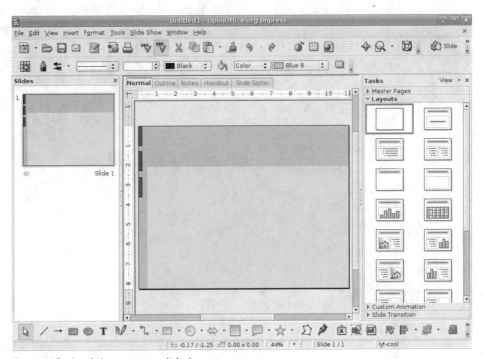

Figure 15–4   *Selecting your slide layout.*

Finally, there's a rather large central pane with five tabs labeled Normal, Outline, Notes, Handout, and Slide Sorter. The normal view is where you do most of your work, creating and editing slides. The Outline view is a kind of bird's eye overview of the whole presentation. You can reorder slides, change titles, and so on. The Notes view does pretty much what you expect; it provides an easy way to add notes to the slides. The Handout view is, I think, very handy. Sometimes, when you are doing a presentation, you are expected to provide printouts of the slides for those in attendance. With Handout, you can define how those printouts look and how many slides fit on a single page. Finally, we have the Slide Sorter, which is just a larger version of the Slides preview pane on the left. With a larger area, sorting slides is just that much easier. For now, we will be working with the Normal view.

You might notice that the various toolbars and menus have some resemblance to those of both Writer and Calc (discussed in the last two chapters). The menu bar sits just below the title bar, and the Standard bar is directly below that. Notice that the Formatting bar has a number of different options unique to working in the Impress environment. Along the bottom is the Drawing bar, which provides quick access to objects, drawing functions, 3D effects, and so on.

Let's jump right in and create a presentation. From the Tasks pane, select the Layouts section, if it isn't already open. Choose the Title, Clipart, Text layout by clicking it and it instantly appears in the main work area in the center (see Figure 15-5).

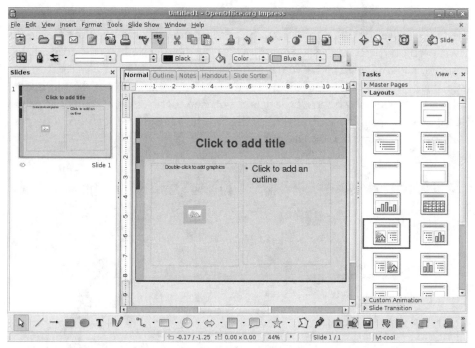

Figure 15–5 Having chosen a slide design, we are now ready to start editing that slide in the central work area.

At any point, you can start the slide show by clicking Slide Show on the menu bar and selecting Slide Show. Pressing <F5> has the same effect. There isn't much to see at this point, but you can do this from time to time to see how your presentation is coming along.

To start editing your slide, click (or double-click for images) the section you want to change. Make your changes by typing into that area. For the title, you might enter **Introducing Linux!** When you are happy with your changes, just click outside of the frame area. On the right, in the frame that says Click to Add an Outline, insert these bulleted points:

- What is Linux?
- Is Linux really free?
- What can it do?
- Advantages?
- Disadvantages?

As you might have noticed, this outline serves as talking points that mirror the first chapter of this book. Now, on the left side, double-click the frame (as instructed on the default slide) and insert a graphic. The Insert Picture dialog appears, allowing you to navigate your folders and look for the perfect image (see Figure 15-6). Once again, this is a pretty standard GNOME file dialog. Take a look over on the lower left and you see a check box labeled Preview. Because you are looking for images, this is a good one to check on. The preview pane appears over on the right.

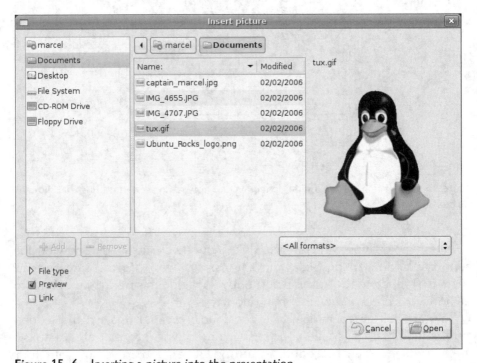

Figure 15–6   Inserting a picture into the presentation.

You can use any image you like here. For my image, I used Firefox to surf over to Larry Ewing's Web site (`www.isc.tamu.edu/~lewing/linux/`), where I picked up my Tux graphic from the source. (I'll tell you more about Tux at the end of this chapter.) You can choose another image if you prefer. When you have your image selected, click Open, and it replaces the default text in the left frame.

Quick Tip Another option is to single-click the default image and press <Delete>. Then you can click Tools on the menu bar, select Gallery, and drag one of the included images onto your slide.

That's it. Your first slide is done. You might want to pause here and save your work before you move on. (Masterpieces must be protected.) Click File on the menu bar, select Save As, and then enter a filename for your presentation. I used Introducing Linux! as my title. Now click Save, and we'll continue building this presentation.

Inserting Slides

At the right end of the Standard bar, there's a button labeled Slide. Clicking this button inserts a new slide after whatever slide you happen to be working on. You can also click Insert on the menu bar and select Slide. Once again, you are presented with a blank slide, ready for your creative vision (as in Figure 15-4). In the left frame, a new blank slide appears below the preview of the completed first slide.

For this second slide, let's select a new slide design. Go back to the Layouts section of your Tasks frame and select the slide design called Title, Text (see Figure 15-7). This is the second design from the top in the lefthand column. Remember to pause over the layout styles and a tooltip identifies them.

Because we had five points (after our introductory slide), let's do a quick add of the next four slides by just clicking the Slide button on the Standard bar. You should now have tabs labeled Slide 1 through Slide 6.

Okay, click the tab for Slide 2, then click the top frame where it says Click to Add Title. Enter the first bullet point from Slide 1. Then repeat the process for the next four slides, inserting the appropriate bullet point as the title.

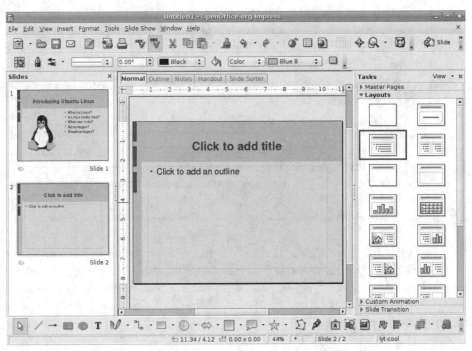

Figure 15–7   With the addition of a second slide, our presentation is starting to take shape.

 Quick Tip You can give those slide labels more useful names by right-clicking them and selecting Rename Slide.

As to what to enter in the text area of each slide, I leave that to either your imagination or your memory of Chapter 1. When you have finished entering all the information you want, save your work. I'm going to show you how to dress up those plain white slides.

Adding Color

Right-click your slide (not the text), and select Slide from the pop-up menu. Now click Page Setup (see Figure 15-8).

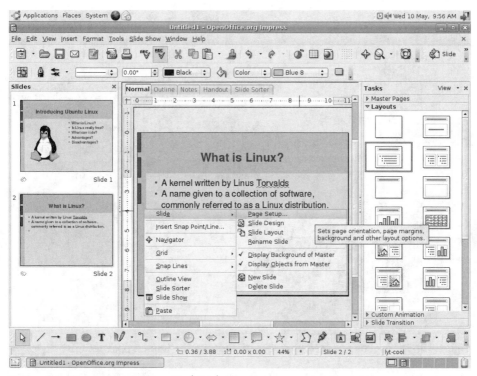

Figure 15–8 Modifying the page (slide) setup in preparation for color.

You see a two-tabbed window (one says Page and the other Background). Click the Background tab. Notice that it's a pretty boring page with nothing but a drop-down list labeled Fill, with None selected. Each item in the drop-down list provides an option for background selection, whether it is plain white, colors, gradients, hatching, or bitmaps. Click each to see the choices that they offer. The example in Figure 15-9 shows the Bitmap selection screen.

For example, you might choose the Linear blue/white gradient (a very business-looking background) or perhaps the Water bitmap. The choice is yours. When you click OK, you are asked whether you want this background setting to be for all slides. For now, click Yes.

All right. You've done a lot of work, so save your presentation. Click File on the menu bar and select Save (or Save As) from the menu. If you choose Save As, you have the opportunity to select the presentation format, whether native OpenOffice.org OpenDocument or Microsoft PowerPoint format.

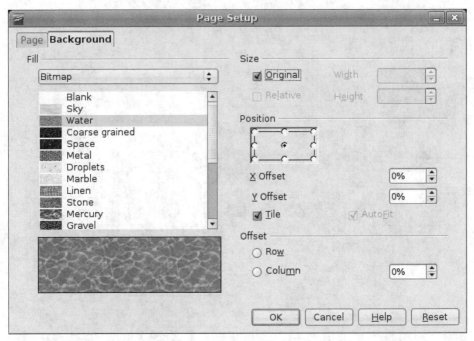

Figure 15–9 *Selecting background decorations from the Impress page setup.*

Now, it's time to see the fruits of your labors. Click Slide Show on the menu bar and select Slide Show. You can also use the <F5> keyboard short-cut. The slides transition with a touch of the spacebar or a mouse click. You can exit the presentation at any time by pressing the <Esc> key.

Printing Your Presentation

As with the other OpenOffice.org applications, click File on the menu bar and select Print; you can also click the small printer icon on the Standard bar. The standard OpenOffice.org print dialog appears, from which you can select your printer of choice.

Instant Web Presentations

Here's something you are going to find incredibly useful. Impress lets you export your existing presentation to HTML format. The beauty of this is that you can take your presentation and make it available to anyone with a Web browser. Best of all, the export functionality takes care of all the details associated with creating a Web site, including the handling of links and forward and back buttons.

To create an instant Web presentation in OpenOffice, here is what you do. Make sure that your current Impress presentation is open and that your work is saved. Click File on the menu bar and select Export. The Export dialog, looking very much like the standard GNOME file selector, appears. Make sure you select HTML Document from the File type drop-down list. Because all the generated pages appear in the directory you choose, it might make sense to create an empty directory, into which to save your files before entering a filename. That filename, by the way, is the HTML title page, normally called index.html. If you would like a different name, choose it here, minus the .html extension (for example, Linux_Intro), and click Save. A new window appears. This is the HTML Export dialog (see Figure 15-10).

Figure 15-10 The HTML export dialog on first run.

If this is your first HTML export, you only have one option on the first screen, and that is to create a new design. Click Next and you are presented with a few additional choices (see Figure 15-11).

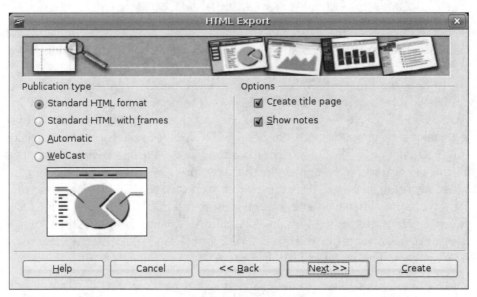

Figure 15–11   It is time to choose the format of your HTML presentation.

You are given the choice of several publication types. The default choice (and probably a very good one) is Standard HTML Format. You can also decide to create an HTML publication with frames, if you prefer. If you want to be totally in control of what your audience sees, you can also elect to create an automatic slide show (using HTML refresh times of whatever you choose) or a WebCast. When you have made your choice, click Next.

On the next window, you must decide the *resolution* of the images created for your Web publication (see Figure 15-12). The default is to use JPG images at 75 percent compression. You can elect to set this all the way up to 100 percent for the best quality possible, but be aware that the higher the quality, the larger the images and the slower the download time. If this presentation is meant to be viewed on your personal office network, it probably doesn't matter. Notice as well that you can choose to use the PNG graphic format instead of JPG.

Tip PNG (Portable Network Graphics) is a lossless, high-quality, and patent-free replacement for the GIF file format of old.

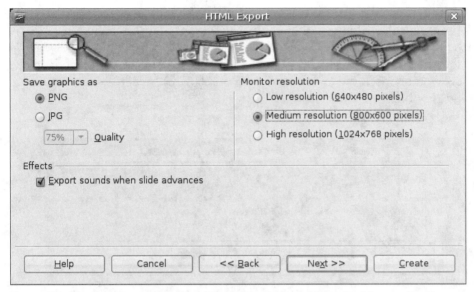

Figure 15–12 Select your image quality and monitor resolution. In this example, I've chosen to use PNG images instead of JPG.

You are also asked to choose the *monitor resolution*. This is an excellent question that is probably worth more than a few seconds of configuration. At some point in your history of surfing, you have come across a Web site where the Web page is larger than your browser window. To view the page, you need to move your horizontal slide bar back and forth just to read the text. Although we are used to scrolling up and down to read text, left to right scrolling is somewhat more annoying. If you want to be as inclusive as possible for your audience, use 640x480. That may be going overboard though. Most personal computer monitors these days will handle 800x600 without any problem and many people run 1024x768 displays. Is there a right answer? Probably not. Consider your target audience, make your decision based on those considerations, and then click Next.

One last thing before we move on. Notice the Effects check box. I'm not a big fan of Web pages that play sounds when I do things. You can choose to export sounds whenever slides advance. The best way to decide what you like is to try both. It's all for fun, anyhow.

On the next window that appears, fill in title page information for the Web presentation. This is the author's name (you), your email address, and a link back to your own Web site, if you want. Click Next, and you then have the opportunity to decide on the graphics you want to use for the forward and back buttons. If you don't want to use graphical buttons, you don't have to. In fact, the default is to use Text Only; so to use a particular button style, make sure you uncheck the check box (see Figure 15-13), select your button style, and click Next.

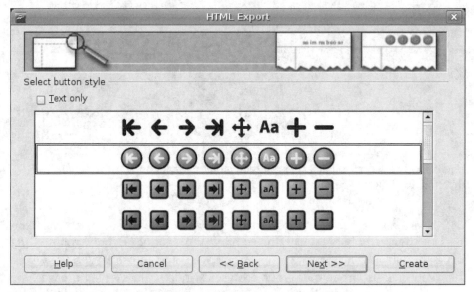

Figure 15–13   Pick a button style, any button style.

We are almost there. The final window lets you decide on the *color scheme* for the presentation. The default is simply to use the colors from the original Impress publication, but you can override this, as well as the color for hyperlinks and the Web page background. Make your choices and click Create. One last window appears, asking you to name the HTML design. This is a free-form text field. Enter a brief description, and click Save.

The process of exporting your presentation may take a few seconds or a few minutes, depending on the speed of your machine and the complexity of your presentation. To view the presentation, open your browser and point to the title page. That is all there is to it.

How About a Little Flash? Shocking!

Before we wrap up, let's revisit that Export dialog one more time. Click File from the menu and select Export. When the Export dialog appears, have another look at the File format selection box, just below the File Name field. The default is to export to an HTML document, but there are other options here. For one, we have a PDF export, the one button export (beside the printer icon on the standard bar) is common to Impress as well.

Notice as well that you have a Macromedia Flash export capability. Isn't that interesting? Enter a filename for your presentation (no need to add the .swf extension). With a single click of the Export button, your presentation is saved to Macromedia's Flash format. Now, your presentation is viewable from any browser with a Macromedia Flash or Shockwave plugin. The advantage of this over the HTML export is that all your animated slide transitions are preserved. Visitors to your site can view the presentation as it was intended.

So What's with the Penguin?

Having made you run off to Larry Ewing's site for a copy of Tux, I suppose I should take a moment to answer one of the most frequently asked questions in the Linux world. After all, every time you look at a Linux book, boxed set, or Web site, you stand a good chance of coming face to face with a fat, smiling penguin. You may well be wondering what Linux has to do with this penguin (see Figure 15-14). Well, for starters, his name is Tux, and he is the Linux mascot. The most famous version of Tux (and there are many) is Larry Ewing's design.

Figure 15–14
Tux, the Linux mascot.

The story behind Tux is the stuff of legend now and, like most legends, a little hard to pin down. Linus Torvalds was asked what he envisioned for a mascot. The answer from Linus was, "You should be imagining a slightly overweight penguin (*), sitting down after having gorged itself, and having just burped. It's sitting there with a beatific smile—the world is a good place to be when you have just eaten a few gallons of raw fish and you can feel another 'burp' coming."

There is also another story where Linus claims he was attacked by a killer penguin at the Canberra Zoo, where he contracted "penguinitis," a disease whose main symptom is that you "stay awake at nights just thinking about penguins and feeling great love towards them."

That's the thing about legends. They tend to get strange over time.

 Some people have told me they don't think a fat penguin really embodies the grace of Linux, which just tells me they have never seen an angry penguin charging at them in excess of 100 mph. They'd be a lot more careful about what they say if they had.

–Linus Torvalds

Extra! Extra!

Before we move away from the classic office applications, I would like to take another moment to address the issue of templates. Although StarOffice, the nonfree commercial sibling of OpenOffice.org, comes with a number of templates for word processing, spreadsheets, and presentation graphics, OpenOffice.org is still quite *light* in this area. As I mentioned earlier, the Impress package includes only a couple of templates.

To that end, I'm going to remind you of the Web sites I mentioned at the end of Chapter 13. They are Travis Bauer's OOExtras site and Scott Carr's OpenOffice.org Documentation Project. Both are excellent starting points for adding to your collection of templates. Look for the links to both in the Resources section.

Perhaps, in time, you too will contribute to this growing body of work.

Alternatives

In the last two chapters, I mentioned that the KDE office suite, KOffice, offers similar components that you may want to consider. These include KWord for word processing and KCalc for spreadsheets. There's also an alternative for presentation graphics and that is KPresenter. As before, you can use Synaptic to search for and install KOffice.

Remember that you do not need to be running KDE to run KOffice or any of its components. These applications work very nicely from the GNOME desktop.

Resources

KPresenter

    http://koffice.kde.org/kpresenter/

Larry Ewing's "Tux" (the Official Linux Penguin)

    http://www.isc.tamu.edu/~lewing/linux/

Linux Logo Links at Linux.org

    http://www.linux.org/info/logos.html

OOExtras

    http://ooextras.sourceforge.net

OpenOffice.org Web Site

    http://www.openoffice.org/

OpenOffice.org Documentation Project

    http://documentation.openoffice.org

Chapter
16

OpenOffice.org Base

Computers have thousands of uses, but in the end, the most important things they do come down to two major and equally important functions. The first is mathematics. More specifically, the computer makes it possible to do complex (or simple) mathematics quickly. The key word here is quickly. Whether it is figuring out ballistic tables to better ensure the trajectory of a missile and cracking complex codes (as was the impetus for the computer's development during World War II) or processing a company's financial information, math is central to every computing operation.

The second most useful function a computer has is storing, sorting, and retrieving data quickly. (Again that word *quickly*.) Search engines like Google or Yahoo! are a testament to the computer's power of sifting through large amounts of information. In doing so, businesses can locate a customer's address in seconds, even though there may be millions of other customer records in the system. A hospital with thousands of patient records can pull up your medical history in a flash and update it with today's visit. The online bookstore maintains your personal information so you can buy a book with a click or two. A year's worth of financial information, arranged into a clear, concise report, appears on the printer seconds after the company accountant requests it.

As my wife, Sally, is fond of saying, "It's all about the data."

Storing data, or *information*, if you prefer, is what a database is all about. That's why the addition of a database into the OpenOffice.org suite is so exciting. OpenOffice.org Base makes it possible to create your own databases, retrieve and modify information, perform queries, create reports, and so on. Base can attach to an existing database engine such as Oracle, Microsoft Access, MySQL, and many others using ODBC or JDBC. If all you need your database to do is simple operations, such as creating and maintaining a mailing list, OpenOffice.org base comes with the built-in HSQL database engine.

The Beginning: Creating a New Database

Because I mentioned mailing lists, let's use that as the basis for our exploration of OpenOffice.org Base. When we are through creating the database, I'll show you how to use it in another OpenOffice.org program, the Writer word processor. We'll take the information from our mailing list and create mailing labels.

To start OpenOffice.org Base, click Applications in the top panel and select OpenOffice.org Base from the Office submenu (command name: `oobase`).

When you start OpenOffice.org Base, you are presented with the Database Wizard (see Figure 16-1). This is a simple wizard with only two screens, the first of which is to select or identify a database. Your options are to Create a New Database, Open an Existing Database File, or Connect to an Existing Database. Let's just go ahead and create a new database by making sure that radio button is selected. Click Next.

The second step is where you must decide how to proceed after saving your database. There are only a few options on the second and final screen, but they are important and worth explaining (see Figure 16-2).

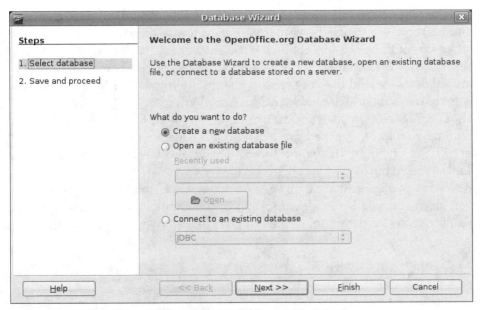

Figure 16–1 The OpenOffice.org Base Database Wizard.

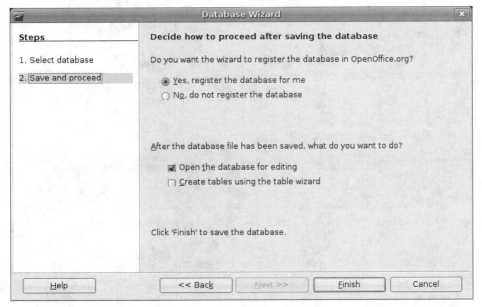

Figure 16–2 The final step in the wizard registers the database so it is easily accessible by other OpenOffice.org applications.

The first option has to do with registering a database. To quickly answer this question, ask yourself whether you want to use this database from inside other OpenOffice.org applications. If the answer is yes, click the radio button Yes, Register the Database for Me. Nothing stops you from creating a nonregistered database and then registering it later, but in this example at least, we want to use the database in OpenOffice.org Writer.

The next section gives you two options. The first, Open the Database for Editing, should be checked (you can create a database and get back to it later). You could, at this point, jump right in and Create Tables Using the Table Wizard but leave that unchecked for now.

When the Save As dialog makes its appearance, select a name and location for the database (see Figure 16-3). For this example, I'm going to create a simple mailing list database, which I'm going to call (wait for it) Mailing List.

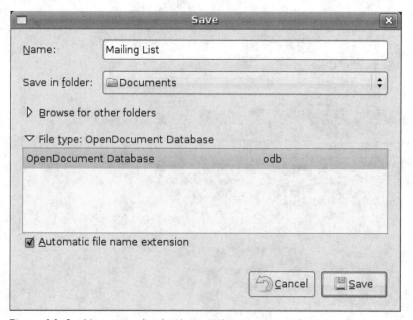

Figure 16–3 You created a database and now you need a name for it.

That's really all you need to do to create the database. Click Save and OpenOffice.org Base's main window appears (see Figure 16-4). By default, the Forms view is selected but that's only so useful if you haven't set up your tables yet. Nevertheless, let's take a look at the interface.

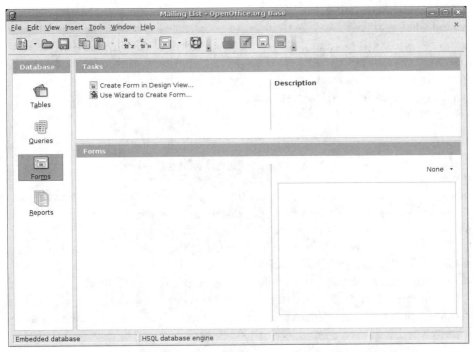

Figure 16-4 The OpenOffice.org Base window immediately upon creating a new database.

Along the top, directly below the menu bar is the Standard bar, looking less standard in OpenOffice.org Base than in any of the other components you have worked with. Running down the left side is an icon bar providing quick access to needed database functions, including Tables, Queries, Forms, and Reports. The main area to the right is divided horizontally into main areas. In the top part, we have Tasks. These tasks are all in some way related to the four database functions in the left sidebar. The bottom part of the window is for Forms.

Tip Pause your mouse cursor over any of the tasks and a description appears to the right of it.

Before we get too deep into all of this, we need to prepare the database to accept data. We do that by creating tables. Simply stated, tables define what our data looks like. You can even define multiple tables that further define bits of data in a master table. For instance, you can have a table that basically is an address list with first and last names, addresses, and so on. A second table might tie in to the person's name, but the information may have to do with the number of hours he worked. The person's name, in this case, might be the key you use to access both tables. A third table, using the same key, might be a list of movie rentals in the last year.

Let's go ahead and create a table.

Setting the Table

Yes, you could even have a table with recipes. Although that sounds like a tasty idea, I started out by saying my database was going to be a mailing list, so we will build an appropriate table.

The easiest way to get started is by using the Table Wizard. To do this, click the Table icon in the left sidebar. Now look at the top in the Tasks section. You see two entries there. The first, Create Table in Design View, is the more advanced approach, when you know what your data looks like. The second option is Use Wizard to Create Table. When you click this item, OpenOffice.org Base's Table Wizard starts (see Figure 16-5).

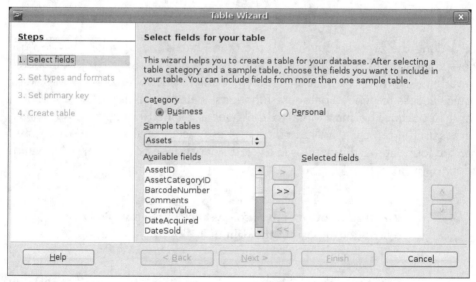

Figure 16–5   The Table Wizard comes with a number of predefined tables for business and personal use.

Tip When selecting the Table Wizard (or any of the Base wizards), you may get a message telling you that you need to turn on the Java runtime. First, you need to make sure you have a Java runtime installed. Luckily, OpenOffice.org automatically discovers its location. Click Tools on the menu bar, and then select Options. On the Options window, click Java from the sidebar, and then check the box Use a Java Runtime Environment.

The Table Wizard comes with a number of predefined tables for common tasks. All of these table definitions are divided into two categories, Business and Personal. Click the radio button for one or the other, then click the Sample Tables drop-down box to browse the table types. Under Business, you find things like Assets, Customers, Employees, Expenses, Projects, Suppliers, and many more. The Personal list has items such as Accounts, CD-Collection, Diet Log, and Household Inventory, to name just a few. For now, click the Personal radio button and select Addresses from the table list. A list of fields appears below the radio button (see Figure 16-6).

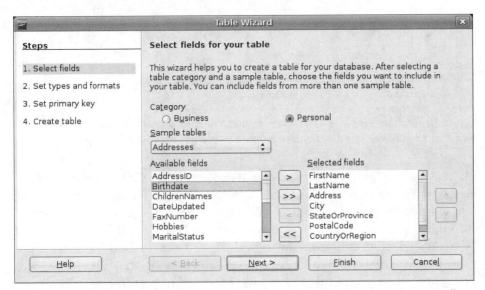

Figure 16-6 Most sample tables have many more fields defined than you may actually want.

If you scroll down that list of available fields, you see a lot more information than you actually need. You can click the double arrow in the middle (the right pointing one) and all the fields are selected. You can also select them one by one, as I have done in Figure 16-6. In the case of a simple mailing list, you may not need anything more than name, address, city, state, phone number, and email address. After you have finished selecting these fields, you can choose to click Finish or click Next to edit the format of each individual field. Let's pretend that the definition and format of these fields are okay. Click Next to move to the primary key selection screen (see Figure 16-7).

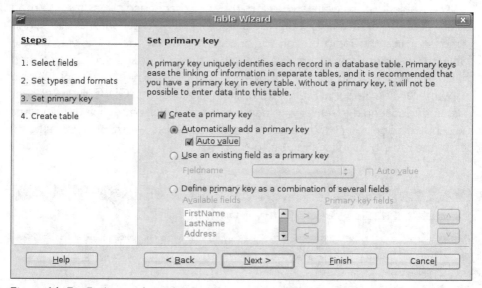

Figure 16–7   Each record in a database requires a unique, primary key. You can choose to base that key on your selected fields or let Base create one for you.

The primary key selection screen is important because a key is how you access and store information in a table. Although you can search on any field, a key needs to be a unique piece of information under which the record is stored. A classic example is the Social Security Number (or Social Insurance Number), which is unique to the individual. You can let Base generate a primary key for you, and that is the default. By checking the Auto Value box, Base automatically generates a key with each record you create.

Your other options are to use an existing field (like that SSN/SIN) or to define a combination of your fields to create that uniqueness.

Let's go with the default for now. Check the Auto Value box as well. Click Next and the final part of the wizard, the Create Table page, appears (see Figure 16-8). If you are using the wizard, Base suggests a name for the table, but you can call it anything you like. I'm going to accept the default of Addresses because that suits me just fine. Keep in mind that although our database is called Mailing List, there can be a lot more associated with a mailing list—the Addresses table is just a small part of it.

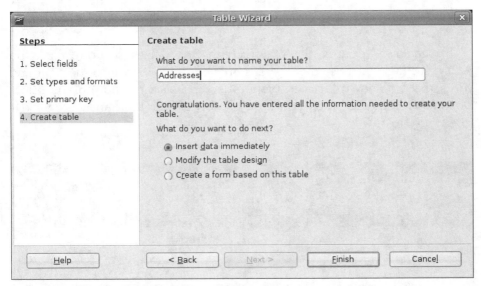

Figure 16–8 The last step of the Table Wizard names your table and gives you the option to start entering data immediately.

We are done with the wizard, but before you click Finish, you have one last choice to make, and three options to choose from. The first is to start adding data (I'll show you that in a moment). The second is to go back and make other changes to the table design. The final choice is to create a form based on this table. I'll show you what happens in both cases, but let's start with the default option, Insert Data Immediately. When you do that, a spreadsheet-like window appears with rows of data and columns representing the fields in your table (see Figure 16-9).

There is one other item I'd like you to look at in the OpenOffice.org Base Tables view. It's not a big deal, but it's kind of cool, so I'm going to tell you about it.

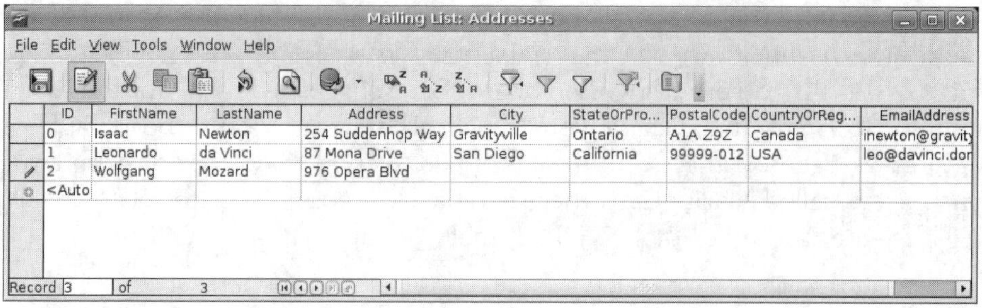

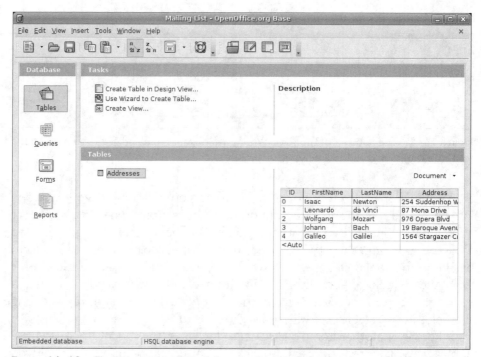

Figure 16–9   Inserting data is as easy as working with a spreadsheet.

In the lower part of the main screen (the Tables section), click the Addresses table (at this time, there is only one). Now, look to the right and you see a drop-down list with None selected. Click the button and select Document. You get a pretty cool little preview of your table and the data in it (see Figure 16-10).

Figure 16–10   The lower part of the left pane lists your tables and provides a small preview of the data when you click a table.

No Wizards for Me!

Before we move on to the next step, I want to touch on the subject of creating a table in design view. There's no question that using the wizard is by far the easiest way to do this, but using the design view isn't much more difficult. It does have the advantage of giving you greater control over the format of your tables, but you have to think about what fields you want, and what you want those fields to look like (see Figure 16-11). In that respect, I recommend it only if you already have some experience in database and table design.

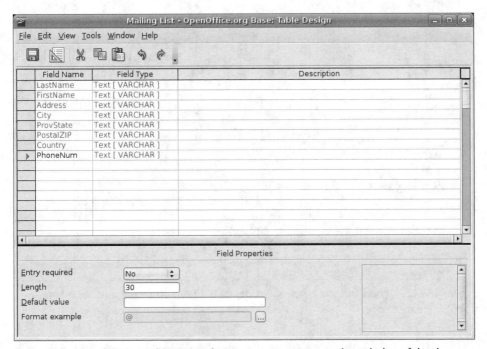

Figure 16–11 Creating tables using design view requires some knowledge of database and table design.

Creating Mailing Labels

Now that we have this great database of names, let's create a sheet of mailing labels. We do this with Writer, the word processor I covered in Chapter 13, but not with OpenOffice.org Base.

To begin, click File on the OpenOffice.org menu bar, and select Labels from the New submenu. You don't have to be running Writer to do this. Any OpenOffice.org application is a perfect starting point for creating labels. A few seconds after making your selection, the Labels dialog appears (see Figure 16-12).

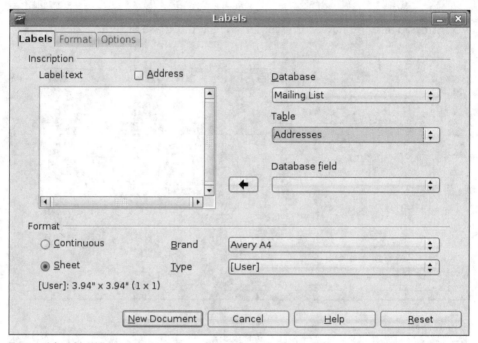

Figure 16–12   When creating a new sheet of labels, OpenOffice.org starts by asking you about the data source.

Start by looking on the right, under the Database heading. This is where registering the database, that little step we did at the beginning, pays off. OpenOffice.org Writer already knows about the various databases and can pick my Mailing List database from the drop-down list. Below that is another drop-down list labeled Table. Click here and select the table from which you will be pulling the information you need. At the bottom of the dialog, you can select the Brand label (for example, Avery Letter Size) and the type (for example, 5961 Address).

To the left, below Label Text, is where we build the label we will be printing. At this moment, there are no fields visible there. Look again to the right to the Database Field drop-down list. Click that list and you see all the fields that make up the records in your table. Select the Database Field you want, and then click the large arrow directly to the left. The field you selected appears in the Label Text window. Put a space after the field name, then select the last name, and click the arrow again. Press <Enter> to go to the next line in the Label Text window. Next is the address, city, and so on. You may want to put a comma between the city and province (or state). Line by line, transfer the fields that you want to have appearing in your finished label (see Figure 16-13).

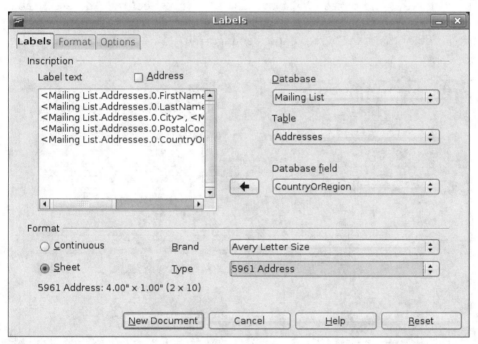

Figure 16–13   As you select fields, they appear in the Label Text window to the left.

Before we move on, let's quickly have a look at the other two tabs, Format and Options. The Format tab allows you to fine-tune your label dimensions. This includes margins, columns, rows, and pitch. If you selected one of the commercial labels from the list, this information will be filled in for you and you shouldn't have to worry about changing anything. Use the Options tab to select whether you are printing a full page of labels or a single label. The most interesting item here is a check box labeled Synchronize Contents. Check this box and you can edit a single label and synchronize the contents of all other labels with a click.

Go back to the Labels tab and click New Document to create your label document. Each label is pre-created with the field labels you selected in the proper place. At this stage of the game, there are no names or addresses in any of the labels, just the data fields. To populate these labels from your Mailing List database, you need to tell the new document where to get its information. To do that, click View on the menu bar and select Data Sources (you can also just press <F4>). The top part of your label document now shows the databases and tables available. Make sure you select the Addresses table from the database list. When you do, the records in that table appear in the right side of the data sources pane (see Figure 16-14).

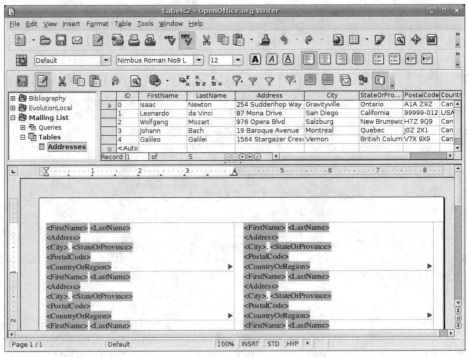

Figure 16–14   The data source for the labels appears directly above the actual label document, in the top-right pane.

To populate your label document, you should now select which records you want included from the Table view at the top right. The easiest way to select them all is to click the button to the left of the top record, press the <Shift> key, then click the last record. You can also select individual records by holding down the <Ctrl> key and clicking the records you want. When you have made your selections, look at the secondary icon bar, directly above the data sources. There's a button fourth from the right that displays a Data to Fields tooltip if you pause your mouse over it (see Figure 16-15).

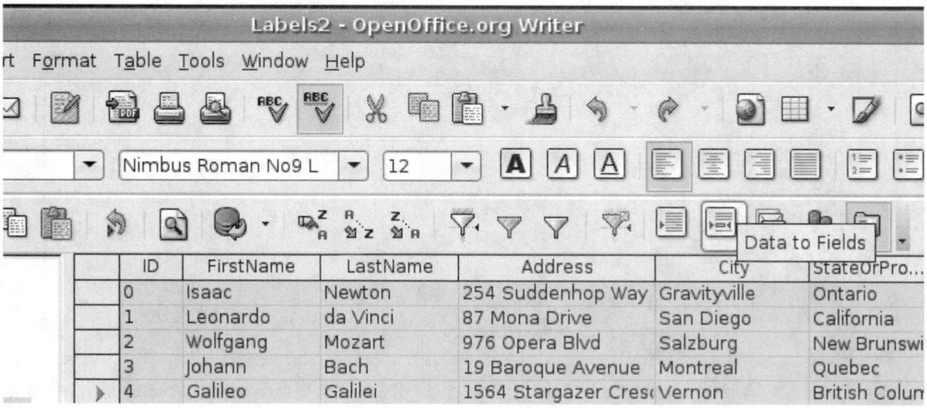

	ID	FirstName	LastName	Address	City	StateOrPro...
	0	Isaac	Newton	254 Suddenhop Way	Gravityville	Ontario
	1	Leonardo	da Vinci	87 Mona Drive	San Diego	California
	2	Wolfgang	Mozart	976 Opera Blvd	Salzburg	New Brunswi
	3	Johann	Bach	19 Baroque Avenue	Montreal	Quebec
▶	4	Galileo	Galilei	1564 Stargazer Cres	Vernon	British Colun

Figure 16–15 Closeup of the Data to Fields button.

Click the Data to Fields button and your document is instantly populated with all of the selected records (see Figure 16-16). You can save this document for later use or you can print the page using your chosen label stock.

Further Exploring

In this chapter, I introduced you to the basics of using OpenOffice.org Base and showed you how to use the database tables in a word processing document. Obviously, this is just the beginning.

Using Base, you can create custom forms for data entry. Wizards make this easy but there is a manual forms creator as well. Simple or complex custom reports are also easily generated using the Report Wizard. You can perform queries, connect to external databases, build indexes, and more. OpenOffice.org Base provides useful database access tools for users at every level.

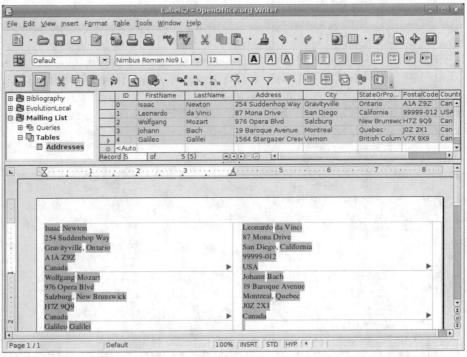

Figure 16–16   With a click, all of the selected record data is transferred to the label form.

Resources

BASE Home Page

    http://www.openoffice.org/product2/base.html

17

Digital Art
with the GIMP

Oddly enough, Linux applications that allow users to work with graphics are among some of the most highly developed in the world. To see the truth in this rather bold statement, turn your eyes to Hollywood. Blockbusters such as Titanic, Star Trek: Nemesis, Shrek, and others use Linux and Linux clusters to create the complex special effects.

In terms of graphical design and photo editing, your Linux system comes with one of the most powerful, flexible, and easy-to-use packages there is, regardless of what OS you are running. It's called the *GIMP.* Allow me to introduce you to some of its many features.

The GIMP is one of those programs that has helped create an identity for Linux. Of course, there are plenty of programs out there, as I'm sure I have demonstrated in the book, but the GIMP is special in some ways. The Linux community has used it to create images, buttons, desktop themes, window decorations, and more. Even the Linux mascot, Tux the Penguin, as created by Larry Ewing (the mascot's best-known incarnation), was a product of the GIMP.

The GIMP is an amazingly powerful piece of software, yet its basic functions are easy-to-use as well. With a little bit of work, a lot of fun, and a hint of experimentation, anyone can use the GIMP to turn out a fantastic piece of professional quality art. You doubt my words? Then follow along with me, and in just a few minutes, you'll create a slick-looking logo for your Web page or your desktop. With time and practice, you may learn to wield the GIMP with the power of a Hollywood special effects master.

Play. Experiment. And don't be afraid.

Ladies and Gentlemen,
Start Your GIMP

Click the Application menu on the top panel and select GIMP Image Editor from the Graphics submenu. You can also use your program quick-start by pressing <Alt+F2> and entering `gimp` into the command field.

When you run the GIMP for the first time, you will get a couple panels, aside from the GIMP's main screen. You will also likely get the GIMP Tip of the Day. As with all such tips, you can elect not to have them appear each time the program starts—just uncheck the Show Tip Next Time GIMP Starts button before you hit Close, and you aren't bothered with them again. What you are likely to see (minus that tip of the day) should look a bit like Figure 17-1.

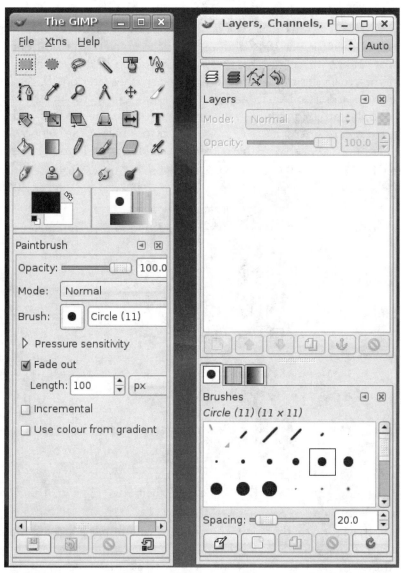

Figure 17–1   First time through, the GIMP starts with the layers and channels dialog (right) open.

The long window on the right is split into two main areas. At the top is the Layers, Channels, Paths dialog. The dialog below has three tabs, one for brushes, another for patterns, and another for gradients. If you choose to close this window, there is no harm done; you end up calling up dialogs as you need them. We'll visit this again when I cover brushes later on.

The most important of those windows is the GIMP toolbox. That's the window to the left in Figure 17-1. The toolbox itself is the top half of the window (see the closeup in Figure 17-2). The bottom half of the window represents the options available to the currently selected tool. If you are using the text tool, you have a choice of fonts, styles, and sizes at your disposal.

Figure 17–2   The GIMP toolbox.

Along the top, directly below the title bar, is a familiar looking menu bar labeled File, Xtns, and Help. Clicking these shows you additional submenus. Below the menu bar is a grid of icons, each with an image representing one of the GIMP's tools. Incidentally, my GIMP toolbox is arranged with six tools per row, but it could just as easily be five—just drag the side of the main toolbox window to increase or decrease the number of tools per row. I will cover all of these things shortly, but first let's take the GIMP out for a spin.

Note The GIMP Help files are not installed on your Ubuntu system, but you can use Synaptic to search for and install them. Search using the term `gimp-help` and you will find the manual in several different languages. You don't actually need to install the help files, however, because the GIMP lets you search the help files online using Firefox.

You may also want to search for `grokking-the-gimp` in Synaptic. This is a book by Carey Bunks, and it is distributed in HTML format.

Easy Logos with the GIMP

The nitty-gritty can wait. I think we should do something fun with the GIMP right now. I'm going to show you how to create a very cool looking corporate or personal logo with just a few keystrokes. If you don't have the GIMP open yet, start the program now. From the main toolbox menu bar, select Xtns, scroll down to Script-Fu, and another menu cascades from it.

Quick Tip Notice that the menus have a *dashed line* at the top. These are menu tear-offs. By clicking the dashed line, you can *detach the menu* and put it somewhere on your desktop for convenient access to functions you use all the time. In fact, all the menus, including submenus, can be detached.

From the Script-Fu menu, move your mouse to Logos. You should see a whole list of logo types, from 3D Outline to Cool Metal to Starscape and more. For this exercise, choose Cool Metal.

Every logo has different settings, so the one you see in Figure 17-3 is specific to Cool Metal. Particle Trace has a completely different set of parameters. To create your Cool Metal logo, start by changing the Text field to something other than the logo style's name. I'll change mine to read Ubuntu Rocks! The font size is set to 100 pixels, and we can leave it at that for now.

In many of these, a default font has been selected for you. You can override the current choice (written on the button itself) and pick something else

Figure 17–3   Script-Fu logo settings for Cool Metal.

by clicking the Font button. The Font Selection window shows you the various fonts available on your system and lets you try different font types, styles, and sizes. A preview window gives you an idea of what the font looks like (see Figure 17-4).

To create my logo, I'm going to choose a font on my system called Kalimati (not sure why, but suddenly I have a taste for Greek salad). You may choose whatever you like. When you have decided on a font, click Close. Then click OK, this time in the Script-Fu:Logos/Cool Metal window. The result should be something similar to my own logo in Figure 17-5.

If you don't like the results, close the image by clicking the Close button in the corner (usually an X unless you have changed your desktop theme or style). A warning box pops up, telling you that changes have been made and you might want to save your work (more on that in a moment). Your options are Save, Don't Save, and Cancel. Click Don't Save and it goes away. Then start over with another logo. You might try changing the background color or the gradient this time. You might even want to try a different type of logo altogether.

Figure 17–4   Script-Fu Font Selection dialog.

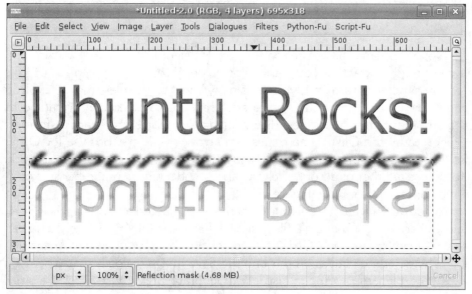

Figure 17–5   Just like that! A professional looking logo.

Saving and Opening Your Work

It is time to preserve your masterpiece. It's also a good time to have another look at the image window—in this case, your logo. Every image created in the GIMP has a menu bar across the top labeled File, Edit, Select, View, and so on. These menus can also be called up by right-clicking anywhere on the image. To save your work, click the File menu, and then select Save As. The Save Image dialog appears (see Figure 17-6).

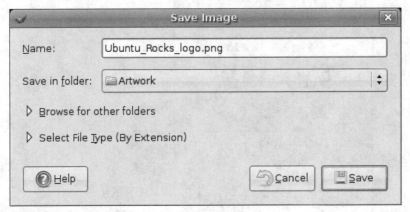

Figure 17–6   It's time to save your creation.

Notice the small arrow beside the words Select File Type (By Extension). If you already know that you want to save your image as a .jpg or a .tif file (or any number of formats), you can simply add it to the filename. The GIMP can figure it out for you. If you prefer to see a list of available formats, click the arrow and the Save Image dialog changes to display the various formats supported by the GIMP. There's also an arrow beside the Browse for Other Folders label. By default, the GIMP uses the current folder to save your work. To choose another directory, click the arrow and a more comprehensive navigation dialog appears (see Figure 17-7).

When you have entered your filename and selected a file type, click Save, and you are done. Opening a file is similar. From the GIMP toolbox menu bar, select Open (or use the <Ctrl+O> shortcut) to bring up the Load Image dialog. The difference between this and the Save Image dialog is that when you click on a filename, you can also click Generate Preview to display a small thumbnail preview in the Open Image dialog.

Figure 17–7 A more comprehensive folder navigation dialog saves your work.

Printing Your Masterpiece

You've created a masterpiece. You are infinitely proud of it, and you want to share it with your friends, who, alas, are not connected to the Internet. It's time to print your image and send it to them the old-fashioned, snail-mail way.

Okay, perhaps you aren't feeling quite that sharing, but there are times when you want to print the results of your work. Simply click File on the image menu bar, and select Print (again, you can right-click your image if you prefer). A printing dialog appears (see Figure 17-8), from which you can specify a number of print options including, of course, which printer you would like to use.

Figure 17–8   Time to print your masterpiece.

 Quick GIMP Trick Want to take a screenshot and open it up to edit in the GIMP? It's easy. Click File on the GIMP toolbox menu bar, move to Acquire, and click Screen Shot. The image size is the same as your screen (for example, 1024×768). Because the GIMP is in the screen shot you take, you may want to minimize it before capturing the image. To make that possible, select an appropriate time delay (for example, five seconds) from the Screen Shot dialog that appears. Minimize the windows you don't want to see, and then wait. After the capture completes, a GIMP image window appears where you can make your modifications.

The Acquire function doesn't limit you to the whole screen. When the Screen Shot dialog appears, you have the option of capturing the entire screen or a single window. Just click the appropriate radio button. The window capture includes the borders for that window and all its decorations.

Tools, Tools, and More Tools

Now that we've had some fun and created some *true art*, it's time to find out what all those icons in the GIMP toolbox do. Before we do this, however, we should look at those two boxes at the bottom of the toolbox, because what they offer affects what the icons do.

The block on the right is the color menu (see Figure 17-9). It gives you quick and easy access to foreground and background colors. The black and white squares on the left can be changed to other colors by double-clicking one or the other. If you click the arrow between the two, you switch between foreground and background colors.

Figure 17–9
The multifunction color, brushes, pattern, and gradient menu.

The box to the right is a quick dialog menu and consists of three different tools: a brush selector, a pattern selector, and a gradient selector. Click any of them to bring up the list of choices each provides. Figure 17-10 shows the Brushes dialog. You may recall that there was a layers and channels dialog in addition to the main GIMP toolbox. At the bottom of that window was the Brushes dialog (as well as gradients and patterns). If you left that window open, the brushes selection will still be there.

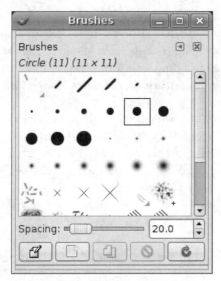

Figure 17–10   The Brushes dialog, on its own.

If you select a different gradient, pattern, or brush from the resulting menus, you see them change on the dialog menu at the bottom of the GIMP toolbox, as well. This gives you a quick visual feedback on what brush, pattern, or gradient is active at the moment.

On to the Tool Icons

In the next few pages, I'm going to cover the GIMP's tools one by one, a row at a time. Each row has six tools, except for the last, which has five. I mention this because this is the default layout. If you decide to resize the GIMP toolbox by dragging one of the sides out, the toolbox widens but the number of tools per row increases as well, so you could have seven tools if you want. The reverse is true should you decide to shrink the width of the GIMP toolbox.

Start by moving your mouse over the various icons, pausing over each one. Tooltips appear, telling you what tool each of the icons represents. (I'll go over these in a moment.) If you click any of these icons, the window below the toolbox changes to present you with that tool's options. For instance, Figure 17-11 shows the tool options for the flip tool.

Figure 17–11 Tool options dialog, in this case for the flip tool.

What are all those icons for? An excellent question. Let's look at them again, one row at a time, starting with—you guessed it—the first row (see Figure 17-12).

Figure 17–12 First icon group.

The first icon, represented by a *dotted rectangle*, lets you select a rectangular area. Just hold down the left mouse button at whatever point you choose for a starting corner, and drag it across your image. A dotted line indicates the area you've selected. If you hold down the <Shift> key at the same time as the left mouse button, your selections are always perfect squares.

Quick Tip To undo changes, press <Ctrl+Z>.

The *dotted circle* icon next to the dotted rectangle is much the same except that it selects a circular or elliptical area. Similar to the rectangular area you selected, you can hold down the <Shift> key along with the left mouse button to select only perfect circles.

Next, we have the *lasso* tool. This is another selection tool, but this one lets you select irregular or hand-drawn regions. Hold down the left mouse button and *draw* your selection around the object.

Quick Tip When you have selected an area on an image, you can right-click, move your mouse cursor over the Edit menu, and select Cut or Copy. You can then Paste your selection back to another part of the image.

Next comes the *magic wand*. This is a strange tool at first glance. It selects an area by analyzing the colored pixels wherever you click. Holding down the <Shift> key lets you select multiple areas. This is a very useful tool but also a little tricky. Double-click the icon to change the sensitivity.

Next, it's over to the *color selection* tool. Using the color selector feels a bit like the magic wand but the functionality is based on color rather than a single area at a time. Select the color picker, click any colored area, and *all* areas matching this color are selected.

Finally, we wrap up this row with another selection tool, the so-called *intelligentscissors*. You select an area by clicking around it. This tool follows curved lines around an object. It does so by concentrating on areas of similar contrast or color. Simply click around the perimeter of the area you want to select and watch the lines magically draw themselves. When you join the last dot, click inside the area to select it.

That wraps it up for the first row of tools. It's time to look at the next set (see Figure 17-13).

Figure 17–13   Second icon group.

The first icon in this row is the *Bezier* tool (also known as the path tool), which takes some getting used to. After you get used to it, however, you'll be impressed with the flexibility it affords you in selecting both straight and curved areas. Click a point outside the area you want to select, and it creates an anchor point. Click again a little further along your outline, and you get new anchor points with a straight line connecting to the original. Click and drag an existing anchor point, and a *bar* appears with control boxes on either end. You can then grab those control points and drag or rotate them to modify the straight line between the points. After you have joined the final point, look at your tool options (the pane below the GIMP toolbox) and click the button labeled Create Selection from Path. You see an animated dotted line, as with the other selection tools.

The second icon looks like an eyedropper. This is the *color picker.* Choosing an exact color can be difficult (if you need to get the tone just right), but if the color you want is on your existing image, click that spot, and you've got it (your default active color changes).

The *magnifying glass* does exactly what you expect it to. Click an area of the screen to zoom in. Double-click the icon to reverse the zoom. This doesn't actually scale the image; it just changes your view of things. Zoom is used to make it easier to work on a small area of the image.

Next in line: the calipers, or *measuring* tool. This doesn't actually change anything on your image. It simple provides information. Click a starting point on the image, then drag the mouse pointer to another part of the image. Now look at the bottom of your image window. You see the distance in pixels from your starting location to where you let go of the mouse pointer. The angle of the line is also displayed.

The fifth icon on the second row looks like a cross with arrows pointing in all directions. This is the *move* tool. It is really quite simple. Click the tool, grab the selected area on the screen, and move it to where you want. If you haven't selected an area, you can move the entire image in the window.

The knife icon is the *crop* tool. If you start working with digital photography in a big way, this is one you will want to know. I use the crop tool all the time when I am trying to get a small part of a larger image. It is what I used to separate the rows of icons from the GIMP toolbox image I captured earlier (refer to Figure 17-2). Click a part of the screen, and drag it to encompass the area you want to select. The space around your selection darkens (see Figure 17-14).

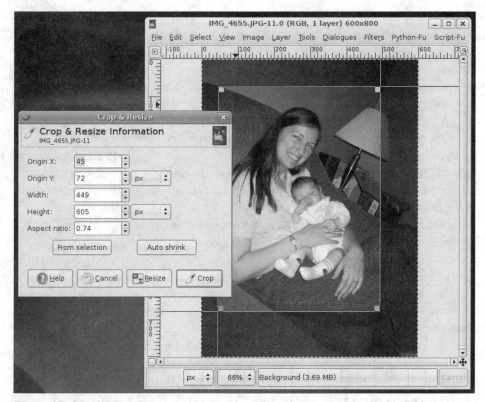

Figure 17–14   When cropping an image, the selected area is emphasized by a darkening around the rest of the image.

Click the Crop button when you are satisfied with your selection. You can also fine-tune the settings (X and Y position, and so on) at this time.

And just like that, it's time to look at row three (see Figure 17-15).

Figure 17–15   Third icon row.

On the left, in the first position, we have the *rotate* tool. Click an image (or a selection), and small square *handles* appear at the corners of your selection. Grab one of these handles (or points), drag the mouse, and the selection rotates. When you have it in a position you like, click Rotate on the pop-up window that appears. The image locks into place.

The second icon, the *scale* tool, is very similar to the rotate tool. Instead of rotating the selected area, you drag the points to resize the selected area. As previously, a pop-up window appears so that you can lock your changes. It's also the place to manually enter your changes if dragging the mouse doesn't offer the control you like.

The *shear* tool is the third on this row and once again, it acts on a previously selected area. This one looks a lot like the last two in terms of functionality, but the effect is more like taking two sides of an object and stretching it diagonally in opposite directions. A square becomes a parallelogram, which gets longer and thinner as you continue to stretch the image. When you're happy with the changes, click the Shear button on the pop-up .

In the fourth position, we have the *perspective* tool. This is one of those that you almost have to try out to understand, but let me try to describe it. Remember your grade school art classes when you first learned about perspective? A road leading off into the distance compresses to a single point in the distance. With the perspective tool, you can take a selected area and pull the points in whatever direction you want to create the perspective effect. Do that with a person's head and the top of his head becomes a sharp little point. As with the last three tools, there's a pop-up where you lock in your changes. Just click Transform.

Next in line is the *flip* tool. By default, it flips the image horizontally. The tool option, in the lower half of the GIMP toolbox, has a check box if you want to flip vertically instead.

Tip Remember that if you close the tool options below the GIMP toolbox, you can always double-click a tool to bring up its options dialog.

The next icon is the *text* tool—that's what the big *T* signifies. Click your image, and the GIMP Text Editor appears. This is where you enter your text. In your tools option is the font selector; the same one that you used for your logo appears. Select a font style, size, and color, and the changes are visible in the image. This makes it easy to change the look and feel on-the-fly, type your text in the preview section, and click OK. Where the text appears on the screen, the move tool is activated, allowing you to place the text accurately. The color of the text is your current foreground color.

The fourth row is next (see Figure 17-16).

Figure 17–16   The fourth row icons.

The paint can represents the *fill* tool. It can fill a selected area not only with a chosen color but with a pattern, as well. To choose between color and pattern fill, double-click the icon to bring up its menu.

The second item on this line is the *gradient fill* tool. Start by selecting an area on your image, and then switch to this tool. Now click a spot inside your selected area and drag with the tool. The current gradient style fills that area. This is one of those tools that you have to use to understand.

Quick Tip Would you like a blank canvas right about now? Click File on the GIMP toolbox menu bar and select New. Those who like using the keyboard can just press <Ctrl+N>.

The third icon of this group looks like a *pencil*. In fact, this and the next three buttons all work with a brush selection (the bottom-right box). This pencil, as with a real pencil, is used to draw lines with sharply defined edges. Try drawing on your image with the different types to get an idea of what each brush type offers.

The next tool icon is the *paintbrush*. The difference between it and the pencil is that the brush has softer, less starkly defined edges to the strokes. Double-click the icon to bring up the paintbrush's menu and try both the Fade Out and Gradient options for something different.

If the next icon looks like an *eraser*, that's no accident. The shape of the eraser is also controlled by the current brush type, size, and style. Here's something kind of fun to try. Double-click the icon to bring up its menu, and then change the Opacity to something like 50 percent. Then start erasing again.

Now it's on to the *airbrush* tool. Just like a real airbrush, you can change the pressure to achieve different results. Hold it down longer in one spot, and you get a darker application of color.

Next is the fifth and final row of icons (see Figure 17-17).

Figure 17–17 The fifth row contains
primarily drawing tools.

The first tool on this line is another drawing tool, the pen, or *ink* tool. Double-clicking the icon brings up a menu that lets you select the tip style and shape, as well as the virtual tilt of the pen. The idea is to mimic the effect of writing with a fountain pen.

Next to the pen is the *clone* tool (the icon looks a bit like a rubber stamp). Sheep? No problem! We can even clone humans. Okay, that's a bit over the top. Where the clone tool comes in handy is during touch-ups of photographs. Open an image, hold down the <Ctrl> key, and press the left mouse button over a portion of the image—the tool changes to a crosshair. Let go of both the mouse button and the <Ctrl> key. This is your starting area for cloning. Now move to another part of the screen, click, and start moving your mouse button (the shape of the area uncovered is controlled by the brush type). As you paint at this new location, notice that you are recreating that portion of the image you indicated with the <Ctrl+mouse-click> combination. Start with someone's head or body, and you can have twins on the screen.

The droplet you see in the third position represents the *convolver* tool. Use it to blur or sharpen parts of an image. You switch between the two operations by selecting the mode in the tool options below the toolbox, or by double-clicking the icon. Change the rate to make the effect more pronounced.

Quick GIMP Trick When you need to zoom in on an image to get some fine work done, press the plus sign on your keyboard. Keep in mind, though: If you zoom in enough, it can get difficult to navigate the larger image. You wind up trying to adjust the scrollbars to locate the area you want. Instead, click the little crosshair icon in the bottom right side of the image editor window. A smaller version of your image window appears with a target area outline that you can move to where you want it.

On to the finger, or the *smudge* tool. . . . Pretend that you are painting. You press your finger on the wet paint and move it around. The smudge tool has exactly the same effect on your virtual canvas or, at the very least, a similar effect.

Finally, the *dodge and burn* tool looks like a stick-pin, but those who have worked in a darkroom might recognize it for something different—a stick with an opaque circle on the end of it. It is used to adjust the brightness or shade of various parts of an image (a photograph might have been partly overexposed).

Touching Up Photographs

I've mentioned the idea of touching up photographs. The GIMP is a wonderful tool for this and more than just a little fun. One of the most common functions I use is changing the light levels on photographs, automagically and instantly. After all, light levels are rarely perfect unless you are a professional photographer and paying attention to every shot. Here's what I do.

Click Image on the Layers menu bar (or right-click the image to bring up the menu), move to the Colors submenu, then select Levels. You should see a window like the one in Figure 17-18. Notice the Auto button? That's where the magic is. I've found that more often than not, you can get a nice, dependable reset of levels just by clicking this one button.

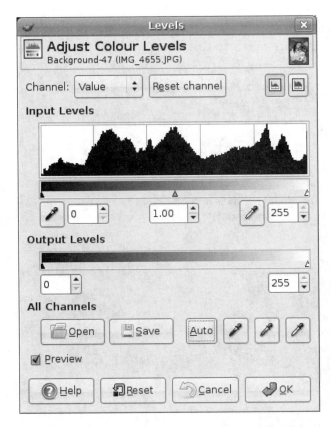

Figure 17–18
Adjusting levels with
the GIMP.

Another very common adjustment you make to your photos, particularly scanned images, is contrast and brightness. You find this dialog in much the same place as Levels (above). Click Layers on the menu bar, then Colors, and finally Brightness-Contrast. To change one or the other, just pull the appropriate slider to the left or right (see Figure 17-19).

There are also those things that are *just plain fun* to do. For instance, open an image in the GIMP, perhaps one you scanned in earlier. If you don't have something handy, grab an image from a Web site. This is just something to play with. Now choose Filters from the image menu bar. A submenu opens with even more options. You might want to detach this menu—you'll certainly want to play with what is there.

Try FlareFX under the Light Effects menu. If you've ever taken a flash picture through a window, you recognize this effect. Then try Emboss under the Distorts submenu. The effect is that of a metal-embossed picture (see Figure 17-20).

Figure 17–19   To adjust brightness or contrast, just pull the sliders.

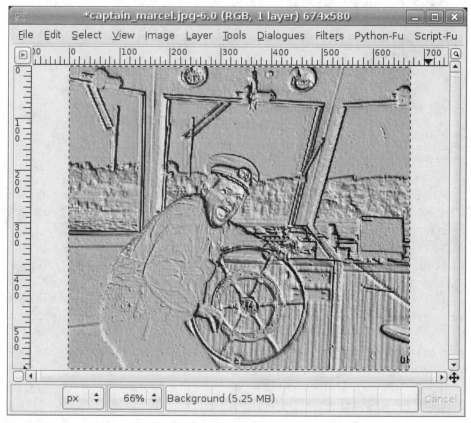

Figure 17–20   Playing with the Emboss filter.

Take some time to try the various filter options. When you are finished, right-click a fresh image and select the Script-Fu menu. There are other interesting effects available here, such as Clothify under the Alchemy sub-menu. Your image look as though it had been transferred to a piece of cloth.

What Is Script-Fu?

Although it sounds like a strange form of martial arts, Script-Fu is in fact a scripting language that is part of the GIMP. With it, you can create scripts that automate a number of repetitive tasks to create desirable effects. When you created your logo, you might have noticed that a number of things were happening as it was being created. Try another logo and watch carefully what is happening. These steps are part of a Script-Fu script.

The GIMP comes with a number of Script-Fu scripts, and these are used for much more than just creating logos. Click Xtns on the GIMP toolbox, and scroll down to the Script-Fu menu. In addition to logos, you see options for creating buttons (for Web pages), custom brushes, patterns, and more. Play. Experiment. Don't be afraid.

Open an image. Then right-click on that image and scroll down to the Script-Fu part of the menu. Another menu drops down with selections such as Alchemy, Decore, Render, and so on. These are all pre-created effects that ordinarily require many repetitive steps. Script-Fu is very much like a command script, where one command follows another. In this case, the commands just happen to be graphical transformations.

Resources

GIMP Web Site

```
http://www.gimp.org
```

Chapter

18

If Music Be the Food of Love . . . (Ubuntu Linux Multimedia)

Playing music on your Linux system is only the beginning of the multimedia experience. After all, multimedia isn't just about music. It represents a cornucopia of sensory experience delivered digitally, comprised of text, audio, video, and endless combinations of the three.

Most modern Linux installations offer an impressive selection of programs to satisfy your cravings for the multimedia experience, from audio to video and everything in between. These programs include sound control systems, CD players, recorders, MIDI programs of varying flavors, music synthesizers, video players, music notation programs, and . . . the list goes on.

In this chapter, I'm going to cover some of the more popular multimedia tools for your Linux system. So, as old William Shakespeare might have said, "If music be the food of love, then multimedia must represent the smorgasbord."

Adjusting the Levels

Think back for a moment to those days of old when Mom or Dad would yell into your bedroom to "TURN THAT NOISE DOWN!" Doesn't that bring back memories? In particular, it brings back the memory that sometimes you just have to crank the tunes.

Most music or multimedia players you are likely to use under Linux have some kind of a volume control. Your speaker system likely has one, as well. There is, however, a third set of controls you should know about: the GNOME volume control. Look over to the right of the top panel and you should see an icon that looks like a speaker. Click that speaker icon and a simple volume slider appears (see Figure 18-1). This provides you with a fast means of making volume-level adjustments.

Figure 18–1   A volume control in your top panel.

Under certain circumstances, you'll want finer control over the levels of certain devices, at least better than the single slider can provide. Either double-click the top panel speaker icon or right-click the icon and select Open Volume Control from the drop-down menu. A Volume Control three-tabbed mixer panel appears with your system sound card's name alongside (see Figure 18-2).

The various sliders correspond to various levels, from that of your hardware's master levels to the PCM output, microphone inputs (under the Capture tab), and so on. Pause your mouse pointer over the sliders and a message describing the slider's function appears at the bottom of the window.

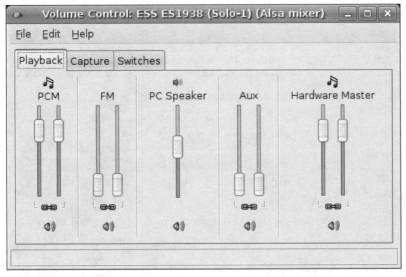

Figure 18–2 The GNOME volume control can be configured to show multiple levels.

 Note The number of sliders and controls vary from sound card to sound card and they may not all be activated by default. Click Edit on the menu bar, then select Preferences. Check boxes representing the possible input and output sources appear. To add one to your mixer control panel, check the appropriate box.

Now that you can easily modify the level of *noise* coming from your speakers, it's time to get some music on.

Playing Audio CDs with the Sound Juicer

Try this. Get your hands on your favorite music CD and pop it into your Ubuntu system's CD drive. As I write this, I've got my Pink Floyd *Echoes* album handy, so I'll use that as an example. A few seconds later, the Sound Juicer application window appears (see Figure 18-3). Sound Juicer, which you can also start from the Sound & Video menu under Applications on the top panel, is the default CD player for Ubuntu.

Figure 18–3   *The Sound Juicer is a multiuse multimedia application. Aside from being the default Ubuntu CD player, it is also a CD ripper.*

Along the top, there are fields identifying the Title of the CD, the Artist, and the Genre. Directly below this information is a list of all the songs on that CD. Because I mentioned that this is the default CD player, I cover this aspect of the program first. Notice that all of the songs are selected when the CD is inserted (the check box to the left of the title).

Click the Play button, sit back, and enjoy the music. Each song on the CD is then played in sequence. As songs are played, the Play button turns into a Pause button. To skip a song, just double-click the song title you want to hear and Sound Juicer abandons your current selection and jumps to the track of your choice. Next to the track number, a little speaker icon appears showing you the song being played. The track title also appears in Sound Juicer's title bar.

Sound Juicer is also a CD ripper, allowing you to make personal copies of your music to play on your Linux system or on a portable player. I'll cover this in detail shortly, but I want to wrap up CD playing. That means I'm going to leave the Sound Juicer behind for a moment so I can tell you about another CD player.

A Simpler CD Player

Although it doesn't come up automatically, and you can't find it in the Applications menu, Ubuntu has another CD player that you might prefer, the GNOME CD player. If all you want to do is play your CDs and you want a simple, easy-to-use interface, look no further. Press <Alt+F2> to bring up your quick-start application starter and type in **gnome-cd**). The CD player launches (see Figure 18-4). Click the Play button, sit back, and enjoy.

Figure 18–4   Gnome CD, a kinder, gentler, CD player.

   Tip   If you can't find the CD player, install it with Synaptic. Look for and install the gnome-media package.

On the left of the player, just above the Pause button, there's a button with a tool icon. Click this button to bring up the CD player preferences dialog. Next to that is the standard list of controls to skip over songs, fast forward, or stop. On the far right of the CD player, there's a vertical slider control. That's a volume control.

After the GNOME CD player has started, look in your top panel's notification area and you see a small icon that looks like a CD. Left-click the icon and the CD player disappears into the panel. Right-click the applet and you have access to the basic CD player controls such as Previous, Next, Stop, Play, and so on (see Figure 18-5).

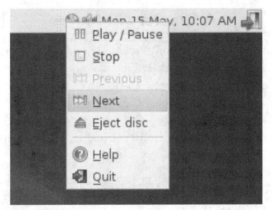

Figure 18–5   The GNOME CD's top panel applet provides some handy, out-of-the-way, controls.

Ripping and Burning Songs

Over the years, we have all purchased a lot of music CDs or, as some of us still call them, *albums*. Many of those albums, unfortunately, had only two or three songs we really liked, so playing the whole album wasn't what we wanted. As a result, we created collections of our favorite songs on tape and played the tapes, instead.

These days, with the help of our Linux systems, we can create our own collections from those albums we purchased and create CD collections of those songs we want to hear. Furthermore, if you have lots of disk space and you spend a lot of time at your computer, nothing beats a collection of songs ready to play without having to change CDs all the time. Pulling songs from a CD and saving them to your system as digital images is what is commonly referred to as *ripping*. The *burning* happens when you take a collection of songs and, well, burn them to a CD.

Intermezzo: Digital Audio Formats

Before I get into the mechanics of ripping and burning songs, I'd like to spend a small amount of time discussing music formats. When you purchase a CD, the songs on that CD are in a format not generally used by your system. In fact, when we copy songs to disk from a CD, we always encode it into another, usually more compact format. The format we transfer to is identified by a three-letter extension on the filename. The most common format extensions are `.wav`, `.mp3`, and (more recently) `.ogg`.

The *WAV* format is one originally created by Microsoft. It is extremely common but not the most efficient in terms of compression. On the other hand, the *MP3* format (from the Motion Pictures Experts Group, a.k.a. MPEG) owes its popularity to the high compression ratio it uses—about 12:1. The newcomer on the block is the *OGG* (or Ogg Vorbis) format. Like MP3, it boasts a high compression rate, but unlike MP3, it is completely unencumbered by patents.

To give you an idea of the compression values, I ripped a 3-minute, 46-second song to WAV format. It came in at 39,866,444 bytes, whereas the same song in OGG format required only 3,438,407 bytes. If you do the math, that is a ratio of 11.6:1. Pretty impressive reasons for not using WAV format files.

Using Sound Juicer as a CD Ripper

Every time you put in a new audio CD, every song is selected, either for play or for extraction by Sound Juicer. Earlier, I had you play the songs, but clicking the Extract button is pretty much all you need to do to get those songs onto your hard drive. Alternatively, you can select individual songs by clicking the check boxes to the left of each song.

When the process starts, the Play button is grayed out and the Extract button changes a Stop button in case you want to cancel the process. At the bottom of the Sound Juicer window, on the left side, is a graphical progress bar. Directly to the right of that, the estimated time is indicated along with the speed at which the process is taking place (see Figure 18-6).

The resulting songs are saved in your home folder using the following format:

```
/home/username/artist_name/album_name/track_title.ogg
```

Figure 18–6   The Sound Juicer is a multiuse multimedia application. Aside from being the default Ubuntu CD player, it is also a CD ripper.

When it's all over, you get a message telling you that your tracks were successfully copied. You can either close the dialog or click the Eject button to pop the CD out.

Now that you have all the basics of ripping songs with the Sound Juicer, let's take a moment to revisit this whole notion of audio formats. Click Edit on the Sound Juicer menu bar and select Preferences. When the Preferences dialog appears (see Figure 18-7), look at the bottom of the dialog. There's a drop-down box labeled Output Format with several formats available. They include two CD quality formats (lossless FLAC and lossy Ogg Vorbis) as well as two voice quality formats (lossless WAV and lossy Ogg Vorbis).

If the music is going to stay on your home computer and you like the idea of patent-free compression format, choose Ogg Vorbis or FLAC. If you own a portable MP3 player and you want to take your music with you, you may still be okay with Ogg Vorbis because it is supported by a number of popular players.

Figure 18–7 When ripping music to disk, you do have a choice of output format, selectable via the Preferences dialog.

Important Legal Tip Regarding MP3 Files Some of you may wonder where the MP3 format is in this list. Because of patent issues (a problem in some jurisdictions, most notably the United States), Ubuntu does not automatically install an MP3 encoder. This is also true of playing MP3s using players such as Rhythmbox, which I will cover shortly. Because this book is distributed worldwide, it may be perfectly legal for you to download and install these encoders and plugins. Consult with your local authorities to find out if playing these formats in your country or state is legal.

To get MP3 functionality (along with several other formats), you need to install the following packages: gstreamer0.10-plugins-ugly and lame. You can do this with Synaptic as described in Chapter 8. Note that you need to have the Universe and Multiverse repositories activated. These only cover MP3 files but there are a handful of other formats that may be considered non-free—again, depending on where you live. To learn about these and how to install the right packages, make sure you visit the following URL:

https://wiki.ubuntu.com/RestrictedFormats

Another, very easy way to add MP3 support (as well as support for many other audio and video formats) is to visit EasyUbuntu at http://easyubuntu.freecontrib.org. Just follow the instructions on the site and you are on your way.

Now, look at your Sound Juicer Preferences window again and click Edit Profiles next to the output format drop-down list. You see the current four formats listed. Now click the New button to the right and enter a name for the new profiles (for example, **CD Quality, Lossy, MP3**). You now have five profiles listed. Click your new MP3 profile and then click the Edit button. A dialog like the one in Figure 18-8 appears.

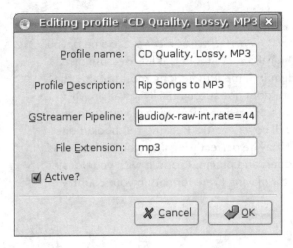

Figure 18–8
To rip your CDs to MP3 format, you need to create an MP3 profile.

It's time to make a few changes. The Profile Name can be left alone, and you can pretty much enter whatever you like as a Profile Description (for example, **Rip songs to MP3**). Under File Extension, enter **mp3**. Because the GStreamer Pipeline information is a little long, I'm going to show it to you on a separate line:

```
audio/x-raw-int,rate=44100,channels=2 ! lame name=enc
```

Click the Active check box, and then click OK to close the dialog. At this point, I would tell you to select your new MP3 encoder from the Output Format list, but on my system, I found that I had to shut down Sound Juicer first and restart it before I could make the change. After that, I was able to rip MP3s without fuss.

Playing Your Songs

This is the easy part. Start up Nautilus and navigate to a folder where your songs are located. If you are looking for a specific song, do a search on it (as described in Chapter 4). In Figure 18-9, you can see that I've done a search on songs with the word Woman, ending with an .mp3 extension.

If you pause over the music file with your mouse cursor, the file starts to play and continues playing as long as your cursor sits there. Not very practical for listening but a great way to make sure this is indeed the song you are looking for. To play it and get back to work at the same time, double-click the song file. The Totem media player appears and your music plays (see Figure 18-10).

Aside from the fact that you can now listen to your track of choice, you have also been introduced to the all-purpose Totem media player. You might also have noticed that while you were listening, Totem was running a pretty cool little light show over in the left pane. It's kind of hard to visualize from the image in Figure 18-10, but it can be rather hypnotic. Press the <F> key (the letter f) and your view switches to full screen. Just sit back, watch the show, and listen. To leave full screen mode, press <F> again or slide your mouse cursor to the top of the screen (a Leave Fullscreen button appears).

At the bottom of the window, you find controls for playing/pausing, previous, and next. There's also a volume control and a slider to position you at any point in the track being played. Notice that your single song selection is listed in the right pane, the one titled Playlist. One song constitutes a fairly small playlist, but you can easily add more songs to the mix. Just click the plus

Figure 18–9   Use Nautilus to find the songs you want to hear.

sign at the bottom of the window and the standard GNOME file selector appears. Select the songs you want and they appear in your playlist. If you like the collection you've created, click the diskette icon at the bottom of the playlist, and you can load it up at a later time.

Tip   To quickly add a number of songs to your playlist, open up a copy of Nautilus, navigate to your music, and then drag and drop the songs of your choice into the playlist window.

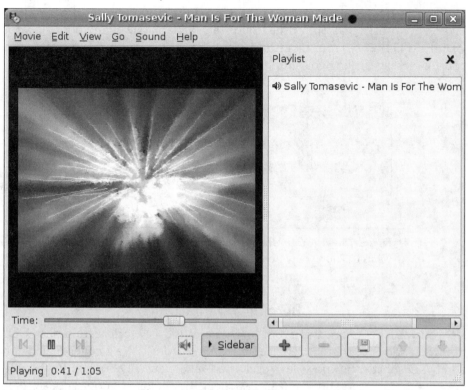

Figure 18–10   The Totem media player starts and plays your songs immediately.

Can You Feel the Burn?

I still find it interesting to consider the terms that have entered the language when referring to creating CDs. We rip, and then we burn. Considering the violent-sounding nature of the process, anything that simplifies the process and makes things a little friendlier is certainly welcome. For this part of the chapter, I'm going to assume that you have already ripped a number of songs and now you want to create a custom collection of your music to listen to in the car or on your living room stereo. I'm also going to tell you how you can use essentially the same process to back up your data.

Try this one. Make sure you have closed the Sound Juicer program and taken your music CDs out of the drive. Take a blank CD-R and pop it in your CD or DVD burner. Your Ubuntu system should recognize this event with a pop-up message asking your intentions for this blank CD (see Figure 18-11).

Figure 18–11   Your Ubuntu system senses a blank CD and wants to know your intentions.

Burning a Data CD

Do you want to ignore this event, create a music CD, or create a data CD? Hmm . . . doesn't that last choice sound interesting? We'll cover making an audio CD shortly. For now, let's click the Make Data CD button. When you do, something interesting appears. A special Nautilus window appears (see Figure 18-12).

 Tip You can bring up the CD/DVD Creator view of Nautilus from any Nautilus window. Click <Ctrl+L> and enter **burn:///** in the location bar or click Go on the menu bar and select CD/ DVD Creator from the menu.

If you are looking to save some files and folders to a CD (or create a backup), the easiest thing to do here is to open another instance of Nautilus from which you can make your selections. Click the files and folders you want and drag them into the Nautilus CD/DVD Creator window. You can also create special folders in this window into which you organize the information you want to burn to a CD. As you add files, the window looks somewhat more populated (see Figure 18-13).

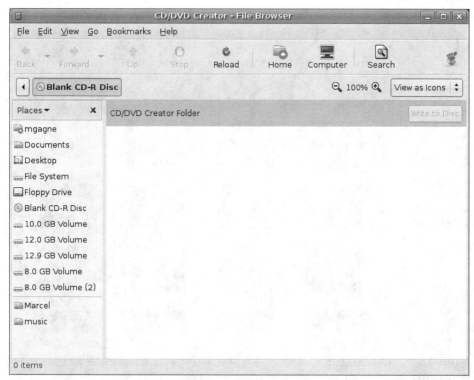

Figure 18–12 GNOME's CD/DVD Creator probably looks pretty familiar right about now. That's right; it's another view of Nautilus.

Repeat this process until you have everything you want, and then click the Write to Disc button in the top right of the Nautilus window. The Write to Disc dialog appears (see Figure 18-14). Before we move on, I should mention that everything I've mentioned up to this point is based on the idea that you started with a blank CD in the drive. If you haven't yet put in a blank CD (that is, you started the CD/DVD Creator manually), this is the time to pop it into the drive.

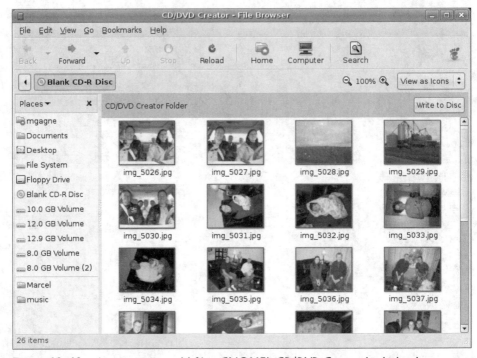

Figure 18–13   As you start to add files, GNOME's CD/DVD Creator looks less barren. When you have all you need, click Write to Disc.

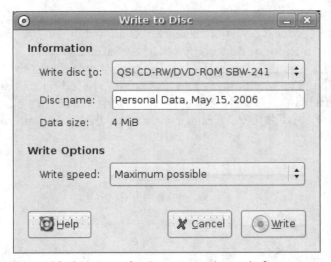

Figure 18–14   Just a few last minute choices before you start burning your CD or DVD.

If you have more than one CD burner (perhaps a CD and DVD burner), you can select from the drop-down list at the top. Directly below that, enter the name of the project you are creating. You can also choose to accept the default of Personal Data followed by the date. The only other thing you might to modify here is the Write Speed. I don't generally find this to be a problem, but sometimes, if I find myself creating more coasters than usual (bad CDs), I turn the burn speed down. This can be caused by CD media that can't handle high write speeds. When you are happy with all your choices, click the Write button. A progress window appears with details of the current burn (see Figure 18-15).

Figure 18–15   The progress dialog tells you whether you have time to make yourself a coffee.

After the CD is complete, another dialog box appears, giving you the opportunity to make another copy or eject the drive.

A Note About Backups

By now you must be thinking, "Hey, if I can copy data directories to my CD, surely this is the perfect way to do backups." It certainly sounds good. CDs allow you to back up roughly 700MB of data, and DVDs a whopping 4GB. Use CD-RWs, and you can create a rotating set of discs for backup purposes. So what's the catch?

Well, for starters, the default Nautilus view does not show hidden files. If you want a complete backup, you need to make sure you get everything.

When navigating Nautilus, make sure you click View on the menu bar, and then select Show Hidden Files.

The second problem has to do with permissions. If you are going to use this system to later restore your data, you need an intermediate step. You need to create an archive of those files. Let's say you had selected a whole collection of configuration files, or email, or anything else for that matter. Right-click the selected files, then select Create Archive. The Create Archive dialog appears (see Figure 18-16).

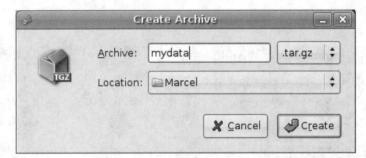

Figure 18–16   An archive not only protects file permissions, but also takes up far less space on your backup device.

The Archive field is where you enter the filename in which you want all this information stored. To the right of the name is a drop-down box with `.tar.gz` selected. This is the default storage format, but several others are also available including `.tar.bz2`, `.zip`, and more. The Location is a folder where this archive file will be written. Click Create and a process dialog appears as files are added and compressed.

When the archive is done, drag that into the CD/DVD Creator window instead of the individual files.

That's it. With your data safely backed up, you can sleep soundly at night.

Burning a Music CD with Serpentine

Data is fine, of course, but I started this chapter talking about music. So let's make ourselves a music CD, shall we? We can start this in two different ways. The first is to pop in a blank CD, wait for the "What would you like to do with this?" message (refer to Figure 18-11), and then select Make Audio CD. This fires up the Serpentine Audio-CD Creator (see Figure 18-17). The second method is to click Applications on the top panel, then select Serpentine from the Sound & Video submenu. Both methods take you to the same place.

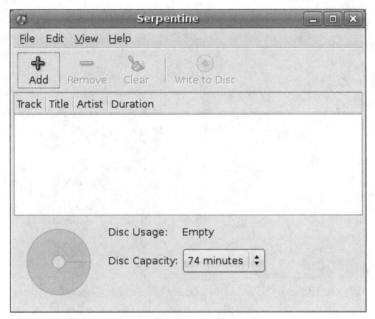

Figure 18–17 *Serpentine is Ubuntu's tool for creating an audio CD of your favorite songs.*

This is a standard interface with a menu bar along the top and an icon bar below. In the large central areas, tracks are listed along with their duration. As you can see, there are no tracks at this time. In the bottom part of the window, the disc usage is reported as empty with a total capacity listed based on the type of CD Serpentine identified. Notice the CD icon to the left. This a graphical progress bar of sorts, showing you how much of your disc is currently full. To add tracks to your CD, click the Add button. The standard GNOME file selector dialog appears from which you can make your selection (see Figure 18-18).

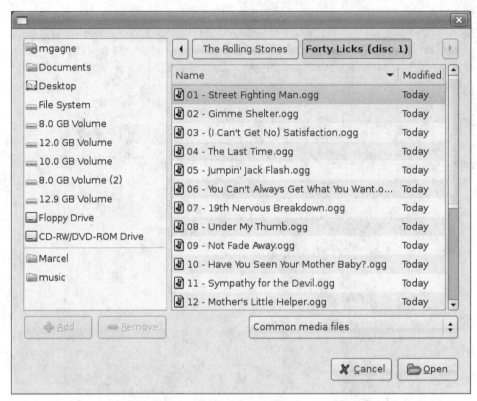

Figure 18–18   To add songs to an audio CD, use the normal GNOME files selector.

Remember, press <Ctrl> and click with the left mouse button to specify which songs you want. When you have what you want, click the Open button. Don't worry about the order in which the songs appear on the list. When you have your selection complete, Serpentine displays the songs and works out the Artist and Title information from the filename (see Figure 18-19). Then, you can simply click on the songs in the middle pane, and move them up or down at will. If the song in position six would make a better opener, drag it up to position one. It is that easy.

Figure 18–19 As tracks are added, Serpentine keeps track of how much space you still have to add new songs.

Notice the disc icon in the lower left. It now shows my CD as being just slightly better than three-quarters full. Feel free to add more songs and rearrange them further. To remove a track, click it then click the Remove button in the icon bar. When you are done, click the Write to Disc icon at the top. A pop-up message appears asking you to confirm that you truly want to burn this music CD. Click the Write to Disc button on the confirmation dialog to begin the process.

As the window appears, you might notice that it looks a little different than the data burn window. For starters, a message appears telling you that the media files are being prepared. That's because your OGG or MP3 files need to be converted back to CD audio first. After the conversion has finished, the same window displays the write progress (see Figure 18-20).

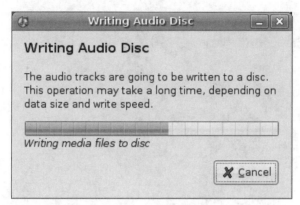

Figure 18–20   A status window keeps you informed
on the progress of your audio CD's creation.

Put Another Nickel In . . .

Ripping songs from your CDs and storing them on your PC so you can listen
while you work (or play) is fantastic. Double-click Start up Totem, pull in a
few songs into your playlist, and enjoy the music. Life couldn't be any better.
Except . . .

You see, all this collecting of music—ripping songs, building huge libraries
of MP3s or OGGs on your computer's hard disk—is eventually going to
become a nightmare to administer. Sure, all those CDs in jewel cases have
disappeared into that virtual space that is your hard disk, but now you have all
these songs in a number of large folders with little or no organization. If you
want to play something, you have to go searching. What you need is a jukebox.

In a much earlier part of my life, I used to make extra money babysitting
some of my parents' friends' children. One of their friends repaired jukeboxes
for a living. Consequently, a real honest-to-goodness jukebox was always in
the house, full of 45 RPM singles. From time to time, the model and type of
machine would change, but with the coin mechanism disabled, I had all the
music I wanted available. Now, that's entertainment! As luck would have it,
your Ubuntu Linux system comes with a very fine jukebox program called
Rhythmbox and you won't have to babysit anybody's kids to use it.

Rhythmbox

You'll find Rhythmbox (command name, `rhythmbox`) by clicking Applications on the top panel, then selecting Rhythmbox Music Player from the Sound & Video submenu. This program integrates nicely into the GNOME desktop, with a notification area icon to drop the application out of sight quickly. It includes support for your MP3 and Ogg Vorbis files, collection and playlist management, tag editing, and much more.

On first start, a Rhythmbox configuration assistant appears to take you through some basic configuration steps. The first of these screens is an intro-duction, so just click Forward and Rhythmbox asks for folders where music is kept (see Figure 18-21). Enter this information manually or click the Browse button to bring up the GNOME file selector, from which you can choose the locations of music on your system. In my case, I have a separate partition called `/mnt/music` where I keep all my music.

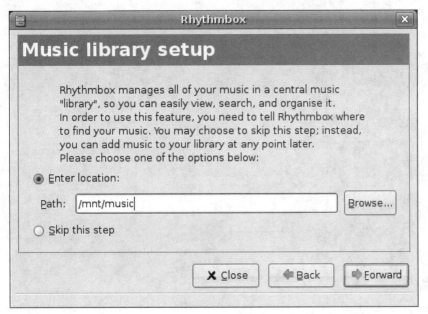

Figure 18-21   Start by adding the names of folders you want Rhythmbox to keep track of.

As the assistant indicates, you can Skip This Step and enter the information at a later time. Click Forward and you are done. On the next screen, click Apply and Rhythmbox starts. The program is smart enough to scan all of your subdirectories for songs so there's no need to list each and every directory where you keep music. You don't want to just scan the entire system, however, because you won't have permissions for many directories. You can add as many folders or file systems as you want.

Rhythmbox starts scanning those folders and builds a base collection. It reads the information tags on each song to try to determine the title, year, and so on of each song. After the process ends, you wind up with a collection list similar to the one in Figure 18-22.

Figure 18–22   Rhythmbox creates a default collection list of all the songs in the folders you specified.

To the left of the interface, there's a vertical pane labeled Source. Several choices are already filled in for you with your dynamically created selection of songs under Library. As the names in that list imply, Rhythmbox is also a way to listen to Internet radio stations, download and enjoy podcasts, and much more. For the moment, let's concentrate on our local music. Most of the action with Rhythmbox happens on the left side with a two-panel music browser in the top half (Artist and Album).

Below is your list of tracks based on the results of your selections in the above browser. By default, all of your songs appear here in the default collection list. Because organization is key, you can create additional playlists by right-clicking the left column, and then selecting *New Playlist*. The new playlist appears in the Source sidebar without a name; click (or right-click) it and rename it to something more appropriate. To populate a new playlist, make sure you have your default playlist selected, then drag and drop song titles into your playlist folder of choice. The titles appear in your new playlist but remain in the master collection as well.

When you added that playlist, you no doubt noticed that there was also an option to add a New Automatic Playlist. This is cool because you can have Rhythmbox create playlists based on criteria you select. Let's pretend that I want a playlist where every song is a song I have played at least 10 times. I might create a playlist called 10 or More that is automatically added to every time I play a particular song more than 10 times (see Figure 18-23). That selection criterion can be anything from artist to words in a title (all songs containing the word *love*) to play count, rating, and so on.

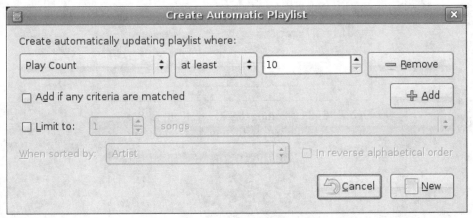

Figure 18–23   Create automatic playlists with Rhythmbox by selecting criteria based on artist, play count, genre, and a whole lot more.

As anyone with a collection of songs on their computer knows, the information contained in the information tags isn't always perfect. To deal with this problem, we have Rhythmbox's tag editor. Right-click a title and select Properties. A two-tabbed window appears (see Figure 18-24), from which you can change basic information about the current track as well as details such as your rating (0 to 5 stars) for the song.

Figure 18–24 Editing tags is easy. Right–click a song, select Preferences, then make the changes you need.

Resources

EasyUbuntu

http://easyubuntu.freecontrib.org

Lame Encoder

http://lame.sourceforge.net

Ogg Vorbis

http://www.vorbis.com

Rhythmbox

http://www.gnome.org/projects/rhythmbox

Ubuntu Wiki on Restricted Formats

https://wiki.ubuntu.com/RestrictedFormats

Chapter

19

Would You Like
to Play a Game?
(Very Serious Fun)

There's plenty to smile about when it comes to taking a little down time with your Ubuntu Linux system. A default GNOME installation comes with a number of games, enough to keep you busy for some time. When you do finally decide that you need additional entertainment, there are literally hundreds of games waiting for you to download.

Expand your mind with one of the many puzzles. Do a little target practice in the arcade. Race down a dizzying mountain slope. Play golf. Sink someone's battleship. Board a space fighter and take on somebody halfway around the world. Play solitaire, backgammon, or poker.

There are tons of games available, and I'm just talking about the ones on your distribution disks. Head off to the Internet and you'll find yourself set for weeks, possibly months.

Sit back, relax, and get ready to enjoy a little fun, Ubuntu Linux style.

Ubuntu Preinstalled Games

You can find most of these under Games in your top panel's Application menu. In each case, I also give you the command name so that you can either run them from the shell or start them with your program launcher <Alt+F2>.

AisleRiot Solitaire

Almost anyone who has held a deck of cards knows about solitaire, a one-person card game whose object is to reorder seven piles of cards, drawn at random, into four ordered piles, by suit and in numerical order. You may also know it as patience (as I did, growing up). There are, in fact, many solitaire or patience card games; the most famous and popular is also known as Klondike.

AisleRiot (command name sol) is more than just Klondike solitaire (see Figure 19-1). Some eighty different games are included (click the Select Game button just below the menu bar), including such favorites as Golf, Clock, Baker's Dozen, and many others.

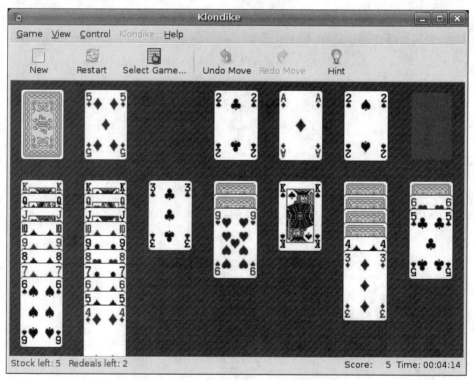

Figure 19–1   AisleRiot, the classic solitaire game, and more.

If the cards look too small for your taste, just grab a corner of the main window and drag. The card table and cards scale accordingly. You can also click View on the menu bar and select Fullscreen (or press <F11>) to hide away any other work that might be nagging you in the background.

Tip I only mention it with AisleRiot, but a number of the games included with Ubuntu also come with a full-screen mode. In all cases, pressing <F11> switches to and from full-screen mode.

Ataxx

Ataxx feels familiar, perhaps because these games, where the object is to conquer opposing pieces and change them to your colors, are so common. Still, Ataxx is no Othello, and it requires substantially more cunning to win. Here's how it works.

When the game starts, there are four pieces on the board, two light and two dark, sitting at opposing corners. When you click one of your pieces, your valid moves are highlighted by a light-colored piece around your own. Click a square right next to one of your pieces and a new piece appears. Click one further away and your current piece jumps to that position, hopping over (but not capturing) other pieces in the process. If your piece lands next to your opponent's piece, or pieces, all of those pieces adjacent to your piece flip and change to your color (see Figure 19-2).

Are the games starting to feel too easy for you? Click Settings on the menu bar and select Preferences to bring up a two-tabbed configuration dialog. Under the Players tab, you see an entry for the light player and one for the dark. One, or both, can be human players, but if you want to play against the computer, select a skill level from either the light or the dark side.

As with a number of these seemingly simple games, there is far more to it than you might initially think. It's also far more addictive than it looks.

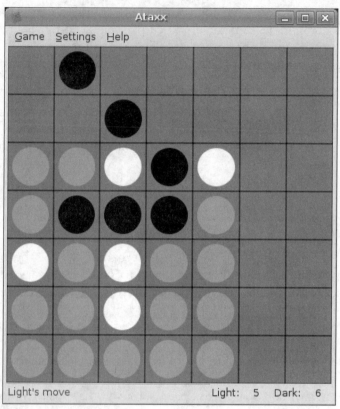

Figure 19–2   Ataxx.

Blackjack

When you play the game for the first time, you may find that it takes a few seconds to get started. The program is busy setting things up for you. You see a message, Computing Basic Strategy . . . , while a progress bar informs you of this process.

What does one say to explain a game like Blackjack? After all, it is a classic that almost everyone (over a certain age) has played. Here's the short version, in case you are among those who have never heard of the game. The idea is simple. The dealer, your computer in this case, deals cards for you and itself. Your job is to get as close to 21 without going over, and getting a higher number than the dealer. Over 21 is a bust and you automatically lose. Face cards are worth 10, and Aces can count as either 1 or 11. When the game starts, you find yourself looking at a casino-like table with your cash chips at the bottom and the cards dealt to the right of center (see Figure 19-3). That's where all the action takes place.

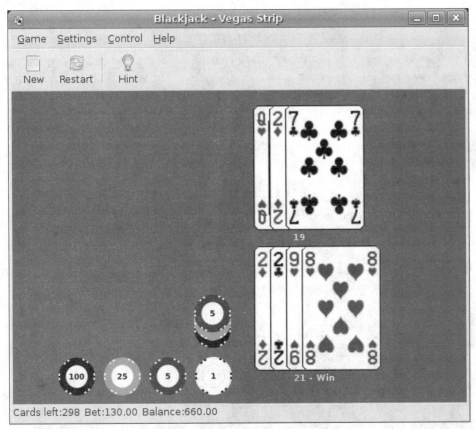

Figure 19-3 Blackjack.

Along the top of the game table, it identifies the game rules as *Vegas Strip*, the default. This particular Blackjack program comes with four different sets of rules including Atlantic City, Ameristar, Vegas Downtown, and Vegas Strip. To change to a different set of rules, click Settings on the menu bar and select Preferences. The configuration dialog lets you change rules and lists the differences in those rules. You can also choose to display the hand probabilities, adjust the delay in dealing, and whether or not you take insurance on a hand.

As anyone who has played this game can tell you, there's more to it than the luck of the draw. While you are busy learning the skills of the game, you can click the Hint button (under the menu bar) at any time to obtain a suggestion from the computer.

Five or More

The idea is simple, line up five or more marbles of the same color. When you do, those marbles disappear and you are rewarded with points. The more marbles you can line up and make disappear, the higher your score. Simple, huh? Let me throw you a few wrinkles.

The game starts with a few marbles randomly positioned on the game grid. Click a marble, then click another square to move that marble. You can move as far away as you want and in any direction, but you must have a clear path to do so. It doesn't even have to be a straight line. In the top right, directly below the menu bar, the program shows you what marbles the computer is about to drop (see Figure 19-4). If you can line up five marbles, you claim an extra turn before the program drops its next batch.

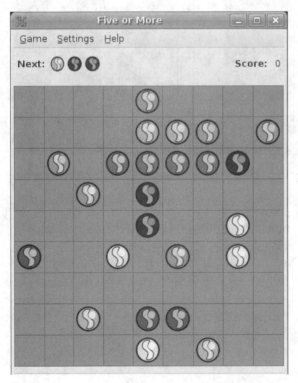

Figure 19–4 Five or More.

Now, I did say "marbles," but perhaps I should have said "objects." Five or More is themeable. Click Settings on the menu bar and select Preferences. The image theme is fairly limited out-of-the-box, but it is possible to create other themes (check the game's Help for details). Your options are colored balls or shapes, different board colors, and different board sizes.

Four-in-a-Row

You've almost certainly played this one as a kid. Back then you probably knew it as Connect Four, a game sold by Milton Bradley. The object is to get four of your colored discs in a row while your opponent tries to do the same. Part of the strategy comes from trying to make sure your opponent is stopped from creating a row of four.

If you have never played, you'll catch on quickly. Drop your colored disc down any row and try to line up four of the same color. This can be a horizontal, vertical, or diagonal row. Whoever gets his four in a row first, wins (see Figure 19-5).

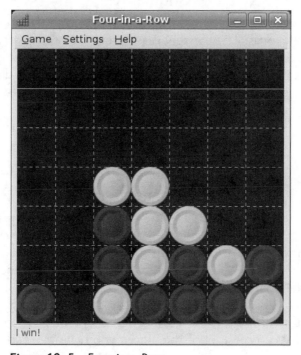

Figure 19–5 Four-in-a-Row.

The game's Settings menu lets you select different themes including balls, glass marbles, blocks, and so on. You can also decide the computer player's skill level.

Freecell Patience

Freecell is just another entry point into the AisleRiot game pack, which I described earlier, so everything I said there applies here. What makes this worth mentioning is how the game is started. If you check the processes and look for the program name sol, you'll see how it's possible to start AisleRiot on a particular game.

```
/usr/games/sol --variation freecell
```

You can use this information to create a quick-start icon on your desktop (discussed in Chapter 5) so that you always start with your favorite solitaire game.

Gnometris

One of the most enduring games of my arcade-playing younger years was something called Tetris. The concept was simple. Colored geometric patterns fall from above, and as they fall, you rotate the pieces so that they fit (like a jigsaw puzzle) into the bottom row. Fill a row and the pieces disappear. Miss too many of the pieces and the top crushes the bottom—you lose. Your Ubuntu Linux system comes with a variation called Gnometris (command name gnometris). If you remember Tetris, you'll find Gnometris an excellent clone (see Figure 19-6).

Iagno

This is another classic game that you probably know as Othello (some also call it Reversi). This is a two-player game where you lay down two-sided discs (white on one side and black on the other) in an effort to control the board (see Figure 19-7). You start out with two white discs and two black in the center of the board. One by one, players put down additional discs. If you trap an opponent's disc between two of your color, you flip the disc to your color. In the situation where there is more than one of your opponent's discs between your two pieces, all of the pieces you have trapped are flipped to your color.

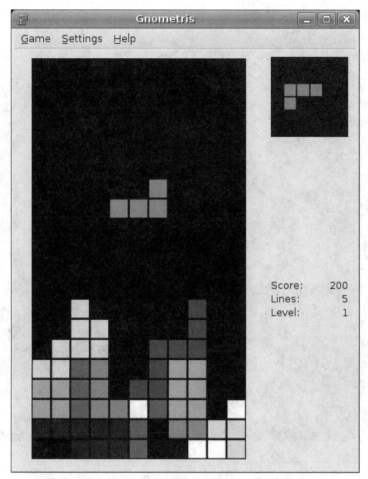

Figure 19–6 Gnometris is a recreation of the classic Tetris game.

To play against the computer, make sure you click Settings, then Preferences, and assign a play level to the computer opponent (by selecting either the light or dark side).

This is a great version of the classic game. Still, I think that one of my favorite things about this particular incarnation of Reversi (or Othello) is the author's explanation of why the game is called Iagno and not something else. This is in Section 1.2 of the Iagno manual (click Help on the Iagno menu bar and select Contents).

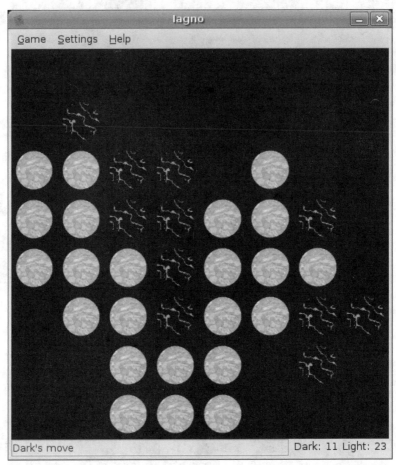

Figure 19–7   Iagno is a disc flipping game you might know as Othello.

Klotski

Klotski is a puzzle game. As with all puzzle games, it looks easy before you start. Here's what happens. You have a two-dimensional box with one door. Inside this box are shapes of different pieces (it starts with large and small squares). One of the pieces is patterned with indents. Outside the box are posts upon which the patterned piece fits. Your job is to get the patterned piece to the posts (see Figure 19-8).

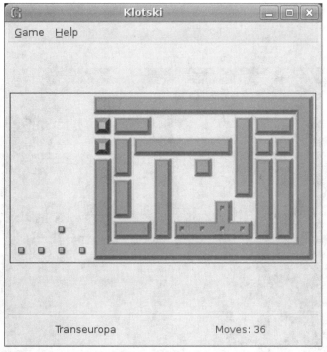

Figure 19–8 Puzzle me this, Klotski. How do you get the patterned piece on to the key posts outside?

The only piece that can pass the jeweled posts at the entrance is the patterned piece that matches the pins. All you have to do is figure out how to manipulate the pieces in order to get your piece out. The first few games seem easy enough, but after about the tenth, I can guarantee a lot of head scratching.

Mahjongg

Mahjongg is an electronic recreation of the classic Eastern tile matching game of the same name, minus the extra trailing g (Mahjong). Mahjong solitaire as a board game is generally a two-player game; however, the computerized version is a single-person puzzler. Each tile is imprinted with a symbol and all of the tiles are arranged in a pattern that partially hides some tiles and covers others completely. The object of the game is to remove all of the tiles two at a time by finding matching symbols (see Figure 19-9).

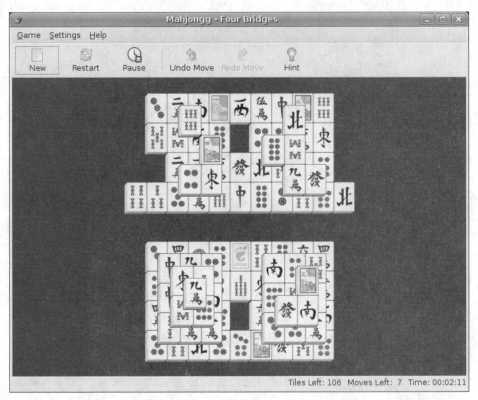

Figure 19–9   Mahjongg contains tons of puzzles and many different levels, and in different maps (or layouts).

If you are thinking there is more to it than this, you are right. You can't remove a tile that is covered by another and you can't remove tiles that are blocked by other tiles on more than one side. As you remove tiles, things start to get easier, at least for the most part. Sometimes, removing the wrong two tiles is enough to stop you from solving the puzzle. Should you find yourself in a position where no more moves are possible, a pop-up window alerts you to that effect.

Tip If the pieces appear too small, just drag one of the game window's corners and the display grows accordingly. This is also a good game to flip into full-screen mode.

Mines

Most people have played some variation of this game going back many years. Early on, it was one of two games included with "that other OS" where you probably knew it as Minesweeper. The idea would be far more nerve-wracking if this were anything but a game. Hidden somewhere beneath the squares on the game board are mines (see Figure 19-10). Step on them and you explode. Sound like fun?

Figure 19–10 It's a good thing Mines is just a game.

You have to uncover the squares that don't contain mines while flagging the ones that do have mines. You uncover mines by clicking a square with the left mouse button, and you flag by clicking with the right. A large, safe area uncovers magically when you click somewhere in the middle. The only hint you get comes from numbers that appear above the square. A 1 on a square indicates that there is one mine hidden in one of the squares adjoining to that square. A 2 means there are two mines in the adjoining squares. Your job is to look at these numbered squares and try to figure out which squares actually have mines.

When the game gets too easy for you, bring up the Preferences menu and change the Field Size from the default Small to Medium, Large, or whatever frightening map you care to imagine.

Nibbles

This one is interesting in that it feels like a few other very similar games I played in my early arcade days. There's even a hint of the light cycles from the movie Tron here, a hint that's particularly felt when you play the game over a network. You and up to three of your friends can play Nibbles online.

As the worm eats more and more of the gems scattered across the playing field, he gets longer and longer. Around the playing field, there are walls, with openings through which the work can pass, making it easier to move from one side of the field to the other. Unfortunately, no matter how clever you are, eventually you are going to run into your own tail (or at least some part of your body), and that's where the game ends.

Robots

Robots is an ancient game—ancient in the computer world, that is—where you try to avoid being killed by an advancing horde of evil robots (see Figure 19-11). Every time you make a move, the robots calculate a way to advance toward you *en masse*. What you need to do to survive is use their weaknesses to your advantage. The robots have the sheer weight of numbers on their side, but they are still pretty stupid; and if they run into anything, they blow up. You can force them to run into each other, thereby destroying them, or push junk piles (also known as previously destroyed robots) in their way.

If the situation appears totally hopeless, hit the Teleport button. The only catch with teleportation is that you have a limited number of safe teleports. That leaves you with the purely Random teleport, which can land you in an even bigger mess.

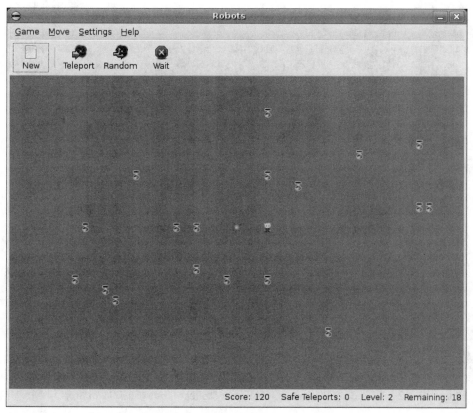

Figure 19–11 *Save yourself from an army of marauding, evil, and downright nasty robots.*

Same GNOME

Same GNOME is one great little puzzle game that takes no time to learn, but forever to master (see Figure 19-12). You start with a grid of brightly colored marbles. When you move your mouse cursor over a marble, all of the similarly colored marbles in a group start to spin. Click that group and the marbles disappear. Any marbles that were above your group fall below. The net effect of this is that you are creating other groupings, which can then be removed. The idea is to clear the grid of marbles in as few moves as possible. A little strategic planning mixed with some good spatial visualization is the key to success. If you don't like the colored marbles, switch to the planets view (my personal favorite).

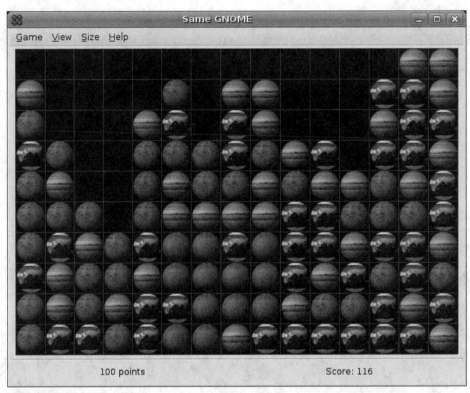

Figure 19–12   The colorful Same GNOME, easy to learn, but tough to master.

Tali

In another universe, you know this game as Yahtzee, or as some of my friends call it, poker dice (see Figure 19-13). The idea is to collect a number of classic poker hands, including a full house, a small and large straight, a three of a kind, four of a kind, and of course, the granddaddy of rolls, the five of a kind or Yahtzee. Whenever the dice are rolled, click the ones you want to roll again, then click the Roll button. You have two chances on each roll to get the score you want. As with the real nonvirtual version of the game, you get an extra 35 points for getting 63 points or more in the top six rows.

The number of players is configurable, so if you don't want to see what the computer drums up when it plays you, change the number of opponents to zero.

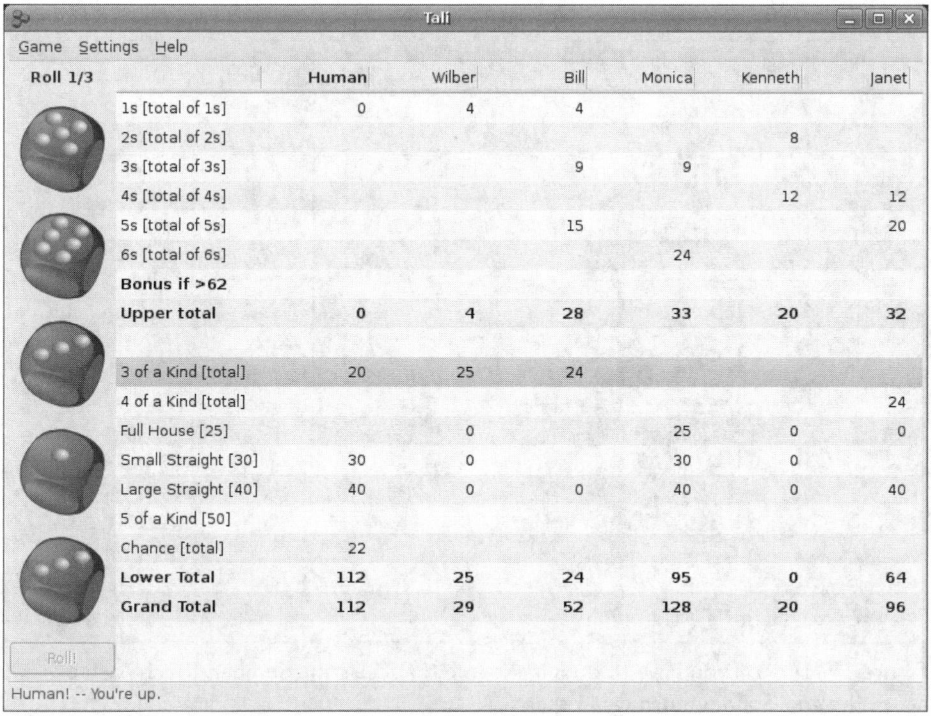

Roll 1/3		Human	Wilber	Bill	Monica	Kenneth	Janet
	1s [total of 1s]	0	4	4			
	2s [total of 2s]					8	
	3s [total of 3s]			9	9		
	4s [total of 4s]					12	12
	5s [total of 5s]			15			20
	6s [total of 6s]				24		
	Bonus if >62						
	Upper total	0	4	28	33	20	32
	3 of a Kind [total]	20	25	24			
	4 of a Kind [total]						24
	Full House [25]		0		25	0	0
	Small Straight [30]	30	0		30	0	
	Large Straight [40]	40	0	0	40	0	40
	5 of a Kind [50]						
	Chance [total]	22					
	Lower Total	112	25	24	95	0	64
	Grand Total	112	29	52	128	20	96

Roll!

Human! -- You're up.

Figure 19–13 Tali, an excellent recreation of the classic Yahtzee game.

Tetravex

Tetravex is a puzzle game using tiles positioned in a grid (see Figure 19-14). The object of the game is to rearrange the pieces so that the same numbers touch each other across the grid (for example, 2 touches 2, and 5 touches 5). When all the squares are arranged so that only the same numbers touch each other, you win. As you play, a timer counts up in the bottom-right corner of the game, so you are playing against time as well. To play the game, you drag pieces from the righthand box and replace them in the left play area. When putting squares into the left play area, the computer stops you from putting pieces down when the numbers don't match up.

If you find it a bit difficult at first, click Size and switch to a 2×2 grid. When you get comfortable, raise the number until you get to the 6×6 grid.

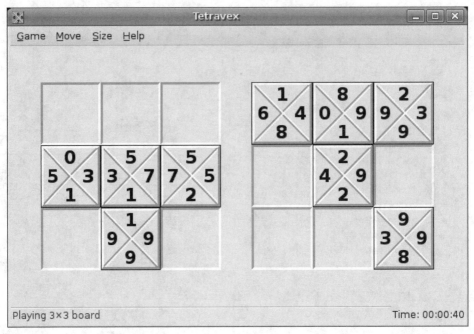

Figure 19–14   All you have to do is make sure that the same numbers touch each other across the grid. Sounds much easier than it is.

Must-Have Linux Games

With Tetravex, we've wrapped up our list of Ubuntu games, at least those that come preinstalled. That is, by no means, the end of your Linux games experience. In fact, we're just softening you up. There are literally hundreds of games that you can download, install, and play for free! So, before I finish up this chapter, I'm going to tell you about a few of my personal favorites.

Frozen-Bubble

Perhaps my favorite arcade-style game under Linux also happens to be one of the most addictive games I have ever run across. It is called *Frozen-Bubble*. This is a bright, beautiful, and colorful game with dozens of levels featuring a great musical soundtrack, cool sound effects, and at least one penguin. You'll just have to trust me on this one—this game is a must-have, and no, age doesn't enter into it. Still with me? Here's the premise.

Frozen, colored bubbles are arranged in various patterns against a wall at the top of your screen. Some kind of hydraulic press behind the wall slowly pushes the bubbles toward you (see Figure 19-15). Your job is to guide your cute little penguin gunner (so to speak) to aim the bubble launcher at the oncoming wall of bubbles. If three of more bubbles of the same color are together, fire a similarly colored bubble at that group, and the arrangement collapses. Destroy all the bubble groups, and you win that level. If any of the bubbles at the wall touch you, everything freezes over, and your penguin cries a river of tears. It's silly. It's fun. You are going to love it.

Figure 19-15   The incredibly addictive Frozen-Bubble.

PlanetPenguin Racer

This is one of my favorite, arcade style, games.

The idea is simple. Tux, the Linux penguin, races down snow- or ice-covered mountains on his belly (see Figure 19-16). As the speed increases, you try to dodge obstacles while picking up herring along the way. The action is fast-paced and exciting, with Tux taking flight off the occasional cliff or ramp. All this happens as you race against the clock.

Figure 19–16   Fast, frozen fun with PlanetPenguin Racer.

You can install this one easily via Synaptic. Search for `planetpenguin-racer`. Make sure you select the `planetpenguin-racer-data` and `planetpenguin-racer-extras` packages when you install. The extras package provides a number of additional courses.

Trust me on this one . . . you don't know the meaning of fun until you race down an ice and snow-covered mountain slope at breakneck speeds. Planet-Penguin Racer is a must!

Armagetron

Remember the 1982 Disney movie called Tron? Inside the computer, programs engaged in gladiatorial battles, fighting for their *users*. One of the deadly sports in this virtual world was a *lightcycle* race. Contestants rode a kind of motorcycle that left a wall of light in its wake. The cycles themselves can't stop. The only thing you can do is ride, avoiding your opponents' walls while trying to get them to crash into yours. The last program standing wins. The popularity of the lightcycle concept has created a number of variations on the theme, including one of my favorites. It's called Armagetron (see Figure 19-17). Think *Armageddon*.

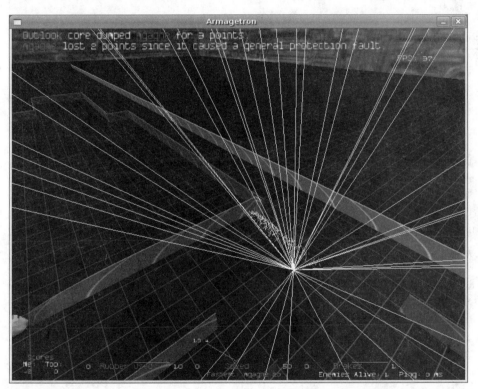

Figure 19–17 Armagetron is an excellent recreation of the classic lightcycle duel.

Armagetron is easily installed using Synaptic. Just search for armagetron. While you are there, take a look for gltron, another fantastic lightcycle game.

More Games! I Need More Games!

In just a moment, I'm going to give you some pointers for locating even more games, but because I mentioned that you already have hundreds of games available with your Ubuntu system, I must give you some pointers on finding them. Here is the short form to using Synaptic to find games. Click Search, then type the word **game** in the search box. The results will have you smiling for a long time (see Figure 19-18). You're welcome!

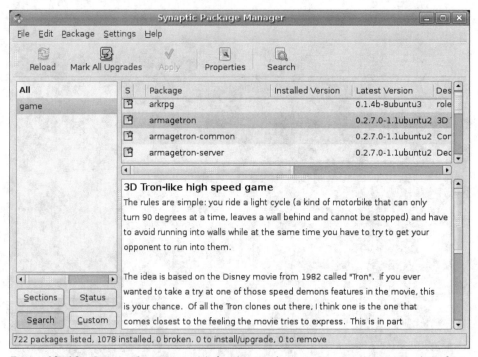

Figure 19–18   Doing a Synaptic search for the word game returns an impressive list of games, ready for you to install with a couple of clicks.

What? You've tried all of those hundreds of games and you still need more? Lucky for you, there really are tons of games out there. Some are commercial packages, and others are free for the download (or compile). Still more are in various stages of development and playability. To satisfy your hunger for Linux games, you might take a little time browsing in one of my favorite sites for Linux games, the Linux Game Tome at happypenguin.org.

Although not a download site, the Linux Game Tome organizes and reviews, and lets users rate games. It's organized and searchable, and it should be on your list when it comes to adding some new diversions to your system. If you find something that sounds interesting, come back and search for it in Synaptic.

Play on!

Resources

Linux Game Tome

```
http://happypenguin.org
```

Tux Games Online Store

```
http://www.tuxgames.com
```

Chapter
20
Turning Ubuntu into Kubuntu

In the Introduction to this book, I mentioned that there are several distributed versions of Ubuntu. These include Edubuntu and Kubuntu, both of which are Ubuntu but with a different default environment. I also introduced you to the concept of desktop environments and told you that GNOME was the default environment for Ubuntu. There is, however, another very popular desktop environment for Linux called KDE. I highly recommend that you introduce yourself to KDE and that you work with it as well. I make that same recommendation for people already working with KDE, by the way. Try out the GNOME desktop as well. You have a choice with Linux. Why not see what works best for you?

Showing you how to work with KDE is beyond the scope of this book, so I won't spend a great deal of time on it, but I will show you how to convert your Ubuntu system to a Kubuntu system. If you want to learn more about KDE, may I suggest that you look at my book, Moving to Linux: Kiss the Blue Screen of Death Goodbye! I cover KDE in detail and the concepts you learn there will serve you well on your Kubuntu system.

Remember, your Ubuntu system will continue to be an Ubuntu system and offer the GNOME desktop you have become familiar with, along with the applications that come with it. However, you will also have access to the KDE desktop and all the applications that come with a Kubuntu system. Best of all, getting the best of both worlds is actually pretty easy.

Ready? Then let's go!

Installing the Kubuntu Desktop

The first step to installing the Kubuntu desktop is to fire up Synaptic. Click System on the top panel and select Synaptic Package Manager from the Administration menu. Because this is an administrative function, you are asked for your password to continue. When the Synaptic interface comes up, click the Search icon directly below the menu bar, and enter **kubuntu-desktop** in the Search field (see Figure 20-1).

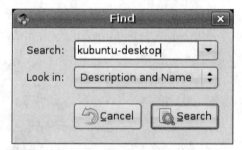

Figure 20–1   Installing Kubuntu begins with a simple search.

This is the easiest way to load Kubuntu. As you might expect, KDE is a collection of many packages, just as GNOME is. Finding all these packages individually could take a great deal of time. It could also introduce the possibility of missing some crucial pieces that correspond to a full Kubuntu system.

Now, click the Search button. You should see just one package listed, but this package is actually multiple packages (as the description tells you). To make things easier, the maintainers of Kubuntu have created a single all-encompassing package that does it all for you (see Figure 20-2).

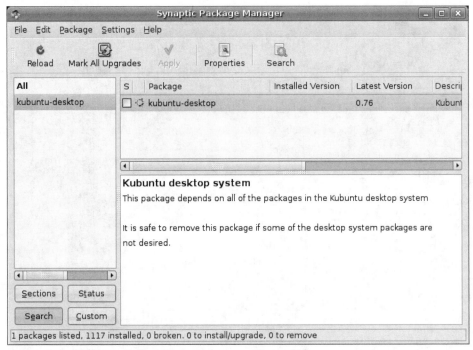

Figure 20–2   The Synaptic window only shows one package listed. However, the description explains what is behind that one package.

Right-click the `kubuntu-desktop` package and select Mark for Installation. The Mark Additional Required Packages dialog appears with a rather long list of packages. This is followed by the summary screen (see Figure 20-3). If you are curious as to what makes up the mega-package that is `kubuntu-desktop`, this is a great time to pause and look things over. Click the arrow beside the To Be Installed label and scroll down the list. You might also want to check out what is removed and what is left unchanged.

Look under the Summary section in the bottom half of this window. You see the number of packages to be installed is a little over 150 and that this will take up just under 500MB of disk space. When you are ready, click Apply and the download begins (see Figure 20-4). The amount of time this takes depends on the speed of your Internet connection.

Figure 20–3   This is a great time to see what packages constitute the Kubuntu desktop. Just click the arrows.

Figure 20–4   The download can take some time, but a progress bar keeps you posted on the details.

After the download is complete, the packages are prepared and the installation proceeds. If you are lucky enough to have a good, high-speed Internet connection, the first part of the Kubuntu desktop installation may have seemed pretty speedy. Now it's time to install the download packages, which can also take a fair bit of time. This might be a good time to take a break, make yourself a cup of your favorite brew, or enjoy a nice glass of wine.

Somewhere in the course of the packages installation, a window pops up asking you to make a decision on your choice of login manager (see Figure 20-5). I covered login managers back in Chapter 3, where we saw the GNOME Display Manager (GDM), GNOME's login manager. The default login manager for KDE is KDM. Either one works fine to start KDE or GNOME, so you can choose to leave things as they are.

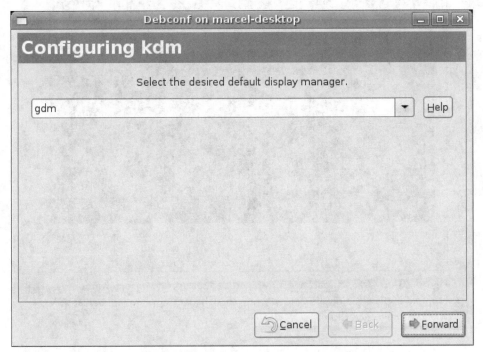

Figure 20–5 Do you stick with the GNOME login screen or do you want to use Kubuntu's KDM?

If you want the complete Kubuntu experience, you may also opt for KDM. Just click the drop-down list and select kdm. Then click Forward to reconfigure. After this process is complete, the installation continues with details scrolling in the progress window's terminal. When the process is complete, you see a nice Changes Applied message in that window (see Figure 20-6).

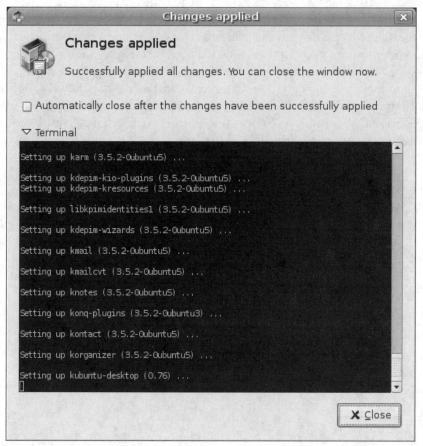

Figure 20–6   As each package is installed and set up, the process window's terminal displays the details below. When the Changes Applied message appears, you can safely click Close.

You're finished. At this point, you can safely log out. You may even want to reboot your system given the number of changes that have occurred. When the login manager comes back up, you have to manually select KDE as your desktop environment; otherwise you are logged in to the last environment you were using. For this example, I'm going to assume that you chose to keep the GDM login screen. To select KDE, click the Options button at the lower left of your login manager and choose Select Session from the pop-up menu. After you do so, a menu appears in the middle of the screen with your available choices (see Figure 20-7).

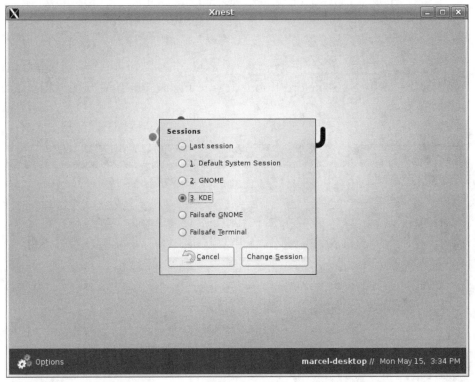

Figure 20–7 To log in to Kubuntu, you need to switch your default session from GNOME to KDE.

Click the radio button to the left of the KDE option, and then click the Change Session button at the bottom. Another message appears asking if you want to make this the new default or whether this is just for the current session. I leave the answer to that question up to you. You may find that you enjoy working in GNOME more than KDE, or the reverse may be true. The great thing here is that you have a choice, and choice is something we are very protective of in the Linux community.

Tip If you choose to use the KDE login manager, things will look different, but the concepts are the same. To select GNOME or KDE for your desktop, click the Session Type button (near the center of the screen) and make your choice from the drop-down list.

Your reward for all this hard work is a shiny new KDE desktop environment and a chance to explore Kubuntu (see Figure 20-8). The fun has just begun!

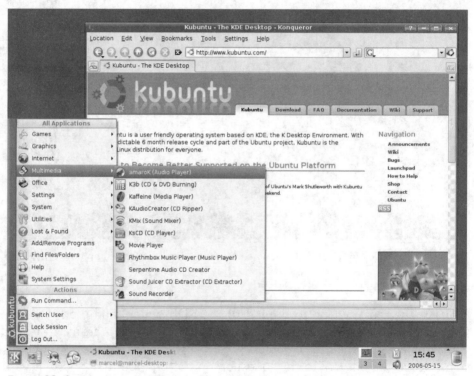

Figure 20–8   Your new Kubuntu desktop. It's time to start exploring again.

Doing It with the Shell

Now that I've had you go through all these installation steps, you may be asking whether there is an easy way to do this from the shell. The short answer is yes. From a terminal shell window, you can type the following:

```
sudo apt-get install kubuntu-desktop
```

Did I just hear a quiet, whispered, "Wow"? Now that you have some appreciation for the power of the shell, turn to Chapter 21 and dig a little deeper.

Resources

KDE Desktop Environment
```
http://www.kde.org
```

Kubuntu Web Site
```
http://www.kubuntu.org
```

Marcel's *Moving to Linux: Kiss the Blue Screen of Death Goodbye!*
```
http://www.marcelgagne.com/mtl2nd.html
```

Chapter

21

Taking Command of Ubuntu Linux

Think of this chapter as an extended Shell Out section. That means it is time to transform you into a master or mistress of the shell. In deciding to join me here, you have identified yourself as one of the bold and curious explorers who really wants to know his Linux systems. Sure, it is possible to work day in and day out with your Linux system and rarely use the command line, but the command line is power. Your reward for continuing to this next level is a deeper understanding of your system and the power to make it do whatever you want.

The things I want to talk about here are basic commands that will serve you well throughout your time with Linux. One of the things I hope to show you is how flexible some of these commands are. With most, you can modify the basic function with command-line switches, flags, or options, and thereby have them yield far more information than a simple execution of the command itself. A little thirst for exploration will open you up to the real potential of everyday commands.

Before I wrap up this chapter, I will also cover editors. Editors aren't a luxury or an option but an eternal necessity in the life of the system administrator. Every once in a while, you will have to edit some configuration file or other in order to get your work done. I'll give you some pointers for making this as simple and painless as possible.

Linux Commands: An Easy Start

When you talk about commands, it invariably means working at the shell level: the command prompt. That's the dollar sign prompt ($), and it is common to many command shells. Some of the commands I will give you require administrative privileges. When this is necessary, I'll have you type **sudo** before the command, at which point you will be asked for your password. It is possible to maintain administrative privileges over the course of several commands by typing **sudo -i**. When you are running in admin mode, you will see a different prompt (#), which goes by many names. In North America, we call it the pound sign or the hash mark. My English lit friends tell me it's an octothorpe. Others call it the tic-tac-toe board.

To exit admin mode, you just type **exit**. However, in my examples, I'll prepend all admin commands with sudo. Whether you choose to enter an extended admin session is something I leave up to you. That said, for most of this chapter, a non-admin, dollar-sign prompt ($) is the way to go. Never run as the administrator unless you need to.

Getting to the Shell

If you are running from a graphical environment, as you likely are, start a Terminal session by clicking Applications on the top panel, and selecting Terminal from the Accessories submenu. The GNOME terminal program supports tabbed shells so you can run multiple shell sessions from one terminal window (see Figure 21-1). Just click File on the menu bar and select Open Tab. You can then click back and forth from one shell to the other. You can even cut and paste between sessions. This is very handy if you are working on multiple systems.

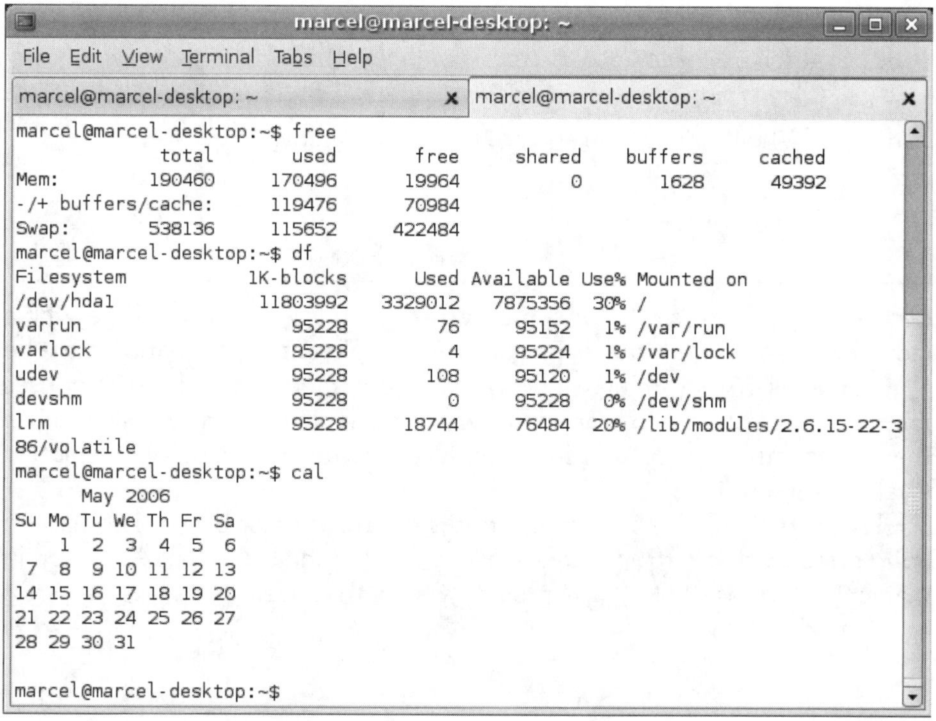

```
marcel@marcel-desktop: ~
File  Edit  View  Terminal  Tabs  Help

marcel@marcel-desktop: ~          x   marcel@marcel-desktop: ~          x

marcel@marcel-desktop:~$ free
             total      used      free    shared   buffers    cached
Mem:        190460    170496     19964         0      1628     49392
-/+ buffers/cache:    119476     70984
Swap:       538136    115652    422484
marcel@marcel-desktop:~$ df
Filesystem         1K-blocks      Used  Available Use% Mounted on
/dev/hda1          11803992   3329012    7875356  30% /
varrun                95228        76      95152   1% /var/run
varlock               95228         4      95224   1% /var/lock
udev                  95228       108      95120   1% /dev
devshm                95228         0      95228   0% /dev/shm
lrm                   95228     18744      76484  20% /lib/modules/2.6.15-22-3
86/volatile
marcel@marcel-desktop:~$ cal
       May 2006
Su Mo Tu We Th Fr Sa
    1  2  3  4  5  6
 7  8  9 10 11 12 13
14 15 16 17 18 19 20
21 22 23 24 25 26 27
28 29 30 31

marcel@marcel-desktop:~$
```

Figure 21–1   Running commands from a bash shell inside the GNOME terminal.

As you work your way through this chapter, you'll notice that I toss in little boxes like the one that follows. If these commands are not already in your arsenal, spend a few minutes playing with them and finding out what they do.

Commands to Know and Love, Part 1

date   Date and time.

df -H   Show me how much free space my disks have, in a nice, human-readable format.

who   Who is logged on to the system?

w   Similar to who but with different information.

cal   Show me a calendar.

`tty`   Identify your workstation.

`echo`   Hello, ello, llo, lo, o, o, o. . . .
            Try typing `echo "Hello world."`

`last`   Who last logged in and are they still logged in?

Working with Files

Let me tell you the secret of computers, operating systems, and the whole industry that surrounds these things: Everything is data. Information is the be all and end all of everything we do with computers. Files are the storehouses for that information and learning how to manipulate them, use and abuse them, and otherwise play with them will still be the point of computers twenty years from now.

The next thing I want to talk about is the three most overlooked files on your system: standard in, standard out, and standard error. A facility in manipulating these "files" will provide you with amazing flexibility when it comes to doing your work.

Commands to Know and Love, Part 2

`ls`   LiSt files.

`cat`   conCATenate files.
            `cat /etc/profile`

`sort`   SORT the contents of a file (or any output for that matter).
            `sort /etc/passwd`

`uniq`   Return only the UNIQue lines—you do this after sorting.

`wc`   Word Count (returns a count of words, characters, and lines).
            `wc /etc/passwd`

`cp`   CoPy files.

`mv`   MoVe, or rename, a file.

`rm`   ReMove, or delete, a file.

`more`   Allows easy paging of large text files.

`less`   Like the `more` command, but with serious attitude.

File Naming Conventions

Valid filenames may contain *almost* any character. You do have to pay some attention to the names you come up with. Your Linux system allows filenames up to 255 characters in length. How you define filenames can save you a lot of hassle, as I will soon demonstrate.

Some valid filename examples include the following:

```
fish
duck
program_2.01
a.out
letter.to.mom.who.I.dont.write.often.enough.as.it.is
.bash_profile
```

Notice the last name in particular. It starts with a dot (or a *period*, if you prefer). Normally, this type of file is invisible with a default listing. Starting a filename with a dot is a way to make a file somewhat invisible. This is good to know if you don't want to burden file listings with a lot of noise. It is also the way that a cracker might hide her tracks should she break into your system— by creating a directory that starts with a dot. To see these so-called dot files, use the ls command with the -d flag (ls -d).

Listing Files with Emotion!

The ls command seems so simple, and yet it has a number of options that can give you tons of information. Change to something like the /etc directory and try these options:

```
cd /etc
ls --color
ls -b
ls -lS
ls -lt
```

The first listing shows different types of files and directories in color. The second (-b) shows octal representations for files that might have been created with control characters. Depending on the terminal you are using, the default is to show question marks or simply blanks. If you need to access (or delete) the file, it helps to know what it is really called. The third and fourth options control sorting. The -ls option gives you a long listing (lots of information) sorted by file size. The last option (-lt) sorts by time with the newest files at the top of the list and the oldest at the bottom.

A Peek at Metacharacters

Metacharacters are special characters that have particular meaning to your shell—the dollar sign or hash mark prompt where you do your work. The two metacharacters I want to look at are the asterisk and the question mark. The following is what they mean to the shell:

*   Match any number of characters

?   Match a single character

Extending our talk of listing files, you could list all files containing ackle by using this command:

```
$ ls *ackle*
hackle hackles tackles
```

Similarly, you could find all the words that start with an h like this:

```
$ ls h*
hackle hackles
```

Now, if you want to see all the seven-letter words in your directory, use this command:

```
$ ls ???????
hackles tackles
```

Each question mark represents a single letter position.

File Permissions in the Shell

In Chapter 4, I showed you how to look at file permissions with Nautilus. When you use the ls -l command, you are doing the same thing; look at basic Linux security at the file (or directory) level. Here is an example of a long ls listing:

```
$ ls -l
total 3
drwxr-x---  5 root     system    512  Dec 25 12:01   presents
-r-xr--r--  1 zonthar  users     123  Dec 24 09:30   wishlist
-rw-rw----  1 zonthar  users     637  Nov 15 09:30   griflong
```

The first entry under the total column shows a directory (I'll talk about the next nine characters in a moment). The first character is a d, which indicates a directory. At the end of each line, you find the directory or filename—in my example, they are presents, wishlist, and griflong. Because the first character in the permissions field is d, presents is a directory.

The other nine characters (characters 2 through 10) indicate permissions for the user or owner of the file (first three), the group (second group of three), and others or everyone else (last three). In the first line, user root has read (r), write (w), and execute (x) permissions, whereas the system group has only read and execute. The three dashes at the end imply that no one else has any permissions. The next two files are owned by the user called zonthar.

Quick Tip Remember user, group, and other (ugo). You will find them useful later when I cover changing file and directory permissions.

Not-So-Hidden Files

When you take your first look at valid filenames, remember that I mentioned that files starting with a period are hidden. As a result, creating directories or files in this way is a favorite trick of system crackers. Get used to the idea of listing your directories and files with a -a option so that you see everything that's there. Look for anything unusual.

Keep in mind, however, that a number of applications create dotted directory names in your home directory so that you are generally not burdened with seeing all these configuration areas. That's great, except that you should know what you've got on your disk. Always balance your need for convenience with a healthy curiosity. A quick ls -a in your home directory shows you some files (and directories) you will become very familiar with as time goes on. Here is an example of what you will see:

```
.Xauthority .bash_history  .bash_profile  .gnupg  .gnome2
```

Strange Filenames That Just Don't Go Away

Every once in a while, you do a listing of your directory and some strange file appears that you just know isn't supposed to be there. Don't panic. It's not necessarily a cracker at work. You may have mistyped something and you just need to get rid of the error. The problem is that you can't. Case in point: I *accidentally* created a couple of files with hard-to-deal-with names. I don't want them there, but trying to delete them does not work. Here are the files:

```
-another_file
 onemorefile
```

Here's what happens when I try to delete them:

```
$ rm -another_file
rm: invalid option -- a
Try 'rm --help' for more information.
```

What about that other file?

```
$ rm onemorefile
rm: cannot remove 'onemorefile': No such file or directory
```

The problem with the first file is that the hyphen makes it look like I am passing an option to the `rm` command. To get around this problem, I use the double-dash option on the `rm` command. Using two dashes tells the command that what follows is not an option to that command. Here I go again:

```
$ rm -- -another_file
$
```

Bravo! By the way, this double-dash syntax applies to many other commands that need to recognize potentially weird filenames. Now, what about the second file? It looked fine, didn't it? If you look very closely, you see that there is a space in front of the leading o, so simply telling `rm` to remove the file doesn't work either, because `onemorefile` is not the filename. It is actually " onemorefile" (preceded by a space). So, I need to pass the space as well; to do that, I give the full name (space included) by enclosing the filename in double quotes.

```
$ rm " otherfile"
$
```

More on rm (or, "Oops! I didn't really mean that")

389

More on rm (or, "Oops! I didn't really mean that")

When you delete a file with Linux, it is gone. If you didn't really mean to delete (or rm) a file, you quickly find out if you have been keeping good backups. The other option is to check with the rm command before you delete a file. Rather than simply typing **rm** followed by the filename, try this instead:

```
rm -i file_name1 file_name2 file_name3
```

The -i option tells rm to work in interactive mode. For each of the three files in the example, rm pauses and asks if you really mean it.

```
rm : remove 'file_name1'?
```

If you like to be more wordy than that, you can also try rm --interactive file_name, but that goes against the system administrator's first principle.

System Administrator's First Principle Simplifying things. If your solution makes things more complicated, something has gone terribly wrong.

Of course, in following the system administrator's first principle, you could remove all the files starting with the word file by using the asterisk:

```
rm -i file*
```

Making Your Life Easier with alias

You might find that you want to use the -i option every time you delete something, just in case. It's a lot easier to type Y in confirmation than it is to go looking through your backups. The problem is that you are adding keystrokes, and everyone knows that system administrators are notoriously lazy people. Then, there's that whole issue of the first principle—that's why we shortened *list* to ls, after all. Don't despair, though—Linux has a way. It is the alias command.

```
alias rm='rm -i'
```

Now, every time you execute the `rm` command, it checks with you beforehand. This behavior is only in effect until you log out. If you want this to be the default behavior for `rm`, you should add the `alias` command to your local `.bashrc` file. If you want this to be the behavior for every user on your system, you should add your `alias` definitions to the system-wide version of this file, `/etc/bashrc`, and save yourself even more time. There may already be `alias` definitions set up for you, even if only one or two. The first way to find out what has been set up for you is to type the `alias` command on a blank line.

```
$ alias
alias ls='ls --color=auto'
```

Using the `cat` command, you can look in your local `.bashrc` file and discover the same information.

```
marcel@ubuntu:~$ cat .bashrc
# enable color support of ls and also add handy aliases
if [ "$TERM" != "dumb" ]; then
    eval "`dircolors -b`"
    alias ls='ls --color=auto'
    #alias dir='ls --color=auto --format=vertical'
    #alias vdir='ls --color=auto --format=long'
fi

# some more ls aliases
#alias ll='ls -l'
#alias la='ls -A'
#alias l='ls -CF'
```

 Note The preceding hash marks (#) represent comments and not the admin command prompt.

As you can see, there are other suggested aliases that you can uncomment by removing that leading hash mark. Incidentally, here are a few I like to add to everyone's `.bashrc` file (or to the global `/etc/bash.bashrc`):

```
alias rm='rm -i'
alias cp='cp -i'
alias mv='mv -i'
```

Isn't this interesting? Notice the two other commands here, the cp (copy files) and mv (rename files) commands, both of which have the -i flag as well. They too can be set to work interactively, requiring your verification before you overwrite something important. Let's say that I want to make a backup copy of a file called important_info using the cp command.

```
cp important_info important_info.backup
```

Perhaps I am actually trying to rename the file (rather than copy it). For this, I would use the mv command.

```
mv important_info not_so_important_info
```

The only time you would be bothered by an "Are you sure?" type of message is if the file already existed. In that case, you would get a message like the following:

```
mv: overwrite 'not_so_important_info'?
```

Forcing the Issue

Inevitably, you're next question is this: What do you do if you are copying, moving, or removing multiple files and you don't want to be bothered with being asked each time when you've aliased everything to be interactive? Use the -f flag, which, as you might have surmised, stands for *force*. Once again, this is a flag that is quite common with many Linux commands—either a -f or a --force.

Imagine a hypothetical scenario in which you move a group of log files daily so that you always have the previous day's files as backup (but just for one day). If your mv command is aliased interactively, you can get around it like this:

```
mv -f *.logs /path_to/backup_directory/
```

Musing Yes, I know that mv looks more like *move* than *rename*. In fact, you do move directories and files using the mv command. Think of the file as a vessel for your data. When you rename a file with mv, you are moving the data into a new container for the same data, so it isn't strictly a rename—you really are moving files. Looking at it that way, it doesn't seem so strange. Sort of.

The reverse of the alias command is unalias. If you want your mv command to return to its original functionality, use this command:

```
unalias mv
```

Standard Input and Standard Output

It may sound complicated, but it isn't. Standard in (STDIN) is where the system expects to find its input. This is usually the keyboard, although it can be a program or shell script. When you change that default, you call it *redirecting* from STDIN.

Standard out (STDOUT) is where the system expects to direct its output, usually the terminal screen. Again, redirection of STDOUT is at the discretion of whatever command or script is executing at the time. The chain of events from STDIN to STDOUT looks something like this:

```
standard in  -> Linux command  ->  standard out
```

STDIN is often referred to as *fd0*, or file descriptor 0, whereas STDOUT is usually thought of as *fd1*. There is also standard error (STDERR), where the system reports any errors in program execution. By default, this is also the terminal. To redirect STDOUT, use the greater-than sign (>). As you might have guessed, to redirect from STDIN, you use the less-than sign (<). But what exactly does that mean? Let's try an experiment. Randomly search your brain and pick a handful of names. Got them? Good. Now type the cat command and redirect its STDOUT to a file called random_names.

```
cat > random_names
```

Your cursor just sits there and waits for you to do something, so type those names, pressing <Enter> after each one. What's happening here is that `cat` is taking its input from `STDIN` and writing it out to your new file. You can also write the command like this:

```
cat - 1> random_names
```

The hyphen literally means `standard in` to the command. The 1 stands for file descriptor 1. This is good information, and you will use it later. Finished with your random names list? When you are done, press <Ctrl+D> to finish. <Ctrl+D>, by the way, stands for EOF, or end of file.

```
Marie Curie
Albert Einstein
Mark Twain
Wolfgang Amadeus Mozart
Stephen Hawking
Hedy Lamarr
^D
```

If you `cat` this file, the names are written to `STDOUT`—in this case, your terminal window. You can also give `cat` several files at the same time. For instance, you could do something like this:

```
cat file1 file2 file3
```

Each file would be listed one right after the other. That output could then be redirected into another file. You could also have it print out the same file over and over (`cat random_names random_names random_names`). `cat` isn't fussy about these things and deals with binary files (programs) just as quickly. Beware of using `cat` to print out the contents of a program to your terminal screen. At worst, your terminal session locks up or rewards you with a lot of beeping and weird characters.

 Quick Tip If you get caught in such a situation and all the characters on your screen appear as junk, try typing `echo` and then pressing <Ctrl+V> and <Ctrl+O>. If you can still type, you can also try typing `stty sane` and then pressing <Ctrl+J>. This works on every system, but some systems, including your Ubuntu system, also provide a command called `reset`, which returns your terminal session to some kind of sane look.

Redirecting STDIN works pretty much the same way, except that you use the less-than sign instead. Using the `sort` command, let's take that file of random names and work with it. Many commands that work with files can take their input directly from that file. Unless told otherwise, `cat` and `sort` will think that the word following the command is a filename. That's why you did the STDIN redirection thing. Yes, that's right: STDIN is just another file. Sort of.

```
sort random_names
```

Of course, the result is that you get all your names printed out in alphabetical order. You could have also specified that `sort` take its input from a redirected STDIN. It looks a bit strange, but this is perfectly valid.

```
marcel@ubuntu:~$ sort < random_names
Albert Einstein
Hedy Lamarr
Marie Curie
Mark Twain
Stephen Hawking
Wolfgang Amadeus Mozart
```

One more variation involves defining your STDIN (as you did previously) and specifying a different STDOUT all on the same line. In the following example, I redirect *from* my file and redirect that output *to* a new file:

```
sort < random_names > sorted_names
```

Pipes and Piping

Sometimes, the thing that makes the most sense is to feed the output from one command directly into another command without having to resort to files in between at every step of the way. This is called *piping*. The symbolism is not that subtle: Imagine pieces of pipe connecting one command with another. Not until you run out of pipe does the command's output emerge. The pipe symbol is the broken vertical bar on your keyboard usually located just below or (depending on the keyboard) just above the Enter key and sharing space with the backslash key. Here's how it works:

```
cat random_names | sort | wc -w > num_names
```

In the preceding example, the output from the `cat` command is piped into `sort`, whose output is then piped into the `wc` command (that's *word count*). The `-w` flag tells `wc` to count the number of words in `random_names`. So far, so good.

That `cat` at the beginning is actually redundant, but I want to stack up a few commands for you to give you an idea of the power of piping. Ordinarily, I would write that command as follows:

```
sort random_names | wc -w > num_names
```

The `cat` is extraneous because `sort` incorporates its function. Using pipes is a great timesaver because you don't always need to have output at every step of the way.

`tee`: A Very Special Pipe

Suppose that you want to send the output of a command to another command, but you also want to see the results at some point. Using the previous word count example, if you want a sorted list of names, but you also want the word count, you might have to use two different commands: one to generate the sorted list and another to count the number of words. Wouldn't it be nice if you could direct part of the output one way and have the rest continue in another direction? For this, use the `tee` command.

```
sort random_names | tee sorted_list | wc -w > num_names
```

The output from `sort` is now sitting in a file called `sorted_list`, whereas the rest of the output continues on to `wc` for a word count.

STDERR

What about `STDERR`? Some commands (many, in fact) treat the error output differently than the `STDOUT`. If you are running the command at your terminal and that's all you want, there is no problem. Sometimes, though, the output is quite wordy and you need to capture it and look at it later. Unfortunately, using the STDOUT redirect (the greater-than sign) is only going to be so useful. Error messages that are generated (such as warning messages from a compilation) go to the terminal as before. One way to deal with this is to start by redirecting STDERR to STDOUT, and then redirect that to a file. Here's the line I use for this:

```
command_name 2>&1 > logfile.out
```

Remember that file descriptor 2 is STDERR and that file descriptor 1 is STDOUT. That's what that 2>&1 construct is all about. You are redirecting fd2 to fd1 and then redirecting that output to the file of your choice. Using that program compilation example, you might wind up with something like this:

```
make -f Makefile.linux 2>&1 > compilation.output
```

 Quick Tip The final greater-than sign in the preceding example could be eliminated completely. When using the 2>&1 construct, it is assumed that what follows is a filename.

The Road to Nowhere

If the command happens to be verbose by nature and doesn't have a quiet switch, you can redirect that STDOUT and STDERR noise to what longtime Linux users like to call the *bit bucket*, a special file called /dev/null—literally, a road to nowhere. Anything fed to the bit bucket takes up no space and is never seen or heard from again. When I was in school, we would tell people to shut up by saying, "Dev null it, will you?" As you can see, we were easily amused.

To redirect output to the bit bucket, use the STDOUT redirection.

```
command -option > /dev/null
```

If, for some strange reason, you want to sort the output of the random_names files and you do not want to see the output, you can redirect the whole thing to /dev/null in this way:

```
sort random_names > /dev/null
```

Using the program compilation example where you had separate STDOUT and STDERR streams, you can combine the output to the bit bucket.

```
make -F makefile.linux 2>&1 /dev/null
```

That's actually a crazy example because you do want to see what goes on, but redirecting both STDOUT and STDERR to /dev/null is quite common when dealing with automated processes running in the background.

Linux Commands: Working with Directories

There is another batch of commands suited to working with directory files (directories being just another type of file).

pwd   Print Working Directory

cd   Change to a new Directory

mkdir   MaKe or create a new DIRectory

mv   MoVe directories, or files, and rename them

rmdir   ReMove or delete DIRectories

One way to create a complicated directory structure is to use the mkdir command to create each and every directory.

```
mkdir /dir1
mkdir /dir1/sub_dir
mkdir /dir1/sub_dir/yetanotherdir
```

You could save yourself a few keystrokes and use the -p flag. This tells mkdir to create any parent directories that might not already exist. If you happen to like a lot of verbiage from your system, you could also add the --verbose flag for good measure.

```
mkdir -p /dir/sub_dir/yetanotherdir
```

To rename or move a directory, the format is the same as you used with a file or group of files. Use the mv command.

```
mv path_to_dir new_path_to_dir
```

Removing a directory can be a bit more challenging. The command `rmdir` seems simple enough. In fact, removing this directory was no problem:

```
$ rmdir trivia_dir
```

Removing this one, however, gave me an error:

```
$ rmdir junk_dir
rmdir: junk_dir: Directory not empty
```

You can only use `rmdir` to remove an empty directory. There is a `-p` option (as in *parents*) that enables you to remove a directory structure. For instance, you could remove a couple of levels like this:

```
rmdir -p junk_dir/level1/level2/level3
```

> *Warning* Beware of the `rm -rf *` command. Better yet, *never use it*. If you must delete an entire directory structure, change the directory to the one above it and explicitly remove the directory. This is also the first and best reason to do as much of your work as possible as a normal user and not root. Because root is all powerful, it is quite capable of completely destroying your system. Imagine that you are in the top-level directory (`/`) instead of `/home/myname/junkdir` when you initiate that recursive delete. It is far too easy to make this kind of mistake. *Beware.*

All the directories from `junk_dir` on down are removed, but *only* if they are empty of files. A better approach is to use the `rm` command with the `-r`, or *recursive*, option. Unless you are deleting only a couple of files or directories, you want to use the `-f` option as well.

```
$ rm -rf junk_dir
```

There's No Place Like $HOME

Yeah, I know. It's a pretty cheesy pun, but I like it.

Because you've had a chance to play with a few directory commands, I'd like to take a moment and talk about a very special directory. Every user on your system has a home directory. That directory can be referenced with the $HOME environment variable. To get back to your home directory at any time, simply type **cd $HOME** and no matter where you were, there you are. Actually, you only need to type **cd**, press <Enter>, and you are home. The $HOME is implied.

The $HOME shortcut is great for shell scripts or anytime you want to save yourself some keystrokes. For instance, say you want to copy the file remote.file to your home directory and you are sitting in /usr/some_remote/dir. You could use either of the next two commands:

```
cp remote.file /home/my_username
cp remote.file $HOME
```

The second command saves you keystrokes, and the more time you spend doing system administration, the more you will love shortcuts like this. To save the maximum keystrokes, you can also use the tilde (~), a special character synonym for $HOME.

```
cp remote.file ~
```

More on File Permissions

What you can and can't do with a file, as defined by your username or group name, is pretty much wrapped up in four little letters. Look at the following listing (using ls -l) for an example. The permissions are at the beginning of each line.

```
-rw-r--r--  1 mgagne mgagne       937 May 17 13:22 conf_details
-rwxr-xr-x  1 root   root   45916220 Apr  4 12:25 gimp
-rw-r--r--  1 root   root        826 Feb 12 09:43 mail_test
-rw-r--r--  1 mgagne mgagne     44595 May 17 13:22 sk_open.jpg
```

Each of these letters can be referenced by a number. They are r, w, x, and s. Their numerical representations are 4, 2, 1, and "it depends." To understand all that, you need to do a little binary math.

Reading from right to left, think of the x as being in position 0. The w, then, is in position 1 and the r is in position 2. Here's the way it works:

2 to the power of 0 equals 1   (x is 1)
2 to the power of 1 equals 2   (w is 2)
2 to the power of 2 equals 4   (r is 4)

To specify multiple permissions, you can add the numbers together. If you want to specify both read and execute permissions, simply add 4 and 1 and you get 5. For all permissions (rwx), use 7.

File permissions are referenced in groups of three rwx sections. The r stands for read, the w means write, and the x denotes that the file is executable.

Although these permissions are arranged in three groups of three rwx combinations, their meaning is the same in all cases. The difference has to do with who they represent rather than the permissions themselves. The first of these three represents the user, the second trio stands for the group permissions, and the third represents everybody that doesn't fit into either of the first two categories.

The commands you use for changing these basic permissions are chmod, chown, and chgrp.

chmod   CHange the MODe of a file (a.k.a. its permissions)

chown   CHange the OWNer of the file or directory

chgrp   CHange the GRouP of the file or directory

User and Group Ownership

Let's pretend you have a file called `mail_test` and you want to change its ownership from the root user to natika. Because root is the only user that can make that change, you need to prepend your command with `sudo`. This is very simple.

```
sudo chown natika mail_test
```

Tip Remember that you can also type **sudo -i** to enter a root shell, should you need to do several administrative commands. Then, just type **exit** to return to the regular non-admin shell.

You can also use the -R option to change ownership recursively. Let's use a directory called test_directory as an example. Once again, it belongs to root and you want to make every file in that directory (and below) owned by natika.

```
sudo chown -R natika test_directory
```

The format for changing group ownership is just as easy. Let's change the group ownership of test_directory (previously owned by root) so that it and all its files and subdirectories belong to group accounts.

```
sudo chgrp -R accounts test_directory
```

You can even combine the two formats. In the following example, the ownership of the entire finance_data directory changes to natika as the owner and accounts as the group. To do so, you use this form of the chown command:

```
sudo chown -R natika:accounts finance_data
```

Quick Tip You can use the -R flag to recursively change everything in a subdirectory with chgrp and chmod as well.

Now, you are aware that files (and directories) are owned by some user and some group. This brings us to the next question.

Who Can Do What?

From time to time, you need to modify file permissions. One reason has to do with security. However, the most common reason is to make a shell script file executable. This is done with the chmod command.

```
chmod mode filename
```

For instance, if you have a script file called `list_users`, you make it executable with the following command:

```
chmod +x list_users
```

That command allows execute permissions for all users. If you want to make the file executable for the owner and group only, you specify it on the command line like this:

```
chmod u+x,g+x list_users
```

The `u` means user (the owner of the file, really), and `g` stands for group. The reason you use `u` for the owner instead of `o` is that the `o` is being used for "other," meaning everyone else. The `chmod +x list_users` command can then be expressed as `chmod u+x,g+x,o+x list_users`. Unfortunately, this starts to get cumbersome. Now let's look at a much more complicated set of permissions. Imagine that you want your `list_users` script to have read, write, and execute permissions for the owner, read and execute for the group, and read-only for anybody else. The long way is to do this is as follows:

```
chmod u=rwx,g=rx,o=r list_users
```

Notice the equal sign (=) construct rather than the plus sign (+). That's because the plus sign adds permissions, and in this case you want them to be absolute. If the original permissions of the file allowed write access for other, the plus sign construct would not have removed the execute permission. Using the minus sign (–) removes permissions. If you want to take away execute permission entirely from a file, you can do something like this:

```
chmod -x list_users
```

One way to simplify the `chmod` command is to remember that `r` is 4, `w` is 2, and `x` is 1, and add up the numbers in each of the three positions. `rwx` is then $4 + 2 + 1$, or 7. `r-x` translates to $4 + 1$, and `x` is simply 1. That monster from the second to last example can then be rewritten like this:

```
chmod 751 list_users
```

Who Was That Masked User?

Every time you create a file, you are submitted to a default set of permissions. Go ahead. Create a blank file using the touch command. I am going to call my blank file fish.

```
$ touch fish
```

Now have a look at its permissions by doing an ls -l.

```
$ ls -l
-rw-r--r-- 1 mgagne mgagne 0 2006-03-10 14:31 fish
```

Without doing anything whatsoever, your file has read and write permissions for both the user and group, and read permission for everybody else. This happens because you have a default file-creation mask of 002. You can discover this using the umask command.

```
$ umask
0022
```

The 2 is subtracted from the possible set of permissions, rwx (or 7). 7 – 0 remains 7, while 7 – 2 is 5. But wait—5 stands for r-x, or read and execute. How is it that the file only shows a read bit set? That's because newly created files are not set executable. At best, they provide read and write permissions for everyone. Another way to display this information is by using the -S flag. Instead of the numeric output, you get a symbolic mask displayed.

```
$ umask -S
u=rwx,g=rwx,o=rx
```

If you have an application that requires you to provide a default set of permissions for all the files you create, change umask to reflect that inside your scripts. As an example, let's pretend that your program or script creates text files that you want everyone to be able to read (444). Because the execute bit isn't a factor anyway, if you mask out the write bit using a 2 all around, everybody will have read permission. Set your umask to 222, create another file (called duck this time), and then do an ls -l to check things out.

```
marcel@ubuntu:~$ umask 222
marcel@ubuntu:~$ touch duck
marcel@ubuntu:~$ ls -l
-r--r--r-- 1 mgagne mgagne 0 2006-03-10 15:26 duck
```

The `setuid` Bit

Aside from those three permission bits (read, write, and execute), there is one other very important one: the s bit, sometimes referred to as the `setuid` or `setgid` bit depending on its position.

The reasoning behind this particular bit follows. Sometimes, you want a program to act as though you are logged in as a different user. For example, you may want a certain program to run as the root user. This would be a program that you want a nonadministrative user to run, but (for whatever reason) this program needs to read or write files that are exclusively root's. The `sendmail` program is a perfect example of that. The program needs to access *privileged* functions to do its work, but you want regular (nonroot) users to be able to send mail as well.

The `setuid` bit is a variation on the execute bit. To make the hypothetical program `ftl_travel` executable by anyone but with root's privileges, you change its permissions as follows:

```
chmod u+s ftl_travel
```

The next step, as you might guess, is to combine full permissions and the `setuid` bit. Start by thinking of the `setuid` and `setgid` bits as another triplet of permissions. Just as you could reference r, w, and x as 4, 2, and 1, you can also reference `setuid` as 4, `setgid` as 2, and other (which you don't worry about).

So, using a nice, complicated example, let's make that command so that it has read, write, and execute permissions for the owner, read and execute permissions for the group, and no permissions for anyone else. To those with execute permission, though, you want to have it `setuid`. You could also represent that command either symbolically or in a numerical way.

```
chmod u=rwxs,g=rx,o= ftl_travel
chmod 4750 ftl_travel
```

The 4 in the front position represents the setuid bit. If you want to make the program setgid instead, you can change that to 2. And, yes, if you want the executable to maintain both the owner's permissions and that of the group, you can simply add 4 and 2 to get 6. The resulting set of permissions is as follows:

```
chmod 6750 ftl_travel
```

Changing the setuid bit (or setgid) is not strictly a case of providing administrative access to nonroot users. This can be anything. You might have a database package that operates under only one user ID, or you may want all users to access a program as though they were part of a specific group. You have to decide.

 Important Note You cannot use the setuid or setgid bit for shell scripts (although there are Perl hooks to do this). This doesn't work for security reasons. If you need to have a script execute with a set of permissions other than its own, you have to write a little C program that wraps around your script and then allows the program rather than the script to have setuid (or setgid) permissions.

The lesson here is that making something setuid immediately raises security issues. Know why you are taking this approach and consider the risks.

Finding Anything

One of the most useful commands in your arsenal is the find command. This powerhouse doesn't get the credit it deserves. Generally speaking, find is used to list files and redirect (or pipe) that output to do some simple reporting or backups. There it ends. If anything, this should only be the beginning. As versatile as find is, you should take some time to get to know it. Let me give you a whirlwind tour of this awesome command. Let's start with the basics:

```
find starting_dir [options]
```

One of those options is `-print`, which only makes sense if you want to see any kind of output from this command. You could easily get a listing of every file on the system by starting at the top and recursively listing the disk.

```
find / -print
```

Although that might be interesting and you might want to redirect that to a file for future reference, it is only so useful. It makes more sense to search for something. For instance, look for all the JPEG-type image files sitting on your disk. Because you know that these images end in a `.jpg` extension, you can use that to search.

```
find / -name "*.jpg" -print
```

Depending on the power of your system, this can take a while and you are likely to get a lot of Permission Denied messages (particularly as you traverse a directory called `/proc`). If you are running this as a user other than root, you likely get a substantial number of Permission Denied messages. At this point, the usefulness of `find` should start to become apparent because a lot of images stashed away in various parts of the disk can certainly add up as far as disk space is concerned. Try it with an `.avi` or `.mpg` extension to look for video clips (which can be very large).

If you are trying to locate old files or particularly large files, try the following example. Look for anything that has not been modified (this is the `-mtime` parameter) or accessed (the `-atime` parameter) in the last 12 months. The `-o` flag is the OR in this equation.

```
$ find /data1/Marcel -size +1024 \
\( -mtime +365 -o -atime +365 \) -ls
```

A few techniques introduced here are worth noting. The backslashes in front of the round brackets are *escape characters;* they are there to make sure the shell does not interpret them in ways you do not want it to—in this case, the open and close parentheses on the second line. The first line also has a backslash at the end. This is to indicate a line break, as the whole command does not fit neatly on one line of this page. If you typed it exactly as shown without any backslashes, it would not work; however, the backslashes in the second line are essential. The preceding command also searches for files that are greater than 500KB in size. That is what the `-size +1024` means because

1024 refers to 512-byte blocks. The -ls at the end of the command tells the system to do a long listing of any files it finds that fit my search criteria.

Earlier in this chapter, you learned about setuid and setgid files. Keeping an eye on where these files are and determining if they belong there are important aspects of maintaining security on your system. Here's a command that examines the permissions on your files (the -perm option) and reports back what it finds.

```
find / -type f \( -perm -4000 -o -perm -2000 \) -ls
```

You may want to redirect this output to a file that you can later peruse and decide on what course of action to take. Now let's look at another find example to help you uncover what types of files you are looking at. Your Linux system has another command called file that can deliver useful information on files and what they are, whether they are executables, text files, or movie clips. Here's a sample of some of the files in my home directory as reported by file:

```
$  file $HOME/*
code.layout:            ASCII text
cron.txt:               data
dainbox:                International language text
dainbox.gz:             gzip compressed data, deflated,
original filename, last modified: Sat Oct 7 13:21:14 2000,
os: Unix
definition.htm:         HTML document text
gatekeeper.1:           troff or preprocessor input text
gatekeeper.man:         English text
gatekeeper.pl:          perl commands text
hilarious.mpg:          MPEG video stream data
```

The next step is to modify the find command by adding a -exec clause so that I can get the file command's output on what find locates.

```
$ find /data1/Marcel -size +1024  \
\( -mtime +365 -o -atime +365 \) -ls -exec file {} \;
```

The open and close braces that follow -exec file mean that the list of files generated should be passed to whatever command follows the -exec option (in other words, the command you will be *executing*). The backslash followed by a semicolon at the end is required for the command to be valid. As you can see, `find` is extremely powerful. Learning to harness that power can make your administrative life much easier. You'll encounter `find` again at various times in this book.

Using `grep`

`grep`: Global regular expression parser.

That definition of the acronym is one of many. Don't be surprised if you hear it called the *gobble research exercise program* instead. Basically, `grep`'s purpose in life is to make it easy for you to find strings in text files. This is its basic format:

```
grep pattern file(s)
```

As an example, let's say you want to find out if you have a user named natika in your `/etc/passwd` file. The trouble is that you have 500 lines in the file.

```
$ grep natika /etc/passwd
natika:x:504:504:Natika the Cat:/home/natika:/bin/bash
```

Sometimes you just want to know if a particular chunk of text exists in a file, but you don't know which file specifically. Using the `-l` option with `grep` enables you to list filenames only, rather than lines (`grep`'s default behavior). In the next example, I am going to look for natika's name in my email folders. Because I don't know whether natika is capitalized in the mail folders, I'll introduce another useful flag to `grep`: the `-i` flag. It tells the command to ignore case.

```
$ grep -i -l natika *
Baroque music
Linux Stuff
Personal stuff
Silliness
sent-mail
```

As you can see, the lines with the word (or name) natika are not displayed—only the files. Here's another great use for `grep`. Every once in a while, you want to scan for a process. The reason might be to locate a misbehaving terminal or to find out what a specific login is doing. Because `grep` can filter out patterns in your files or your output, it is a useful tool. Rather than trying to scan through 400 lines on your screen for one command, let `grep` narrow the search for you. When `grep` finds the target text, it displays that line on your screen.

```
$ ps ax | grep getty
4779 tty1       Ss+    0:00 /sbin/getty 38400 tty1
4780 tty2       Ss+    0:00 /sbin/getty 38400 tty2
4781 tty3       Ss+    0:00 /sbin/getty 38400 tty3
4782 tty4       Ss+    0:00 /sbin/getty 38400 tty4
4783 tty5       Ss+    0:00 /sbin/getty 38400 tty5
4784 tty6       Ss+    0:00 /sbin/getty 38400 tty6
3083 pts/9      S+     0:00 grep getty
```

Here, the `ps ax` command lists the processes, and then the `|` pipes the output to the `grep` command. Notice the last line that shows the `grep` command itself in the process list. You use that line as the launch point to one last example with `grep`. If you want to scan for strings other than the one specified, use the `-v` option. Using this option, it's a breeze to list all processes currently running on the system but ignore any that have a reference to root.

```
ps ax | grep -v root
```

And speaking of processes . . .

Processes

You are going to hear a lot about processes, process status, monitoring processes, or killing processes. Reducing the whole discussion to its simplest form, all you have to remember is that any command you run is a process. Processes are also sometimes referred to as *jobs*.

Question: So what constitutes a process?
Answer: Everything.

The session program that executes your typed commands (the shell) is a process. The tools I am using to write this chapter are creating several processes. Every terminal session you have open, every link to the Internet, every game you have running—all these programs generate one or more processes on your system. In fact, there can be hundreds, even thousands, of processes running on your system at any given time. To see your own processes, try the following command:

```
# ps
  PID TTY            TIME CMD
 3119 pts/11     00:00:00 su
 3120 pts/11     00:00:00 bash
 3132 pts/11     00:00:00 ps
```

For a bit more detail, try using the u option. This shows all processes owned by you that currently have a controlling terminal. Even if you are running as root, you do not see system processes in this view. If you add the a option to that, you see all the processes running on that terminal—in this case, revealing the subshell that did the su to root.

```
# ps au
USER      PID %CPU %MEM   VSZ   RSS TTY     STAT START   TIME COMMAND
root     4755  3.4  9.1 65376 41288 tty7    Ss+  Feb21 858:59 /usr/X11R6/bin/
mgagne  24156  0.0  0.1  4540   824 pts/2   Ss   Mar03   0:00 /bin/bash
mgagne  24449  0.0  0.2  4540  1200 pts/3   Ss   Mar03   0:00 /bin/bash
mgagne  24462  1.3  3.5 63260 15916 pts/3   Sl   Mar03 132:09 ./skype
mgagne  10069  0.0  0.2  4540  1148 pts/5   Ss   Mar07   0:00 /bin/bash
mgagne  15479  0.0  0.1  5096   824 pts/5   S+   Mar07   0:00 ssh -X -l mgagn
root     3119  0.0  0.2  3696  1192 pts/11  S    15:31   0:00 su
root     3120  0.0  0.4  4024  1876 pts/11  S    15:31   0:00 bash
root     3134  0.0  0.2  2396  1020 pts/11  R+   15:31   0:00 ps au
mgagne  26060  0.0  0.2  4544  1188 pts/1   Ss+  Mar09   0:00 /bin/bash
```

The most common thing you will do is add an x option. This shows all processes, controlled by your terminal or not, as well as those of other users. The administrator also wants to know about the l option, which stands for long. It is particularly useful because it shows the parent process of every process, because every process has another process that launched (or spawned) it. This is the parent process of the process ID. In sysadmin short form, this is the PPID of the PID. When your system starts up, the first process is called init. It is the master process and the superparent of every process that comes until such a time as the system is rebooted. Try this incarnation of the ps command for an interesting view of your system:

```
# ps alxww | more
F UID   PID PPID PRI NI  VSZ RSS WCHAN  STAT TTY  TIME COMMAND
4   0     1    0  16  0 1568 524 -       S    ?   0:04 init [2]
1   0     2    1  34 19    0   0 ksofti  SN   ?   0:00 [ksoftirqd/0]
1   0   653    6  10 -5    0   0 serio_  S<   ?   0:00
5   0  1886    1  17 -4 2424 892 -       S<s  ?   0:01 /sbin/udevd --daemon
1   0  2630    1  20  0    0   0 -       S    ?   0:00 [shpchpd_event]
1   0  2643    6  10 -5    0   0 gamepo  S<   ?   0:00 [kgameportd]
4   0  3371    1  15  0 1680 488 syslog  Ss   ?   0:00 /bin/dd bs 1 if /proc/kmsg of
                                                       /var/run/klogd/kmsg
1 103  3373    1  17  0 2424 956 pipe_w  Ss   ?   0:00 /sbin/klogd -P /var/run/klogd/kmsg
5 104  3392    1  16  0 2188 836 -       Ss   ?   0:03 /usr/bin/dbus-daemon --system
4 108  3428 3408  16  0 2008 860 -       S    ?   0:26 /usr/lib/hal/hald-addon-storage
1   0  3447    1  15  0 1928 656 -       Ss   ?   0:00 /sbin/dhcdbd --system
```

Again, this is a partial listing. You noticed, of course, that I threw a couple of new flags in there. The double w, or ww, displays each process's command-line options. A single w truncates the options at a half a line.

The columns you see tell you a bit more about each process. The F field indicates the process flag. A 040 in that position indicates a process that forked, but didn't exec, whereas a 140 means the same, but that superuser privileges were used to start the process. The UID field represents the user ID, whereas PID and PPID are the process and parent process ID that I covered earlier. PRI and NI (priority and nice number) are featured later when I discuss performance issues. In fact, there are quite a number of information flags for the ps command. Every system administrator should take some time to read the man page. More importantly, play with the command and the various flags. You will be enlightened.

Forests and Trees

With all the information displayed through ps, you are forgiven if your head is starting to hurt. It is a little like trying to see the forest but being overwhelmed by the sheer number of trees. And yet, all these processes are linked in some way. Luckily, your stock Linux distribution contains tools to make this easier. One of them is called pstree. Here's a sample of what you get by simply typing the command and pressing <Enter>:

```
init--|--NetworkManager
      |--NetworkManagerD
      |--atd
      |--bonobo-activati
      |--clock-applet
      |--cron
      |--cupsd
      |--2*[dbus-daemon]
      |--dbus-launch
      |--dd
      |--dhcdbd
      |--esd
      |--events/0
      |--fish-applet-2
      |--gconfd-2
      |--gdm----gdm--|--Xorg
      |                |-x-session-managssh-agent
      |--6*[getty]
      |--gksu----synaptic
      |--gnome-cups-icon----{gnome-cups-icon}
      |--gnome-keyring-d
      |--gnome-panel----{gnome-panel}
      |--gnome-power-man
      |--gnome-screensav----fuzzyflakes
      |--gnome-settings----{gnome-settings-}
      |--gnome-terminal--|--bash
      |                  |--gnome-pty-helpe
      |                  |--{gnome-terminal}
      |--gnome-vfs-daemo----{gnome-vfs-daemo}
```

This is only a partial listing, but notice that everything on the system stems from one super, ancestral process called `init`. Somewhere under there, I have a login that spawns a shell. From that shell, I start an X window session, from which spawns my GNOME display manager, then my login, and so on.

If you want a similar output, but in more detail, you can go back to your old friend, the `ps` command. Try the `f` flag, which in this case stands for forest, as in forest view. The following output is the result of my running `ps axf`. Again, this is a partial listing, but unlike the `pstree` listing, you also get process IDs, running states, and so on.

```
$ ps axf

 3356 ?     Ss     0:00 /bin/dd bs 1 if /proc/kmsg of /var/run/klogd/kmsg
 3358 ?     Ss     0:00 /sbin/klogd -P /var/run/klogd/kmsg
 3377 ?     Ss     0:00 /usr/bin/dbus-daemon --system
 3392 ?     Ss     0:02 /usr/sbin/hald
 3393 ?     S      0:00  \_ hald-runner
 3410 ?     S      0:49      \_ /usr/lib/hal/hald-addon-storage
 3666 ?     Ss     0:00 /usr/sbin/gdm
 3674 ?     S      0:03  \_ /usr/sbin/gdm
 3679 tty7  Rs+ 1548:41      \_ /usr/bin/X :0 -br -audit 0 -auth /var/lib/gd
 4850 ?     Ss     0:02      \_ x-session-manager
 4892 ?     Ss     0:00          \_ /usr/bin/ssh-agent /usr/bin/dbus-launch -
 3737 ?     Ssl    0:00 /usr/sbin/hpiod
 3746 ?     S      0:01 python /usr/sbin/hpssd
```

In the Linux world, you can find a number of programs devoted to deciphering those numbers, thereby making it possible to find out what processes are doing and how much time and resources they are using to do it and making it possible to manage the resultant information.

Interrupting, Suspending, and Restarting Processes

Once in a while, I start a process that I think is going to take a few seconds—like parsing a large log file, scanning for some text, extracting something else, sorting the output, and finally sending the whole thing to a file. All of these are very ad hoc in terms of reporting. The trouble is this: Two and a half minutes go by and I start to get a little impatient. Had I thought that the process would take a while, I might have started it in the background.

When you start a process (by typing a command name and pressing <Enter>), you normally start that process in the foreground. In other words, your terminal is still controlling the process and the cursor sits there at the end of the line until the process completes. At that point, it returns to the command or shell prompt. For most (not all) processes, you can run things in the background, thus immediately freeing up your command line for the next task. You do this by adding an ampersand (&) to the end of the command before you press <Enter>.

```
$ sh long_process &
```

However, I've already confessed that I wasn't thinking that far ahead and as a result, I am sitting looking at a flashing cursor wondering if I did something wrong and just how long this process will take. Now, I don't want to end the process, but I would like to temporarily pause it so I can look at its output and decide whether I want to continue. As it turns out, I can do precisely that with a running process by pressing <Ctrl+Z>.

```
$ sh long_process
Ctrl-Z
[1]+  Stopped                      sh long_process
```

The process is now suspended. In fact, if you do a `ps ax` and you look for `long_process`, you see this:

```
5328 ?          RN    2267:04 ./setiathome -nice 19
11127 tty       1S       0:00 rxvt -bg black -fg white -fn fixed
11128 pts/0     S        0:00 bash
11139 pts/0     S        0:00 ssh -l www website
11177 ?         S        0:00 smbd -D
11178 ?         S        0:00 smbd -D
11219 pts/2     T        0:01 sh long_process
```

 Quick Tip Do you want to see what jobs you have suspended? Try the `jobs` command.

I added a few processes in the preceding command snapshot because I wanted to show the state of the processes. That S you see in the third column of most of these processes means they are sleeping. At any given moment or snapshot of your system, almost every single process are sleeping and a small handful show up with an R to indicate that they are currently running or runnable, sometimes referred to as being in the run queue. The T you see beside the suspended process means that it is *traced*, or suspended.

Two other states you might see processes in are D and Z. The D means that your process is in an uninterruptible sleep and it is likely to stay that way (usually not a good sign). The Z refers to a process that has gone *zombie*. It may as well be dead and will be as soon as someone gets that message across.

Getting back to the suspended process, you have a few choices. You can restart it from where it left off by typing **fg** at the shell prompt; in other words, you can continue the process in the foreground. The second option is to type **bg**, which tells the system (you guessed it) to run the suspended process in the background. If you do that, the process restarts with an ampersand at the end of the command as it did earlier.

```
$ bg
[1]+ sh long_process &
```

Your other option is to terminate the process, or kill it.

Killing Processes

You can usually interrupt a foreground process by pressing <Ctrl+C>, but that does not work with background processes. The command used to terminate a process is called kill, which is an unfortunate name for a command that does more than just terminate processes. By design, kill sends a signal to a job (or jobs). That signal is sent as an option (after a hyphen) to a process ID.

```
kill -signal_no PID
```

For instance, you can send the SIGHUP signal to process 7612 like this:

```
kill -1 7612
```

Signals are messages. They are usually referenced numerically, as with the ever popular kill -9 signal, but there are a number of others. The ones you are most likely to use are 1, 9, and 15. These signals can also be referenced symbolically with these names.

Signal 1 is SIGHUP This is normally used with system processes such as xinetd and other daemons. With these types of processes, a SIGHUP tells the process to hang up, reread its configuration files, and restart. Most applications just ignore this signal.

Signal 9 is SIGKILL, an unconditional termination of the process. Some administrators I know call this "killing with extreme prejudice." The process is not asked to stop, close its files, and terminate gracefully. It is simply killed. This should be your *last resort* approach to killing a process and it works 99 percent of the time. Only a small handful of conditions ever ignore the -9 signal.

Signal 15, the default, is SIGTERM, a call for normal program termination. The system asks the program to wrap it up and stop doing whatever it was doing.

Remember when you suspended a process earlier? That was another signal. Try this to get a feel for how this works. If you are running in an X display, start a digital xclock with a seconds display updated every second.

```
xclock -digital -update 1 &
```

You should see the second digits counting away. Now, find its process ID with ps ax | grep xclock. Pretend the process ID is 12136. Let's kill that process with a SIGSTOP

```
kill -SIGSTOP 12136
```

The digits have stopped incrementing, right? Restart the clock.

```
kill -SIGCONT 12136
```

As you can see, kill is probably a bad name for a command that can suspend a process and then bring it back to life. For a complete list of signals and what they do, look in the man pages with this command:

```
man 7 signal
```

If you want to kill a process by specifying the symbolic signal, you use the signal name minus the SIG prefix. For instance, to send the -1 signal to xinetd, you could do this instead:

```
kill -HUP `cat /var/run/xinetd.pid`
```

Note that those are backward quotes around the previous command string.

Working with Editors

Now on to the wonderful world of editors. I'm talking here about computerized line editors, as opposed to those who want to know whether your book will be delivered in time for the original deadline.

There are times when you need to work with an editor, whether to edit a configuration file, write a script, or do some quick edits on the company Web site. In the Linux world, there are many alternatives, and your Ubuntu system comes with a few. Let me introduce you to a friendly new member of the family.

Meet gedit

Your GNOME desktop comes with a very nice and powerful editor called gedit (command name gedit). With colorful language-sensitive syntax highlighting (sh, C, C++, Perl, HTML, and others), tabs, and a spell checker, gedit is easy and fun to work with. To see gedit in action, look at Figure 21-2. You can start gedit on its own or specify a filename to start with. Notice that I started my session using gksudo because I was editing a system script.

```
gksudo gedit /etc/profile
```

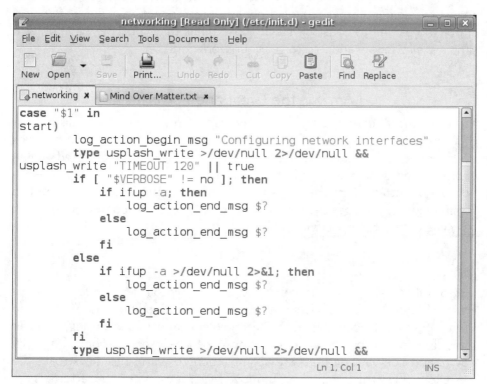

Figure 21–2 gedit is an easy-to-use editor that supports tabs so you can work on multiple files simultaneously.

Tip In the preceding example, I use `gksudo` instead of `sudo`. This is a graphical frontend to `sudo`. It's also the best (and correct) way to run a graphical command that requires administrative privileges via the <Alt+F2> quick-start.

As you can see by looking at Figure 21-2, gedit supports tabs, thereby making it simple to work on multiple files at the same time. Just click the tab to select the file you want to edit. Basic editing functions like cut, paste, find, and replace, are available directly below the menu bar. To edit a file without starting from a command line, click the Open icon, which opens up the standard GNOME file selector.

For years, I've been a fan of `vim`, the next editor I will discuss, but I appreciate the beauty of a simple, friendly editor like gedit. It's easy-to-use with a learning curve close to zero. Still, there may be times when you don't have access to gedit and times when a slow, remote connection makes a graphical editor too painful to consider. It's at those times that you'll be thankful for a simple shell window and `vim` to get your work done.

I Am **vi**, the Great and Powerful

You can almost hear a fearsome voice echoing eerily around the walls of your office or home. If there is one editor that strikes fear in the hearts of newbies everywhere, it is certainly `vi` (or `vim`), the visual editor. `vim` stands for *vi improved* and is the version of `vi` that you find in your Linux system. Anyhow, pay no attention to that fearsome voice behind the program. `vi` is not so frightening after you get to know it. To start `vi`, enter the command name on its own or start it by specifying a filename.

```
vi /tmp/test_file
```

To start entering information, press <i> to go into insert mode. Type several lines and then press <Esc> when you are done editing. Moving around with `vi` is easy. Depending on the terminal emulator you are using, you can typically use your cursor keys. In the absence of cursor key control, the up, down, and sideways motions are all implemented with single keystrokes. To move left, press the letter <h>. To move right, press <l>. The letter k is up, and j is down.

A little further on, I've included a quick cheat sheet.

When you work with vi, the <Esc> key is your friend. If you don't know where you are or what mode you are in (insert, replace, or append), press the <Esc> key. You go back to normal vi command mode. Your second best friend is u or U, which stands for undo. The uppercase undo undoes every change to the current line and the lowercase undo undoes the last change only.

:q, :w, :wq, and ZZ

Finished editing? When it comes time to save your work, press <Esc> (to get out of whatever mode you are in) and type **ZZ**. Another way to exit is to type **:wq** (write and quit). At any time during an editing session, you can type **:w** to save your current work. Finally, if you really don't want to save anything you have done, type **:q!** The exclamation point essentially says that you won't take no for an answer. Had you modified the file and simply typed **:q**, vi would warn you that you were trying to exit from a modified file without having saved your changes.

Keystrokes for Functions

Function	Keystroke
These commands let you move around:	
Line (or cursor) up	k
Line (or cursor) down	j
Single character (or cursor) right	l
Single character (or cursor) left	h
Move one word right	w
Move one word left	b
Move cursor to the first character in a line	^
Move cursor to the very beginning of a line	0
Move cursor to the end of a line	$
Jump to the end of a file	G

Keystrokes for Functions *(Continued)*

Function	Keystroke
Jump to the beginning of a file	gg
(You can also type a number followed by gg and jump to that line.)	
These commands let you start inserting text in various ways:	
Start inserting text before the current character	i
Start inserting text at the beginning of the line	I
Start inserting text after the current character	a
Start inserting text after the last character in the line	A
Open a blank line below the current position	o
Open a blank line above the current position	O
These commands let you delete or change characters, lines, and so on:	
Delete a single character	x
Delete three characters	3x
Delete a whole line	dd
Delete 20 lines	20dd
Delete a word	dw
Change an entire word (press <Esc> to finish)	cw
Change five words (press <Esc> to finish)	5cw
Replace a single character	r
Start replacing text (until you press <Esc>)	R

Quick Tip Need help while in `vi`? Make sure you aren't in insert or replace mode, and then type **:help**.

I urge you not to let vi frighten you. Get to know it. The likelihood that you will ever log on to a modern Linux (or UNIX) system that doesn't have some form of vi installed is virtually nonexistent. That said, if you need more information than I've given you here, consider the vi tutor. This little tool is distributed as part of the vim documentation. It is essentially a text file that tells you what to do and how to do it as you read it. To start the tutor, type the following command:

```
vimtutor
```

When the tutorial starts, you should see a picture like the one in Figure 21-3. The entire tutorial takes between 25 and 30 minutes for most people to complete.

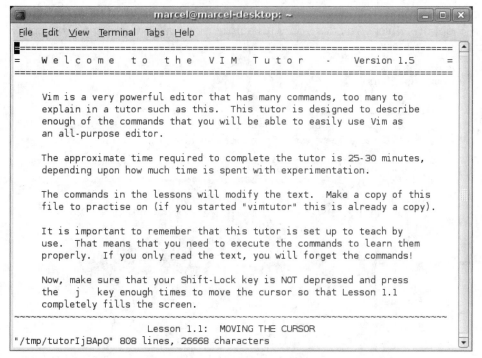

Figure 21–3 Learning vi or vim from the vimtutor.

Recovering a **vi** Session

From time to time, you may find yourself trying to edit a file, but someone else, maybe you, is already editing it. That session may be open or something may have happened to terminate it accidentally. As a result, you get a nice, long-winded message along the lines of "swap file found" and a whole lot of information on what you can do about it. Here's a shortened version of that message:

```
E325: ATTENTION
Found a swap file by the name "textfiles/.listing1.swp"
          owned by: mgagne   dated: Sun Dec 28 14:43:20 2003
          file name: ~mgagne/textfiles/listing1
```

To locate these files, you can use the famous find command and look for anything with a .swp extension. Another and better way is to have vi report on these for you. You can check for the existence of swap files by using the -r option, which provides you with a little more information than the simple find.

```
Swap files found:
    In current directory:
1.    .linux_companies.swp
          owned by: mgagne   dated: Mon Sep 15 14:38:55 2003
          file name: ~mgagne/textfiles/linux_companies
          modified: YES
          user name: mgagne   host name: francois
          process ID: 2266
2.    .sas.swp
          owned by: mgagne   dated: Mon Sep  8 09:49:02 2003
          file name: ~mgagne/textfiles/sas
          modified: no
          user name: mgagne   host name: ultraman
          process ID: 6340
    In directory ~/tmp:
    -- none --
    In directory /var/tmp:
    -- none --
    In directory /tmp:
    -- none --
```

Power **vi**: Start-Up Options

The next time you need a reason to use vi over one of the other editors, consider some of these tricks for getting to what you want as quickly as possible.

```
vi +100 ftl_program.c
```

This takes you right to line 100 in the file called (in this case) ftl_program.c. This can be a great timesaver when you are compiling programs and something goes wrong, as in the following example:

```
gcc  -O2 -Wall  -c -o ftl_program.o ftl_program.c
ftl_program.c:100: parse error before `<'
make: *** [ftl_program.o] Error 1
```

Another useful start flag is the same one you use to search for text inside a file: the forward slash (/). In the next example, I want to get back to the same place I was working on in my file. To mark my place, I had written my name on a blank line. This vi starter gets me right to where I was working:

```
vi +/Marcel ftl_program.c
```

Note the plus sign before the slash.

Other Editor Options

gedit and vi (or vim) represent only two of many, many different editors available to the Linux user. Your Ubuntu Linux system comes with a few others. One of my old favorites is another nongraphical editor that makes a nice alternative for people who, having gotten up close and personal with vim, would prefer something else. It's called Nano (command name nano), an enhanced editor based on Pico (in case you are curious). Nano, by the way, stands for Nano's ANOther editor.

Yeah, I know.

Resources

PINE Information Center (the home of Pico)

```
http://www.washington.edu/pine/
```

Nano's Home Page

```
http://www.nano-editor.org
```

vim Home Page

```
http://www.vim.org/
```

The GNU General
Public License

This is a copy of the GNU General Public License (GPL). Those wanting to see the original can do so by visiting the Free Software Foundation Web site. The direct link to the license is as follows:

```
http://www.gnu.org/copyleft/gpl.html
```

On that Web site, you may also want to check out the comparative list of license types (both commercial and noncommercial) and how they compare with the GNU GPL. Most interesting here is the definition of whether a license qualifies as free and whether it is compatible with the GPL. That address is

```
http://www.gnu.org/philosophy/license-list.html
```

Note As this book was going to print, a new version of the GPL was in the late stages of preparation, along with a great deal of discussion regarding its final form. For more on the GPL version 3, the first change to the GPL since 1991, please visit the following address:

```
http://gplv3.fsf.org/
```

Now, without further adieu, here is the current incarnation of the GNU GPL, version 2.

GNU General Public License

Version 2, June 1991
Copyright © 1989, 1991 Free Software Foundation, Inc.
59 Temple Place, Suite 330, Boston, MA 02111-1307 USA

Everyone is permitted to copy and distribute verbatim copies of this license document, but changing it is not allowed.

Preamble

The licenses for most software are designed to take away your freedom to share and change it. By contrast, the GNU General Public License is intended to guarantee your freedom to share and change free software—to make sure the software is free for all its users. This General Public License applies to most of the Free Software Foundation's software and to any other program whose authors commit to using it. (Some other Free Software Foundation software is covered by the GNU Library General Public License instead.) You can apply it to your programs, too.

When we speak of free software, we are referring to freedom, not price. Our General Public Licenses are designed to make sure that you have the freedom to distribute copies of free software (and charge for this service if you wish), that you receive source code or can get it if you want it, that you can change the software or use pieces of it in new free programs; and that you know you can do these things.

To protect your rights, we need to make restrictions that forbid anyone to deny you these rights or to ask you to surrender the rights. These restrictions translate to certain responsibilities for you if you distribute copies of the software, or if you modify it.

For example, if you distribute copies of such a program, whether gratis or for a fee, you must give the recipients all the rights that you have. You must make sure that they, too, receive or can get the source code. And you must show them these terms so they know their rights.

We protect your rights with two steps: (1) copyright the software, and (2) offer you this license which gives you legal permission to copy, distribute and/or modify the software.

Also, for each author's protection and ours, we want to make certain that everyone understands that there is no warranty for this free software. If the software is modified by someone else and passed on, we want its recipients to know that what they have is not the original, so that any problems introduced by others will not reflect on the original authors' reputations.

Finally, any free program is threatened constantly by software patents. We wish to avoid the danger that redistributors of a free program will individually obtain patent licenses, in effect making the program proprietary. To prevent this, we have made it clear that any patent must be licensed for everyone's free use or not licensed at all.

The precise terms and conditions for copying, distribution, and modification follow.

GNU General Public License
Terms and Conditions for Copying, Distribution, and Modification

0. This License applies to any program or other work which contains a notice placed by the copyright holder saying it may be distributed under the terms of this General Public License. The "Program," below, refers to any such program or work, and a "work based on the Program" means either the Program or any derivative work under copyright law: that is to say, a work containing the Program or a portion of it, either verbatim or with modifications and/or translated into another language. (Hereinafter, translation is included without limitation in the term "modification".)

Each licensee is addressed as "you."

Activities other than copying, distribution, and modification are not covered by this License; they are outside its scope. The act of running the Program is not restricted, and the output from the Program is covered only if its contents constitute a work based on the Program (independent of having been made by running the Program). Whether that is true depends on what the Program does.

1. You may copy and distribute verbatim copies of the Program's source code as you receive it, in any medium, provided that you conspicuously and appropriately publish on each copy an appropriate copyright notice and disclaimer of warranty; keep intact all the notices that refer to this License and to the absence of any warranty; and give any other recipients of the Program a copy of this License along with the Program.

    You may charge a fee for the physical act of transferring a copy, and you may at your option offer warranty protection in exchange for a fee.

2. You may modify your copy or copies of the Program or any portion of it, thus forming a work based on the Program, and copy and distribute such modifications or work under the terms of Section 1 above, provided that you also meet all of these conditions:

    a. You must cause the modified files to carry prominent notices stating that you changed the files and the date of any change.

    b. You must cause any work that you distribute or publish, that in whole or in part contains or is derived from the Program or any part thereof, to be licensed as a whole at no charge to all third parties under the terms of this License.

    c. If the modified program normally reads commands interactively when run, you must cause it, when started running for such interactive use in the most ordinary way, to print or display an announcement including an appropriate copyright notice and a notice that there is no warranty (or else, saying that you provide a warranty) and that users may redistribute the program under these conditions, and telling the user how to view a copy of this License. (Exception: if the Program itself is interactive but does not normally print such an announcement, your work based on the Program is not required to print an announcement.)

These requirements apply to the modified work as a whole. If identifiable sections of that work are not derived from the Program, and can be reasonably considered independent and separate works in themselves, then this License, and its terms, do not apply to those sections when you distribute them as separate works. But when you distribute the same sections as part of a whole which is a work based on the Program, the distribution of the whole must be on the terms of this License, whose permissions for other licensees extend to the entire whole, and thus to each and every part regardless of who wrote it.

Thus, it is not the intent of this section to claim rights or contest your rights to work written entirely by you; rather, the intent is to exercise the right to control the distribution of derivative or collective works based on the Program.

In addition, mere aggregation of another work not based on the Program with the Program (or with a work based on the Program) on a volume of a storage or distribution medium does not bring the other work under the scope of this License.

3. You may copy and distribute the Program (or a work based on it, under Section 2) in object code or executable form under the terms of Sections 1 and 2 above provided that you also do one of the following:
    a. Accompany it with the complete corresponding machine-readable source code, which must be distributed under the terms of Sections 1 and 2 above on a medium customarily used for software interchange; or,
    b. Accompany it with a written offer, valid for at least three years, to give any third party, for a charge no more than your cost of physically performing source distribution, a complete machine-readable copy of the corresponding source code, to be distributed under the terms of Sections 1 and 2 above on a medium customarily used for software interchange; or,
    c. Accompany it with the information you received as to the offer to distribute corresponding source code. (This alternative is allowed only for noncommercial distribution and only if you received the program in object code or executable form with such an offer, in accord with Subsection b above.)

The source code for a work means the preferred form of the work for making modifications to it. For an executable work, complete source code means all the source code for all modules it contains, plus any associated interface definition files, plus the scripts used to control compilation and installation of the executable. However, as a special exception, the source code distributed need not include anything that is normally distributed (in either source or binary form) with the major components (compiler, kernel, and so on) of the operating system on which the executable runs, unless that component itself accompanies the executable.

If distribution of executable or object code is made by offering access to copy from a designated place, then offering equivalent access to copy the source code from the same place counts as distribution of the source code, even though third parties are not compelled to copy the source along with the object code.

4. You may not copy, modify, sublicense, or distribute the Program except as expressly provided under this License. Any attempt otherwise to copy, modify, sublicense or distribute the Program is void, and will automatically terminate your rights under this License. However, parties who have received copies, or rights, from you under this License will not have their licenses terminated so long as such parties remain in full compliance.

5. You are not required to accept this License, since you have not signed it. However, nothing else grants you permission to modify or distribute the Program or its derivative works. These actions are prohibited by law if you do not accept this License. Therefore, by modifying or distributing the Program (or any work based on the Program), you indicate your acceptance of this License to do so, and all its terms and conditions for copying, distributing or modifying the Program or works based on it.

6. Each time you redistribute the Program (or any work based on the Program), the recipient automatically receives a license from the original licensor to copy, distribute or modify the Program subject to these terms and conditions. You may not impose any further restrictions on the recipients' exercise of the rights granted herein. You are not responsible for enforcing compliance by third parties to this License.

7. If, as a consequence of a court judgment or allegation of patent infringement or for any other reason (not limited to patent issues), conditions are imposed on you (whether by court order, agreement or otherwise) that contradict the conditions of this License, they do not excuse you from the

conditions of this License. If you cannot distribute so as to satisfy simulta-neously your obligations under this License and any other pertinent obli-gations, then as a consequence you may not distribute the Program at all. For example, if a patent license would not permit royalty-free redistribu-tion of the Program by all those who receive copies directly or indirectly through you, then the only way you could satisfy both it and this License would be to refrain entirely from distribution of the Program.

If any portion of this section is held invalid or unenforceable under any particular circumstance, the balance of the section is intended to apply and the section as a whole is intended to apply in other circum-stances.

It is not the purpose of this section to induce you to infringe any pat-ents or other property right claims or to contest validity of any such claims; this section has the sole purpose of protecting the integrity of the free software distribution system, which is implemented by public license practices. Many people have made generous contributions to the wide range of software distributed through that system in reliance on consis-tent application of that system; it is up to the author/donor to decide if he or she is willing to distribute software through any other system and a lic-ensee cannot impose that choice.

This section is intended to make thoroughly clear what is believed to be a consequence of the rest of this License.

8. If the distribution and/or use of the Program is restricted in certain coun-tries either by patents or by copyrighted interfaces, the original copyright holder who places the Program under this License may add an explicit geographical distribution limitation excluding those countries, so that dis-tribution is permitted only in or among countries not thus excluded. In such case, this License incorporates the limitation as if written in the body of this License.

9. The Free Software Foundation may publish revised and/or new versions of the General Public License from time to time. Such new versions will be similar in spirit to the present version, but may differ in detail to address new problems or concerns.

Each version is given a distinguishing version number. If the Program specifies a version number of this License which applies to it and "any later version", you have the option of following the terms and conditions either of that version or of any later version published by the Free Software Foundation. If the Program does not specify a version number of this License, you may choose any version ever published by the Free Software Foundation.

10. If you wish to incorporate parts of the Program into other free programs whose distribution conditions are different, write to the author to ask for permission. For software which is copyrighted by the Free Software Foundation, write to the Free Software Foundation; we sometimes make exceptions for this. Our decision will be guided by the two goals of preserving the free status of all derivatives of our free software and of promoting the sharing and reuse of software generally.

No Warranty

11. BECAUSE THE PROGRAM IS LICENSED FREE OF CHARGE, THERE IS NO WARRANTY FOR THE PROGRAM, TO THE EXTENT PERMITTED BY APPLICABLE LAW. EXCEPT WHEN OTHERWISE STATED IN WRITING THE COPYRIGHT HOLDERS AND/OR OTHER PARTIES PROVIDE THE PROGRAM "AS IS" WITHOUT WARRANTY OF ANY KIND, EITHER EXPRESSED OR IMPLIED, INCLUDING, BUT NOT LIMITED TO, THE IMPLIED WARRANTIES OF MERCHANTABILITY AND FITNESS FOR A PARTICULAR PURPOSE. THE ENTIRE RISK AS TO THE QUALITY AND PERFORMANCE OF THE PROGRAM IS WITH YOU. SHOULD THE PROGRAM PROVE DEFECTIVE, YOU ASSUME THE COST OF ALL NECESSARY SERVICING, REPAIR OR CORRECTION.

12. IN NO EVENT UNLESS REQUIRED BY APPLICABLE LAW OR AGREED TO IN WRITING WILL ANY COPYRIGHT HOLDER, OR ANY OTHER PARTY WHO MAY MODIFY AND/OR REDISTRIBUTE THE PROGRAM AS PERMITTED ABOVE, BE LIABLE TO YOU FOR DAMAGES, INCLUDING ANY GENERAL, SPECIAL, INCIDENTAL OR CONSEQUENTIAL DAMAGES ARISING OUT OF THE USE OR INABILITY TO USE THE PROGRAM (INCLUDING BUT NOT LIMITED TO LOSS OF DATA OR DATA BEING RENDERED INACCURATE OR LOSSES SUSTAINED BY YOU OR THIRD PARTIES OR A FAILURE OF THE PROGRAM TO OPER-

ATE WITH ANY OTHER PROGRAMS), EVEN IF SUCH HOLDER OR OTHER PARTY HAS BEEN ADVISED OF THE POSSIBILITY OF SUCH DAMAGES.

END OF TERMS AND CONDITIONS

How to Apply These Terms to Your New Programs

If you develop a new program, and you want it to be of the greatest possible use to the public, the best way to achieve this is to make it free software which everyone can redistribute and change under these terms.

To do so, attach the following notices to the program. It is safest to attach them to the start of each source file to most effectively convey the exclusion of warranty; and each file should have at least the "copyright" line and a pointer to where the full notice is found.

<one line to give the program's name and a brief idea of what it does.>
Copyright © <year> <name of author>

This program is free software; you can redistribute it and/or modify it under the terms of the GNU General Public License as published by the Free Software Foundation; either version 2 of the License, or (at your option) any later version.

This program is distributed in the hope that it will be useful, but WITH-OUT ANY WARRANTY; without even the implied warranty of MER-CHANTABILITY or FITNESS FOR A PARTICULAR PURPOSE. See the GNU General Public License for more details.

You should have received a copy of the GNU General Public License along with this program; if not, write to the Free Software Foundation, Inc., 59 Temple Place, Suite 330, Boston, MA 02111-1307 USA

Also add information on how to contact you by electronic and paper mail.

If the program is interactive, make it output a short notice like this when it starts in an interactive mode:

Gnomovision version 69, Copyright © year name of author
Gnomovision comes with ABSOLUTELY NO WARRANTY; for details type "show w." This is free software, and you are welcome to redistribute it under certain conditions; type "show c" for details.

The hypothetical commands "show w" and "show c" should show the appropriate parts of the General Public License. Of course, the commands you use may be called something other than "show w" and "show c"; they could even be mouse-clicks or menu items—whatever suits your program.

You should also get your employer (if you work as a programmer) or your school, if any, to sign a "copyright disclaimer" for the program, if necessary. Here is a sample; alter the names:

Yoyodyne, Inc., hereby disclaims all copyright interest in the program "Gnomovision" (which makes passes at compilers) written by James Hacker.

<signature of Ty Coon>, 1 April 1989
Ty Coon, President of Vice

This General Public License does not permit incorporating your program into proprietary programs. If your program is a subroutine library, you may consider it more useful to permit linking proprietary applications with the library. If this is what you want to do, use the GNU Library General Public License instead of this License.

Resources

Linux Documentation Project

`http://www.tldp.org`

Linux.org List of LUGs

`http://www.linux.org/groups/index.html`

Index

BOOKS ONLINE

ENABLED

THIS BOOK IS SAFARI ENABLED

INCLUDES FREE 45-DAY ACCESS TO THE ONLINE EDITION

The Safari® Enabled icon on the cover of your favorite technology book means the book is available through Safari Bookshelf. When you buy this book, you get free access to the online edition for 45 days.

Safari Bookshelf is an electronic reference library that lets you easily search thousands of technical books, find code samples, download chapters, and access technical information whenever and wherever you need it.

TO GAIN 45-DAY SAFARI ENABLED ACCESS TO THIS BOOK:

- Go to **http://www.awprofessional.com/safarienabled**
- Complete the brief registration form
- Enter the coupon code found in the front of this book on the "Copyright" page

Addison
Wesley

If you have difficulty registering on Safari Bookshelf or accessing the online edition, please e-mail customer-service@safaribooksonline.com.

DVD Warranty

Addison-Wesley Professional warrants the enclosed DVD to be free of defects in materials and faulty workmanship under normal use for a period of ninety days after purchase (when purchased new). If a defect is discovered in the DVD during this warranty period, a replacement DVD can be obtained at no charge by sending the defective DVD, postage prepaid, with proof of purchase to:

Disc Exchange
Addison-Wesley Professional
Pearson Technology Group
75 Arlington Street, Suite 300
Boston, MA 02116
Email: AWPro@aw.com

Addison-Wesley Professional makes no warranty or representation, either expressed or implied, with respect to this software, its quality, performance, merchantability, or fitness for a particular purpose. In no event will Addison-Wesley Professional, its distributors, or dealers be liable for direct, indirect, special, incidental, or consequential damages arising out of the use or inability to use the software. The exclusion of implied warranties is not permitted in some states. Therefore, the above exclusion may not apply to you. This warranty provides you with specific legal rights. There may be other rights that you may have that vary from state to state.

More information and updates are available at:
http://www.awprofessional.com/